THE CLEGG
COUP

BRITAIN'S FIRST
COALITION GOVERNMENT
SINCE LLOYD GEORGE

Jasper Gerard

GIBSON SQUARE

For Eleanor, who gave birth to my liberalism
3 May 1929 — 1 November 2010

First published in 2011 by

Gibson Square

Tel: +44 (0)20 7096 1100

info@gibsonsquare.com
www.gibsonsquare.com

ISBN 9781908096098 HB

CONTENTS

ACKNOWLEDGEMENTS

This book is not "authorised" but is unashamedly celebratory about the revival of a political movement I love. Some were wary but I hope they will now be reassured. It was a collaborate project written with help from an eclectic cast.

It is not possible to thank everyone, not least because significant numbers preferred to donate their information anonymously. However, special mention must go to the following: Monica Allen, Paddy Ashdown, Julian Astle, Norman Baker, Jeremy Browne, Duncan Brack, Malcolm Bruce, David Butler, Sir Menzies Campbell, Greg Clark, Ken Clarke, Nick Clegg, Miriam Clegg, Bobbie Cummines, Lord Fearn, Tony Gallagher, Nick Harvey, Paul Holmes, Chris Huhne, David Laws, Andrew Lownie, James Lovelock, Ian McFadyen, Ben Macintyre, Paul Marshall, Glen Owen, Martin Pierce, Lance Price, Lord Rennard, Edward Roussel, Jackie Rowley, Andrew Russell, Mark Sainsbury, Neil Sherlock, Keith Simpson, Rachel Sylvester, Louis Theroux, Martin Tod, Eddie Vaizey, Frank van den Wall Bake, Paul Whiteley, Marie Woolf, Patrick Wintour and Ian Wright.

Posthumously, I would like to thank Jo and Laura Grimond, Nancy Seear and the painfully missed Russell Johnston.

Finally, this book would not have been written without my children Emilia and Freddie keeping a daily word count to monitor my often painful progress and my wife Diana who assured me constantly that one day this book would be finished.

13 September, 2011

THE VOTERS HAVE SPOKEN

As Nick Clegg's chauffeur-driven Jaguar purred through the media jungle, its every turn was captured through telescopic sights from a pack of hunting helicopters. This stately prowl, eased by police outriders clearing a path through the morning herd, looked suspiciously like a presidential motorcade, or grander still, Lord Sugar on his way to the studio. Could this really be a Liberal Democrat's tootle to work? For here was a political movement apparently so insignificant that, an opponent once hooted, its parliamentary party could meet in the back of a taxi. So it was an arresting image for Clegg to project, all that sleek muscle in pursuit of its prey. David Cameron, as a Conservative, might have been rendered more humble by bicycling to the office, but to strike a note of favourable surprise Clegg needed to convey the opposite: "now I matter. I'm no lap dog, I'm the big cat. And I'm about to bare my teeth."

Just 21 May days had apparently transported "Nick Who?" from a man unrecognised in his local shop to Westminster's kingmaker. His performances in the live television debates had turned him into something of a Politician Idol. According to the *British Election Study*, voters agreed Clegg had fought by far the strongest campaign. He had been hailed the most popular party leader since Churchill and commentators speculated he was about to become the most powerful Liberal since Lloyd George.

As the world's press jostled on ladders outside his Westminster HQ to witness the denouement of "Clegg-mania", something genuinely momentous was happening, and this was dawning through the exhausted morning light on less sleep-starved members of the establishment. They found it as terrifying, in its way, as when the mob bayed at the window of the Tuileries Palace for Marie Antoinette. For if there was one verity Labour and Conservative could agree upon most cordially, it was that civilisation as they both enjoyed it would be at an end if that damnable interloper Clegg should ever be in the puffed up position to decide which of them to do out of jobs. And here he was, apparently snarling over the prone bodies of both Prime Minister and Leader of the Opposition.

British elections typically produce clear winners, but in 2010 a country of 60 million people had trudged to the polls to elect a new government in a campaign costing over £100 million—and had marked their collective ballot paper "don't know". And so it appeared to fall to just one man to decide what their enigmatic verdict had meant. And thanks to his domination of the campaign, denying the two "major" parties their customary majorities, that was Clegg. The day after polling the leader of Britain's "third party" is normally sucked back into the vortex of anonymity from whence he came, but not this time. Rolling news programmes demanded to know how Britain was to be governed. Historians were hauled from their beds to answer the question of when we had last seen anything quite like this. Was it 1974, the most recent election to give an inconclusive result, or 1918, when the last peace-time coalition was formed? Or was it 1906, or 1895, or even—a frightening thought, this, for defenders of the status quo in the two old parties—never? Nobody knew, because Clegg hadn't announced what he intended to do. All that could be predicted was that there were going to be fireworks lighting up the political landscape, but as to their likely colour, that remained a secret known only to Clegg.

Both David Cameron and Gordon Brown had drawn consider-able satisfaction from variously bullying, patronising and ignoring the leader of what they liked to term the "minor" party. How careless the taking of those pleasures must have seemed on this most singular of mornings, every jeer and jibe played back before the shaving mirror as their statesmen-ly fates hung limply in Clegg's jaws. One of them was toast—it was simply a question of which one to devour.

Wasn't this the decision, as delicious as it was daunting, Clegg chewed over in the back of his bullet-proof limousine?

Well, if that is how it will be written up by historians, it wasn't how it felt at the time. For the exhausted figure slumped on the back seat, fiddling distractedly with his BlackBerry, was very far from jubilant. As the Jaguar slunk into its Cowley Street lair, the triumphs of entering government and the travails of governing were miles further down the track. On a morning when even dawn seemed a faded-day grey, Clegg looked no master of the universe. There was little satisfaction from taking in the chauffeur-driven pomp of the cavalcade; nor schaudenfreude, imagining gnawing the political carcass of Brown—whom he quietly loathed—or Cameron, whom he faintly despised as an all-too predictable product of his class.

Most immediately, he was physically and emotionally exhausted after three adrenalin-charged, sleep-deprived weeks, which had followed two years without a day off. And all culminating in the chaotic delay of his Sheffield count. For party leaders the hope of polling day morphs with sickening slowness into the cruellest night, awaiting a verdict both highly public and deeply personal. And it is in this groggy, grotty almost grotesque state that they are expected to take on the even greater challenge of forming a government. Paddy Ashdown discloses: "Cameron was flat on his back; friends tell me he was devastated"; Clegg was scarcely on top form, either.

According to one who telephoned, Clegg apologised and said he had "let the party down". Another intimate found him "close to tears and talking of resigning," though perhaps this was more cry of pain than careful plan. It was of only limited consolation to Clegg that, if anything, Brown and Cameron felt worse.

"Clegg-mania" had proved a media phenomenon now more time-ravaged than the Parthenon. Voter excitement hadn't translated into electoral victory. Indeed, the Liberal Democrats came out of the campaign with just 23.5 per cent of the vote and 57 MPs, five fewer seats than in 2005 and about 30 below private expectations. True, the party had only once in the modern era grabbed a higher electoral share, but this had promised to excite not contended sighs from the wise heads of the Liberal Democrat History Group, but a new future. Worst of all it was messy, with only a Lib-Con coalition able to command a majority in the House, a Lib-Lab cohabitation requiring the taking in of some decidedly unsavoury lodgers, perhaps even those strange men in orange sashes from the Democratic Unionists. Clegg knew many in his party would find power-sharing with "the Tories" unpalatable. No wonder Ashdown was heard to wonder if the electorate had invented an ingenious game of torture for his party.

After such exulted expectations it felt suspiciously like a loss, and the war metaphors were soon whizzing and whirring across the televisual battlefield like bullets in a Benghazi back alley. Had the Lib Dems won the air war but lost the ground war? Or won mere skirmishes and lost the war entirely? Brown may have been a hopeless, hapless Captain Mainwaring, but the morning after election night he was hardly showing the greatest urgency to telephone Pickfords. Instead he remained, browned-off in his "bunker", apparently without the obligatory glass of whisky and pearl-encrusted revolver.

As Clegg rose from his car with as much spring as he could muster, flashbulbs mocked the very spectacle they had earlier sensationalised. Shattered Lib Dem toilers were shoved into the street to crowd round Clegg and form a victorious doughnut, but looked suspiciously like a cake that had failed to rise.

Clegg's disarming, rueful shrug scarcely disguised his disappointment. He resisted any temptation to play the lion king, growling that power was somehow his. Instead he came across as modestly subdued, aided by chronic sleep deprivation. In line with his pre-poll formula, he said it now fell to the Conservatives, as the largest party, to see if they could form a government able to call on the support of the House. As aides eased him from the gentlemen of the press and swung shut Number 4's reassuringly solid door, at last Clegg found respite from TV crews that had stalked him on the train from Sheffield, asking how he felt. Now, though, he had to thank party workers from the first floor landing. By the close of his speech he was choking back tears, and whispered to his confidant David Laws that it was the hardest address he'd ever made.

He then stepped into a conference room with key members of his pack. Tactfully, the champagne had been removed, unopened. Instead strong coffee and sobering biscuits appeared. The celebration was looking like a crisis.

But it was one for which Clegg was prepared. The Lib Dems, the only party unashamedly hoping for a "balanced" parliament, had devoted the most time before the election to figuring out what they might do after it. Just as Clegg had trained harder than rivals for the public pugilism of the TV debates, now he was in the best shape for the private wrestling of the negotiations.

Everywhere lurked dangers, but as Clegg ran through the options with senior colleagues the gloom gradually lifted—opening up an enticing view of opportunity. Laws has said: "We might not have had the seats we wanted, but we had the leverage we needed." And that was the point. Clegg had invited the Conservative leader to make the first attempt at forming a government—somewhat against the conventions of the constitution, as power supposedly remains with the incumbent Prime Minister—but neither Cameron nor Brown were going to kiss the hand of the Queen unless Clegg gave his consent. Our next government was going to be decided upon by the Lib Dems sitting round this table. Indeed, there was even the possibility that those present might sit in it.

So would this government wear a reddish hue, which this party of progressive orange might find a closer match, or blue, as the numbers seemed to indicate? Or—and this was the massive prize, hard even to imagine for any post-war Liberal—could it be an entirely new colour, a mixing of the political palates in a ground-breaking coalition? All scenarios were possible, because Clegg had transformed his party and dragged it to the centre ground. What the political and media class had monumentally missed was that Clegg had quietly turned this vague movement of left-wing protest into a genuinely centrist, liberal party of government with a credible political programme. This might compliment a re-invigorated Labour Party led by David Miliband, but also—and this was the game changer—one led by a more moderate, modern Conservative such as Cameron.

As Clegg outlined his negotiating strategy, the Cowley Street phones grew hotter. Privately, sharper brains in both rival parties began to realise that all lines led to Clegg. Not that their dinosaurs got it, stuck in the now-outmoded binary world of Westminster politics. They took to the airwaves demanding that Clegg meekly submit to whatever was offered. They couldn't comprehend that there were few advantages to being the smallest of three parties, but that by making itself marginally less disagreeable than the other two, the Lib Dems were the only party either could work with.

Here was the first Liberal leader since the guns still smouldered on the Western Front without whom Britain's next government could not realistically be formed. Clegg had won the ace in the pack, and it would be up to him how he played it.

INTRODUCTION

"J: kindly have David Steel's dead animal removed from my wall. P."
Such was the note, dashed off with an impatient fountain pen,
awaiting me on my first day toiling for Paddy Ashdown. It was 1988
and Ashdown had just been "crowned" leader of Britain's newly
created third party, thanks largely to his appearing less boring than
his rival, Alan Beith. The missive referred to a buffalo skin presented
to Ashdown's predecessor by the great warrior chief and anti-
Apartheid campaigner, Chief Buthelezi—but as I staggered from the
leader's shady Commons office, the dead animal in my arms felt suspiciously like the corpse of centre politics.

As a 20-year-old research assistant I found my new employer, the
Liberal Democrats, unveiling its emblem, a bird, which newspapers
dubbed "the dead parrot". And you could see their point. The party
enjoyed an approval rating of just four per cent, with Greens and
even Monster Raving Loonies in hot pursuit. As polling companies
threatened to attribute our support to a sampling error, the public
clearly wasn't observing too many signs of vitality in Liberalism's
body politic.

But if the party looked as if it might soon cease to be, Ashdown's
leadership was to inspire one youthful mind. Ashdown first
encountered this precocious talent when it laboured writing speeches
for the Conservative European Commissioner, Lord Brittan. Brittan
had told Ashdown that this boyish creature with the winning smile
was quite the most promising individual he had met in politics.
However, for some unfathomable reason, it had recently woken up
one morning and—perhaps not feeling entirely well—discovered
that it had turned into a Liberal.

On a visit to Brussels Ashdown met this rare specimen and was
equally wowed, marking down his new acquaintance as a future
Liberal Democrat leader. And so, just as Ashdown had earlier

nurtured the Liberalism of this student, he now found an altogether more talented protégé determined to breathe fresh life into Liberal England: Nick Clegg.

Ashdown warned that it was hard enough simply gaining election as a Liberal Democrat MP. As for attaining high office wearing an orange rosette, well, that was the stuff of fantasy—or so it had proved these last eight decades or so.

Yet none of this deterred Clegg, which suggests he could be accused of much—insanity would be an obvious charge—but hardly of opportunism. You would have gained generous odds on him being elected to parliament, let alone on him becoming the second most important figure in the country.

That Clegg believed this was achievable speaks of a pretty extraordinary determination. Liberalism had continued to attract adherents through its wilderness decades, but many were dreamers, nostalgics or purely local campaigners. Clegg, with his European outlook, was not tied to old nostrums about British Liberal Democrats being decent old sticks that banged on about worthy causes and then lost. Call it arrogance or even ignorance but very early on Clegg saw the Liberal Democrats as a vehicle of government. And few who knew him were in any doubt he would be at the wheel.

Incontrovertibly it had not been a political corpse I'd lugged from Ashdown's study all those years before. I had come to learn that British Liberalism had been receiving more premature obituaries than Oscar Wilde, from as far back as 1935 in George Dangerfield's brilliant study, *The Strange Death of Liberal England.* Naturally we had to accept that the patient had endured grave illnesses, but the body still twitched. Indeed, on the wilder shores of medical opinion, some voices were even venturing that it could make a complete recovery and lead a relatively normal life. Three quarters of a century on, not only did I feel Dangerfield's book could use an update, I also saw that, through Clegg, Liberalism could rise again.

I was given the idea for this book on a train back from the launch of Clegg's leadership campaign in Sheffield in 2007. Neil Sherlock, a mercurial fixer at the heart of the party who had the distinction of beating Boris Johnson to the presidency of the Oxford Union, had called to ask how the day had gone. He rung off saying "you do realise, don't you, that you're in the perfect position to write the Clegg book?"

I'd become an admirer of Clegg's from the moment he entered parliament two years before, and had helped in small ways to raise his profile. He was so obviously the talent to take the party forward my only frustration was that many were slow to see it. But it simply hadn't occurred that this thoughtful, amusing, likeable man I occasionally lunched would soon warrant a book. A small group of us had certainly identified in him the personality and intellect to lead the revival, but even I hadn't dared hope these qualities would bloom quite so dramatically in the TV debates, leaving his more established opponents looking like they had just been dead-headed.

If the political and media elite has taken to regarding Liberal Democrats as a devilishly subversive addition to government, it had dismissed them in opposition as harmless cranks. At the point Clegg was challenging for the leadership I had to work overtime to have a mere article published about him, so an entire book? A former editor of the *Sun*, David Yelland, has admitted—after leaving his post, naturally—that for years Britain's best selling newspaper operated a ban on stories about the Liberal Democrats that were not salaciously negative. Even during leader conferences at *The Times* I discovered that the Lib Dems served as a kind of shared joke, giving journalists of left and right something they could finally agree on. A Liberal Democrat columnist could feel very like a fifth columnist.

And publishers were, if anything, less enquiring. In explaining the modern Conservative and Labour Parties, entire Amazonian rainforests had been felled to feed Amazon. But where was the critique of Liberal Democracy? You would have been lucky to find one, except in the "history" or perhaps "humour" section. Since the death of Roy Jenkins, author of definitive works on Asquith and Lloyd George, no writer had even tried to understand the third great political movement in Britain.

Now, thanks to Clegg's breakthrough, the only question is why no one has written this book already. It's virtually nine decades since

Britain's last peace-time coalition government and almost as long since the last serious, mainstream study attempted to describe the state of Liberalism. Pushier sorts than Liberal Democrats might consider that a bit remiss, with the party a pivotal force in government. Like the buffalo, the Liberal had been hunted to the verge of extinction, but against the odds, survived—and it makes for a surprisingly powerful beast.

To those who fear the future marching over the horizon, this must feel suspiciously like enemy occupation. Liberal Democrats, with their new and sinister continental ways, have seized power. If conservative opinion believed it had the measure of Labour, it can't quite get to grips with Britain's newest rulers. For not only are Liberal Democrats in office for the first time, they have given us an apparently foreign form of government, a coalition.

Traditionalists are in uproar about this apparently "un-British" set up. Such is the fear of peacetime partnership, where two united parties put aside past perfideries. All has now changed, yet few seem to grasp why our coalition has come about, how it works, or even quite who half the axis is. This ignorance needs to be challenged because, whatever you think of the Liberal Democrats, you do need to think of them. And with the once impregnable fortress of the two-party system reduced to a smouldering ruin, the Liberal Democrat standard could be flying for some time.

Even now, the establishment is in denial. The right considers it an affront that it is not enjoying unfettered power, able to simultaneously impose on the country its contradictory prescription of authoritarian social dogmas and libertarian economic cruelties.

The left is equally outraged. In power it broke promise after promise to build a "progressive consensus", but still expected the Liberal Democrats to loiter like an unloved mistress in a drab St John's Wood bed-sit, until her faithless lover felt in the mood to swing by.

But is there any basis for resentment? There is a very simple point forgotten by deprecators of the coalition in both Conservative and Labour circles: the party of the right received just 36 per cent of the vote, the party of the left 29 per cent. In the general election of 1951, 97 per cent of voters had backed one of the two great battalions of state, with only 2.5 per cent rallying behind the Liberal resistance. But since then, the forces of Conservatism and socialism have been driven back to their heartlands. By 2010 the voting share of the two "major" parties had fallen to just 65 per cent, with the so-called "third party" dominating the campaign. The Lib-Con alliance might have been formed in response to a crisis pounding at the City's gates, but coalition forces have been pushing this way for six decades.

Their ranks have been swelled by an increasingly educated and thus free thinking population, more inclined to vote according to fresh argument than tired class prejudice. The injustice is not that Liberal Democrats have finally overthrown Whitehall's ruling class. The scandal is that a two-party cabal clung to power for decade after decade—despite nearly two-thirds of the people regularly voting against the party that declared itself the "winner".

How in 2010 could one party possibly have claimed legitimacy with scarcely a third of the vote? But hogging power was precisely what many Conservatives wanted. Had Cameron agreed, and Britain was somewhere hot and far away, the United Nations would surely have muttered about election monitors. All that could be said for British democracy prior to the coalition was that it was very, very old. And under the Con-Lab hegemony, archaic antagonisms festered as both parties took turns to punish their "class enemy". The effect on our economy and our society was clear, an almost Third World gulf between affluent "non-doms" and unemployed "no hopes".

In 2010, none of the parties could claim the consent of the public, or the control of parliament, least of all to make unpopular yet vital decisions to tackle the debt crisis. As the party that lit up the campaign and was most willing to compromise in the national interest, the Liberal Democrats had to be part of the solution. For all the manure hurled at the coalition, we have a Conservative-Liberal Democrat administration because that was the only outcome that could lay any claim to represent the will of voters.

Cameron realises this, even if his more carnivorous cheerleaders do not. If he were to call an early election without the elusive economic upturn, the most likely scenario would be outright Labour victory. Even with recovery he might be punished because voters would want to know why he was reneging on his commitment to work in coalition for five years.

If Cameron had sought to lead a minority administration he would have found the City in flames of panic and our inner cities burning with rage—not merely with the consumerist looting of August 2011, but with political intent. While Cameron would have done his emollient best to placate a rioting nation rebelling against "Tory cuts", George Osborne would have needed approval for budgets from John Redwood and every other flapping white coat on the Tory backbench.

The real reason the Tory irreconcilables lambast Liberal Democrats with quite so much vim and vitriol ("yellow bastards" is a favoured term of endearment) is to either drive Cameron to the right—or to exit, stage left. Either scenario, they intuit, would allow them to introduce robustly Thatcherite policies that, for reasons not apparent to many of us, the country apparently craves. But what is it that makes them think they can ignore the wishes of the people? Despite Conservatives having their most appealing leader in years, facing a monumentally unpopular Labour government, 64 per cent of voters still took one look and said "no thanks". Actually, many probably didn't even look, they just said: "Tory? Yuk. No way."

The left doesn't get it either. Short of storming Number 10, the public could scarcely have made it plainer that it had endured enough hard Labour. The Liberal Democrats had been even clearer: in the event of a "balanced" parliament, they would seek to govern with the party that had done least badly. That they did. What Labour can't forgive the Liberal Democrats for is telling the truth. Yet Labour had 13 years in power to honour Tony Blair's commitment to unite Britain's "progressive majority", by introducing electoral reform and inviting the Liberal Democrats into government. If Blair and Gordon Brown had been less tribalistic and more pluralistic they might have avoided disaster, the Blair Iraqi adventure, the Brown boom in statist welfare, the pair's botched reforms of our public services. If realignment of the centre-left is dead, it was their haughty neglect that killed it.

Suppose Liberal Democrats had spurned Cameron's overtures and cobbled together a deal of the defeated with Labour. Then those irreconcilables in the Conservative press that have picked off Liberal Democrats one by one in a series of confected scandals would have declared all out war. Labour's negotiating team offered no serious proposal to tackle the deficit or public sector pensions. The markets would have revolted, and it is at least conceivable there would have been a rush on the pound to make Black Wednesday look like a spot of light cloud cover over the outer courts of Wimbledon.

Further, a Lib-Lab coalition would have commanded no majority, opening it to the financial extortion of the nationalist parties and the mercurial ambitions of Alex Salmond. It is hard to imagine such a government prospering, and in any ensuing general election voters would almost certainly have held their noses and returned the Conservatives with a thumping majority. And without the Liberal Democrats standing in the way, it would have been the poor receiving the hardest thump.

Far from being some trick on the electorate, coalitions have more legitimacy than the single party governments we had been lumbered with after every election since the war, always after a majority had just rejected the "winning" party at the ballot box. It is no coincidence that leaders reach out to other parties at times of crisis: the coalition of World War One and its aftermath; the national government of the great depression and then World War Two; even the Lib-Lab pact of the 1970s when the country faced economic oblivion; and now a coalition for the near-collapse of the global banking system.

Not only do coalitions foster unity, they draw on strengths of two parties. Crudely, the traditional perception was that Conservatives were competent but thoroughly nasty, Liberal Democrats nice but thoroughly incompetent. Nobody is running up the bunting to celebrate the coalition just yet, but international observers have given guarded praise for its macro-economic decisions, while at home its painful cuts have been ameliorated by substantial assistance for disadvantaged citizens. The Lib Dems have de-toxified the Tories; perhaps the Tories have helped de-"woolify" the Lib Dems. With policy there has been an intriguing synthesis, with Tory ideas of choice, individualism and self-reliance melding with Liberal Democratic themes of empowering the poor to help themselves, community decision making and civil liberties. Take "free schools". Conservatives might have been right that we needed new schools, unburdened by the bureaucracy of education authorities. But Liberal Democrats were surely also right to insist that such schools should first serve deprived children, not the financial interests of private companies.

There is a more trivial advantage to coalition, a conclusion I hope readers arrive at by the close of this book. The dynamic of government with two parties is hugely more compelling, as rival traditions with enmities stretching back centuries suddenly find they must compromise. As well as the political there is the personal, as friendships forge and fragment, within parties and between them, as the shrewd politician fashions new alliances. The story of how this historic experiment came about and has progressed, driven by a group of still largely-unknown leaders, has fascinated me; I hope it will you.

But above all this is the story of one man and his very personal revolution. It is, I would suggest, the great untold story of British politics.

It will show how just five years before Nick Clegg stood in the Downing Street rose-garden to announce the formation of an historic coalition, he had been an anonymous private citizen in Sheffield. Now he is effectively joint Prime Minister, but in 2005 he was sleeping nightly in a hospital wondering if his wife Miriam would pull though as she lay in intensive care after giving birth to their second son. Clegg, meanwhile, was nursing his eldest critically ill with pleurisy. While not rushing between two hospital beds Clegg was, in brief moments of respite, daring to wonder if he could win election as a humble MP.

Politically the change he oversaw was more dramatic still. Within three years of being elected Liberal Democrat leader in 2007, Clegg had turned this hitherto peripheral, almost comical, outfit into a party of government, infused with exciting ideas and professional discipline. After negotiating a coalition agreement which contained 75 per cent of his manifesto commitments such as tax cuts for the low paid and more resources for the education of under-privileged children, he gave modern Britain her first taste of continental, consensual coalition politics.

When readers fully understand Clegg's achievement in remodelling not only his party but the way we have done politics in this country for the best part of a century, they will see that at the very least this stands comparison with the far more comprehensively documented revolutions wrought by Blair and Cameron.

But first we should understand a little of Clegg's background—as turbulent and dramatic as anything he later found at Westminster.

1

NOBLEMEN, EVIL MEN AND
WAYWARD WOMEN

Swaddling-clothes, more than statecraft, defines politicians in the public mind. And the grimmer the childhood the better: a council house is promising but an orphanage sweeter; a single mother engenders sympathy, but what of a single mum who struggles to hold down three jobs while simultaneously teaching the future politician the difference between right and wrong? Throw in a spot of domestic violence from a drunken father or some horrific war leaving civilian misery, and a politician looking to play the populist card cannot lose; you just cannot buy that sort of poverty. In the deprivation of his family Bill Clinton mined electoral gold. If it cannot be horrible it helps if it is at least humble, preferably captured by a single motif. For Margaret Thatcher, like Harry Truman, it was the small town shop, for John Major the (failed) garden gnome business, for Lloyd George the village of Llanystumdwy in Wales.

When out on the stump it is trickier for Nick Clegg to grow quite so Monty Python-esque about his background. This is partly due to his family's elitism but also its sheer exoticism, with ancestors ranging from aristocrats murdered by their own serfs to KGB spies who befriended Stalin. When he was elected leader of the Liberal Democrats, he was called a "young Turk", but Turkey is actually one of the few countries not to have provided some Clegg blood.

Dutch, not English, was the first language round the family breakfast table, though it could as easily have been Russian. Nick, or "Nickje" to family, was the third of four children. He has described boyhood in Chalfont St Giles as "all catapults and scuffed knees", which bathes it in a warm *Swallows and Amazons* glow. But it would be harder to gain much traction in a Gateshead drop-in centre from recollections of sojourns in the family retreat near Bordeaux, or in the ski chalet which boasts only marginally fewer bedrooms than a Holiday Inn. It is, then, less rags-to-riches than a riches-to-robes story.

One newspaper even felt moved to describe the house on a hill overlooking the hamlet of Curac in South West France as an "imposing ten-bedroom chateau". "Chateau" is coming-it a pinch as Clegg's parents bought the tumbledown farmhouse as a retirement project. Still, now restored, it's not a bad pad: "The house is approached by a long, straight drive bordered by poplar trees which lead to iron gates... By any reckoning it is an impressive pile and one that, were it in England, would undoubtedly fall foul of the Lib Dem's proposed mansion tax on properties worth more than £2 million." Ignoring that the tax was Cable's brainchild, the article concluded: "It is possible Clegg dreamt up the tax while in Curac, splashing about in the pool or strolling through its gardens."

Meanwhile, during the general election voters learned that the chalet contains "20 rooms". Actually it is jointly owned with Dutch relations, and what contradiction it revealed in Clegg wasn't clear. Clegg had never attacked ethically-earned wealth. Nor has he ever "done a Blair" by claiming to be "prolier than thou" (you recall how Blair would tout his membership of the Deaf Hill Working Men's Club and claim—except when in Islington—that his favourite food was fish and chips). If the Clegg stories contained any significance it was probably that those who didn't want Liberal Democrats in power were now worried.

That said, the occasional Clegg flourish can invite teasing, such as the Lib Dem leader's assertion during the campaign that he was "the only one of the three leaders who actually comes from one of our great cities in the North." Even friends have raised a discreet eyebrow when Clegg has extolled "my city of Sheffield". Certainly few voters would sigh mournfully about his father's career in the City. Clegg was clearly aware there were few votes in hailing from a banking clan, or even in having once met a banker, so settled for describing papa as "an old fashioned banker", distancing himself from what Cable calls "casino capitalism".

But Nicholas Clegg CBE was no provincial bank manager, doling out home improvement loans to kindly grannies before slinging some clubs in the back of the Rover and toddling off for a swift nine holes and a snifter at the 19th. He was chairman of United Trust Bank, a major supplier of funding to property developers—suggesting a certain contrast to Nick's life, which includes a masters evaluating "deep green thinking" and addressing environmentalists often opposed to building developments. Clegg snr was also director of Hill Samuel, now a subsidiary of Lloyds TSB and a major vehicle for off-shore private banking: legitimate, but hardly the virtuous capitalism to win plaudits from Mr Cable.

Clegg snr was also chairman of Daiwa Europe Bank PLC, where he worked with the former chancellor Ken Clarke, one of several Tory grandees to help Clegg jnr's march on Downing Street. Indeed, Clarke has told me of his admiration for Clegg jnr and expressed bafflement he isn't a Conservative. During the campaign Clarke suggested Clegg's father was a Tory, before venturing, unkindly, that Clegg snr was disappointed Nick had rejected his "wisdom" and "serious politics". This was not my impression observing a father's pride as he clapped his son at a Liberal Democrat conference. Banking, it seems, is in the blood. Clegg's maternal grandfather was also a banker.

But while Cameron's upbringing included tutorials with Prince Edward followed by Bullingdon Club japery, Clegg's parents did not regard free thought and argument as dangerous or rude. Smartness was measured in brains, not braying. Clegg snr remains intellectually agile and leaves messages on Nick's phone declaring "son, it's your father," before launching into an opinion on a major question. He doesn't expect his boy to agree, but does want him to engage. This interest in ideas provided space for Clegg's later free-thinking liberalism and internationalism.

While the Cleggs may appear the apogee Anglo-Saxon rectitude, they are a product of the great European Diaspora, as war and revolution scattered millions across the continent, with the lucky few finding sanctuary in liberal England. "There is simply not a shred of racism in me," Clegg has said "as a person whose whole family is formed by flight from persecution, from different people in different generations. It's what I am. It's one of the reasons I am a liberal."

His family's history is so chequered it could be from the pages of Chekov, brimming with stories of troubled Russian noblemen brought down by tragedy. "War and revolution have had a huge effect on my family," he has told me, "and certainly affected what we talked about round the kitchen table." This, Clegg has said, also imbued his family with resilience.

During the war his Dutch mother, Hermance van den Wall Bake, had been interned and half starved with her mother Louise and two sisters in a Japanese concentration camp in Jakarta. She had been born in 1936 in Palembang in the Dutch East Indies, now Indonesia, where her father Hemmy worked for Shell. When the Japanese invaded in 1942, a Japanese soldier rounding up the family kicked Louise so hard she developed an ulcer that failed to heal for the war's duration.

After Hemmy was dragged off, the females of the family spent three years incarcerated at Tjideng, regarded as one of the worst Japanese internment camps and "hell on earth." There was scarcely enough food, and what there was Hermance grew too ill to eat. To this day Hermance will not suffer fussiness over meals. Her mother told her later that if the war had dragged on another month, Hermance would not have survived. Through it all they would witness prisoners being beaten to a pulp or dragged into the night.

Hermance never spoke in detail of this to her children, and they only learned the full horror when in 2010 she gave an interview to a Dutch magazine for survivors. "The camp commandant, Sonei, was a cruel lunatic who made us stand on parade for hours, day and night, so we could be counted," she recalled. "We had to make a very deep bow, in the direction of Japan, with our little fingers on the side seams of our skirt. If we didn't do it properly, we were beaten." Her family would squash into a bug-infested bed and dodge open sewers.

"Our worst fear was that we would lose each other,' *Aanspraak* quoted her saying, "so my sister and I were very worried about my mother's tropical ulcers. She was covered with them. For her sake, we would go out early in the mornings and gather cherries that had fallen from the trees in the night. When the war ended she only weighed 36 kilos. I was listless by that time and unable to eat anything at all."

Louise was a powerfully protective presence, insisting her daughter learned to read while prisoners were taken out and shot. Mama even made the girls a dictionary and bartered her already inadequate food supplies for maths lessons.

One of Clegg's Dutch cousins, Frank van den Wall Bake, who sees Clegg when the entire clan enjoys a re-union every five years near Amsterdam, reflects: "The war was a terrible time for the family. The children were with their mother but they could only see their father on the other side of the barbed wire."

At the end of the war Hemmy demanded the guards open the gate and was the first Dutchman in the camp. He scarcely recognised his bed-bound wife.

Frank remarks: "They all survived but Hemmy retained a profound hatred for the Japanese." However, other family figures say his daughter Hermance never expressed bitterness. Indeed, her husband (Nick's father) gained his CBE promoting Anglo-Japanese relations.

Either way, the family's ordeal did not end there. Indonesian freedom-fighters shot at a train of Dutch colonialists as it entered a tunnel. Louise remained granite-cool, telling the girls: "Stay very calm and you won't need so much air." Hemmy took the hint and got his family home, via Cairo, where the Red Cross gave them their first proper tuck in years.

In Holland the family slowly recovered and Hemmy rose to become president of the Dutch banking giant, ABN. The Netherlands re-embraced the clan so tightly the family became friends with Dutch royalty. Hermance uprooted herself again in 1956, travelling to Cambridge, where she intended to pick up English, but instead found a Cambridge undergraduate, Clegg snr. Louise died in 2000, nine years after her husband Hemmy, who is remembered by grandchildren as a veritable giant, full of stories about tiger hunts in the East Indies.

In interviews Clegg casts his mother, a special needs teacher, as no-nonsense Dutch, impatient with class divisions she found in Britain, which glosses over her adult prosperity. Yet no one toils with special needs children and remains oblivious to the travails of those less blessed by the bonus ball lottery of birth. And this social concern was passed to her son. "I became a liberal not in a library, but over the dinner table, in the car, in the park, in conversation with my mum," Clegg has said. He has also remarked: "I'm not going to pretend we sat around the kitchen table mournfully talking about concentration camps and the Bolsheviks. It was a happier childhood than that, but there was this feeling that big things mattered and there was something precious about Britain as a place of liberty and security."

This historical truth was learned first-hand by his ancestors. His paternal grandmother, Kira von Engelhardt, a baroness of Russian, German and Ukrainian extraction, was among White Russians fleeing the Bolshevik revolution for England. Another ancestor, Count Johann von Benckendorff, a tsarist diplomat, was slaughtered by his own serfs on his Estonian estate—a family boast open to few previous Liberal leaders. The count was discovered by the young Kira and her British nanny, a Mrs Wilson, on the path where he had been shot. When Clegg visited Estonia on EU business he went in search of the house by the frozen lake he had heard so much about. The pile survived, as an agricultural college, and Clegg found the path and a monument to the count. Clegg, suited but immersed in snow to his knees, was overcome by emotion.

Kira eventually escaped to England where she became a life-long Liberal and married Nick's grandfather, Hugh. But it was her blood-line that interested a Moscow newspaper, reporting during the general election: "Russian aristocrat wants to be British Prime Minister."

Further back, Clegg's great-great grandfather was a Ukrainian nobleman, Ignaty Zakrevsky, the Imperial Russian senate's attorney general and a leading mason. He travelled to Egypt as ambassador in 1898 and sent home material for a brick pyramid, built in the garden of his estate as a mausoleum.

"He was a man of liberal views and European education," says Valentina Gonchar, who runs a museum in the small village of Berezova Rudka. Tsar Alexander III sacked him from the senate in 1900 after he wrote to *The Times* supporting Alfred Dreyfus, the French officer victim of anti-Semitic prejudice in a notorious miscarriage of justice. It is a stand Clegg would surely admire, though this liberalism did not impress the Bolsheviks when judging his family. "Clegg's family were class enemies," says Gonchar. "Every second aristocrat perished." Zakrevsky at least escaped the gulag. After dying in Cairo in 1906 he was embalmed, brought home and buried in his mausoleum.

The ancestor who really intrigues is his great-great aunt, Baroness Moura Budburg, whose "unbelievably feline" beauty and advanced attitudes to sex captivated half the great figures of Europe. In Clegg's Wikipedia entry she is referred to as a "writer", which is like calling Winston Churchill a bricklayer, or Albert Camus a goalkeeper; factually true, but hiding a rather more interesting life behind thick, billowy curtains.

Her accomplishments included stints as KGB spy and lover of H.G. Wells. She may also have spied for Britain, and even Nazi Germany. Over a 40 year career this alleged super-sleuth is said to have herself been spied on by virtually every security service in Europe. All we know for sure, courtesy of British documents released in 2002, is that as early as 1922 spooks deemed her a Soviet agent. Meanwhile, the British embassy described her as "a very dangerous woman".

Dangerous in a fun way, too, fitting in affairs with Maxim Gorky and Robert Bruce Lockhart, the celebrated British spy. An old-fashioned sort, Bruce Lockhart managed to conduct his espionage entirely for his own side. His romance with Moura inspired the 1934 film *British Agent.*

As the starting pistol was fired on the Russian revolution, she was a dilettante of 25, daughter of an Anglophile tsarist politician and married to a Russian diplomat, Johann von Benckendorff. When he fled, abandoning her in St Petersburg with her terminally ill mother, she had to rely on her guile and mastery of several languages—not so very different from the young Clegg, perhaps.

Bruce Lockhart, erroneously described as inspiration for James Bond, was the apogee of the dashing spy. He visited Russia in 1918, either to destabilise the Bolsheviks or lure them back into the war. There was also suspicion he was behind an assassination attempt on Lenin. Whatever his mission, he began an affair with Moura. One allegation is she then joined the Cheka, forerunner of the KGB, and betrayed her lover.

By that summer the couple were sharing a flat in Moscow while tsarists fled and streets flared. The Bolshevik boot was coming down on dissenters with thudding force. In September Bruce Lockhart was arrested—according to some accounts, while he lay in bed with Moura—and held in the Kremlin, accused of organising a counter-revolution. Moura was also hauled in and interrogated by Yakov Peters, deputy head of the Cheka who Moura likened to "Dracula". She later claimed he threatened to have her shot in 24 hours unless she told him everything. She claimed to have replied: "All I can talk about is Lockhart's sexual prowess. I don't know anything else."

Given her response, frank for the time, it is hardly surprising a trade was agreed: he gave her a visa, she gave him herself. Peters then brought her back to see Bruce Lockhart in his cell, presumably to tease a confession. Instead Moura signalled and slipped a note in one of Bruce Lockhart's books: "say nothing and all will be well." Bruce Lockhart recorded how her visit filled him with hope, but it was his reporting of it—and in particular her companion—that led British authorities to suspect her.

Soviet files suggest that if she was working for anyone then, the Russians thought it probably the British, but that her involvement was at most minimal. However, consorting with a notorious spy and possibly introducing him to dissidents left her compromised.

Bruce Lockhart was eventually swapped for the Soviet ambassador in London. But Moura had already moved on to the writer Gorky, his reputation tarnished as a mouthpiece for the regime. He observed: "She knows everything, and is interested in everything." This curiosity certainly applied to powerful men.

After he introduced her to Lenin and Stalin, she befriended both, giving the latter an accordion.

But was her brush with Bolshevik nomenklatura this innocent? The Russian novelist Nina Berberova, who shared a house with Gorky and was quite possibly jealous, later claimed Moura stole a suitcase of incriminating letters written to Gorky by Lenin's opponents, including Trotsky and Bukharin. If Moura really was complicit in the purges that followed it would place her well beyond the moral pale of even the most indulgent nephew. However, both KGB and Gorky archives contain nothing to support the allegation and it seems unlikely such a potentially bountiful cache would go unrecorded.

But the story doesn't end there. Clegg's first cousin Dimitri Collingridge, who has researched Budburg's history, suggests she was in contact with Genrikh Yagoda, notorious for helping organise purges. A former KGB official paid by Collingridge to fish in the murky waters of historical Soviet secret service files produced documents suggesting Moura had been in contact with Yagoda, and used his offices to gain visas.

Collingridge speculates she might have provided information on Gorky's circle, pointing out she would have needed to offer something. Undeniably she aroused as much suspicion as ardour. After Collingridge examined her MI5 file at the Public Records Office in Kew, he remarked: "The entries run from 1921 to 1952. Words jumped out: 'Double agent for the Bolsheviks and Germans in 1922-31... July 1941: Nazi agent... November 1942: instigator of plot to remove General de Gaulle as head of the Free French Movement... July 1951: Soviet agent.'"

Moura spent the thirties in London with Wells and grew as immersed in his circle as she had in Gorky's. He put a kinder interpretation on her machinations, suggesting she harboured sensitive information to protect friends. But her secret visits to the ageing Gorky in Russia would leave Wells infuriated—even though his grounds for outrage were not strong, as Gorky had introduced them while the Russian was still with Moura. When Somerset Maugham asked Moura what she saw in the "clapped-out" Gorky, nearly 30 years her senior, she cooed: "He smells of honey."

As for Wells, he was spellbound: "She was wearing an old khaki British army waterproof and shabby black dress; her only hat was some twisted-up piece of black—a stocking, I think—and yet she had magnificence."

In between great men and gruesome events she married an Estonian playboy, Baron Nikolai Budberg, who, though handsome, was a gambling-fixated wastrel. It didn't take her long to dispense with the husband, even if she took better care of the title.

While it is easy to cast her as a Mata Hari figure, she is more interesting than the *femme fatale* of cheap fiction. For surface beauty was combined with intellectual depth, reflected in her later writings. She was not a great one for rouge and scent; her costumes were frequently ad-hoc affairs, thrown together from fragments. Virtually all men she was linked with were exceptional, delighted to find a woman who dared provide mental as well as physical stimulation.

Moscow was a dangerous place for aristocratic revolutionaries, but London has always secretly enjoyed socialist socialites. Here she blossomed, dispensing stiff vodka-based cocktails and "cheeselets" from her Kensington flat in Ennismore Gardens, where she held a salon every evening. A Russian Orthodox church, centre of much intrigue through the Cold War, shared her street. She remained under suspicion of British intelligence until the fifties and was followed frequently, though nothing more incriminating was discovered than a penchant for shopping and drinking. This prompted much security debate over whether the vast surveillance bill was necessary. "She drinks like a fish — gin," noted one report, almost admiringly, contriving to err even about her preferred tipple. "She can drink an amazing quantity without showing any slow-up in her mental processes."

One officer was alarmed to note that a frequent visitor was Guy Burgess, though the agent drew spectacularly muddled conclusions, noting with as much pomposity as unintentional hilarity that Moura was "not a desirable acquaintance for someone of his character".

She was interviewed by Peter Ustinov's father, the British agent

Jona Ustinov, who in the cosy way of the times was a friend. During this exchange she denounced Anthony Blunt, keeper of the queen's pictures, as a member of the Communist Party—12 years before the security services suspected. "Such things only happen in England," she said of Blunt's dual role, a truth later mined with comic genius by Alan Bennett in *A Question of Attribution*. Her claim was dismissed as she was not viewed as "sufficiently reliable". Her friend John Julius Norris said he "adored" her, though found her stories as wildly extravagant as they were entertaining. She claimed to have been present at Rasputin's death, and even suggested rats sung to her while in prison. Given this exuberance perhaps we can understand in part the scepticism of the sleuths.

Quite what Moura's motives were in denouncing Blunt remain cloudy. Collingridge suspects her guiding principle was expediency, so to embark on some search for the source of her ultimate loyalty would be futile. Clegg's father bristles at suggestions there was anything terribly wicked about her.

Certainly her *Times* obituary of 1974 was warm: "This fantastic woman was unique. For nearly four decades she was in the centre of London's intellectual, social and artistic life." She had variously written, translated, acted and advised on films, but what fascinates is her quite extraordinary ability to build the least likely of coalitions.

Clegg was seven when Moura died. At their last meeting she fixed on him the same eye that had trained on Lenin, Stalin, Bruce Lockhart, Gorky, Wells and Burges. "Boy," she appraised him. "You mumble too much." Given her alarming presence, the boy could probably have been forgiven.

This exotic clan blew into the sturdily English Clegg family through the marriage of Moura's niece, Baroness Kira von Engelhardt, to Hugh Clegg in 1932. Hugh was Nick's grandfather who went on to edit the *British Medical Journal* (*BMJ*) for 35 years. Kira, like Moura, harboured intriguing ambiguities. Most genealogists contend she was born in Russia, but there are also documents signed in her hand suggesting the warmer breezes of Nice. One form also states she was born in 1918 rather than 1909, improbably rendering her 14 at the time of her marriage. She and her two children left England during the Blitz for Canada but returned. She died in London's Hammersmith in 2005.

Hugh Clegg was the third son of a Huntingdonshire clergyman and headmaster. After attending his father's school in Lowerstoft, St Ives Grammar, Hugh progressed to Westminster, before gaining an exhibition to Cambridge—a route his grandson was to follow. Hugh later became a senior scholar at his old college, Trinity, and possessed a stellar mind, taking a first in natural sciences before entering St Bart's for clinical training. He rose to become registrar at Charing Cross Hospital with a special interest in chests, but joined the *BMJ* in 1931.

By the outbreak of war, Clegg had become *de facto* editor, just when medical provision was growing political. During the writing and implementation of the Beveridge Report which led to the formation of the full NHS, Clegg's leading articles were, according to his obituary, "widely regarded as the authentic voice of medicine." Impressive, this, as half way through writing he often had to duck into an air-raid shelter. Beveridge was a Liberal who believed the NHS would be unaffordable unless individuals made contributions. He also warned against it becoming a Whitehall run Leviathan. Fittingly these arguments were revived in controversial fashion more than half a century later by Nick Clegg's friend, David Laws, in *The Orange Book,* a collection of essays which inspired the party's intellectual revival. Less well-read politicians than Laws and Clegg frequently discuss these ideas as if they were "new", but they would have sounded eminently familiar to Hugh Clegg. However, there has been debate over which side of the argument on NHS reorganisation this Clegg would now sit. The *BMJ* defended consultants who, controversially, won the right to treat private patients in NHS beds. Clegg snr reputedly told one medical writer that he might be more comfortable at the *Lancet,* as it was more "left wing".

Hugh also wrote many of those stirring "pull your socks up" wartime propaganda booklets, now re-published as Christmas stocking fillers for humorous effect. One was called *How to Keep Well in Wartime.* Of more lasting significance, perhaps, were the two major reports he crafted for the Royal College of Physicians in 1971 and 1977, the first official attempts to face the medical damage caused by smoking.

Though a portrait depicts Hugh Clegg as slightly austere, there is more than a little of him in Nick. The *BMJ* obit avers that Hugh saw his weekly publication as a "vehicle for the free expression of thought for members of a liberal profession." He was praised for both "organisational ability" and innovative thinking, a rare combination (his use of statistical analysis when contributors favoured rhetoric was considered radical). His internationalist outlook showed when he helped establish the World Medical Association. Its Declaration of Helsinki set out agreed principles on ethics in medical experimentation. Another colleague remarked: "He was dedicated to the belief that through the exchange of ideas medicine as a humanitarian calling was peculiarly fitted to transcend national and ethnic boundaries." Replace "medicine" with "politics" and that's pure Nick Clegg.

After Hugh stepped down in 1965, the Royal Society of Medicine invited him to set up an office to spread medical findings around the Commonwealth. He resigned when his ambitious plans for expansion were rejected. However, colleagues also reported that "occasionally he courted trouble unnecessarily".

Another concluded: "Hugh was a fighter. He would attack anything or anyone who seemed to threaten [the *BMJ* or medicine]—whether strikes by printers, Ministry mandarins, or the bumbling in-consequences of committee men. At close quarters he was knowledgeable and often wickedly amusing, though not always easy to work with. His stature was undoubted." You don't need great foresight to predict the grandson's obituary will one day brim with similar reflections.

While Hugh's son went into banking, his daughter became a doctor. And so Nick's father bought a large house near Chalfont St Giles, Buckinghamshire. This was the posher end of Julian Barnes's *Metroland*, where the middle class could enjoy country cream while earning City crusts. It is a well-fed patch. A neighbour who, usefully for Nick's later career, became a family friend was Lord Carrington.

Incidentally, legend has it that as Foreign Secretary Carrington only made one visit to Chevening—now Clegg's official country residence—because it was apparently smaller than his own house.

Metroland was a starchy place for a future radical, a "gin and Jag" stretch of the Home Counties. *Midsomer Murders* was filmed locally. The Tory statesman Disraeli derived his earldom from neighbouring Beaconsfield, and Bucks is in the very bosom of Conservatism. Yet perhaps it is not entirely barren for budding Liberals.

This is the area where John Milton wrote *Paradise Lost*, one of the great tracts of British Liberalism. His *Areopagitica* is an argument against censorship, as sweetly phrased as it is argued:

> … as good almost kill a Man as kill a good Book; who kills a Man kills a reasonable creature, Gods Image; but hee who destroyes a good Booke, kills reason it selfe, kills the Image of God, as it were in the eye. Many a man lives a burden to the Earth; but a good Booke is the pretious life-blood of a master spirit, imbalm'd and treasur'd up on purpose to a life beyond life.

It was one of the old Liberal Party's more touching traditions that an increasingly battered copy of the *Areopagitica* was handed to the incoming party president. Milton also argued people should be able to print what they liked in a powerful call for a free press.

A further Liberal hero from the otherwise Tory-voting commuter village was William Penn, who established Pennsylvania and is buried at the local Quaker meeting house. President Reagan said of him: "William Penn, as a British citizen, founded the Commonwealth of Pennsylvania in order to carry out an experiment based upon representative government; public education without regard to race, creed, sex, or ability to pay; and the substitution of workhouses for prisons. He had a Quaker's deep faith in divine guidance, and as the leader of the new colony, he worked to protect rights of personal conscience and freedom of religion. The principles of religious freedom he espoused helped to lay the groundwork for the First Amendment of our Constitution."

The Cleggs originate from Yorkshire, which was handy for Clegg when he ran for a Sheffield seat. This branch was decidedly less grand than the Russian side. It also tended to be more upstanding, and so less interesting. The only possible fall from respectability was a Gertrude Wilson—born Hull, 1861—who was "illegitimate". A Simeon Clegg was a butcher from Bramley in Yorkshire, born in 1844. Other ancestors included master joiners, mariners and a collier, mainly from that fine, no nonsense county.

The family's bloodline was transformed dramatically, first by its Russian, then Dutch and now Spanish infusion. Even the Christian name of Nick's father is actually the Russian "Nicolas" without the "h". "Nickje", like generations of Cleggs, was known at school as "Clog".

It is the foreign fruit that provides the richer pickings for the biographer, particularly the Russian family tree. In the wake of the Bolshevik revolution Clegg's ancestors fled to Luxembourg, France, Germany and America. Budberg's daughter Tania published a memoir *A Little of All These*, quoting the line from Hermann Keyserling: "I am not a Dane, not a German, not a Swede, not a Russian nor an Estonian, so what am I? A little of all these." Such little parts form a large part of Clegg.

Given the family diaspora, it seems inconceivable the Deputy Prime Minister could be anything but an internationalist. It is probably why arguments about integrated transport networks will, to him, always be secondary. Questions that raise his passions on a platform are about freeing people from persecution, and the role Europe can play in ensuring a more secure future for its citizens after a bloody past.

When you know a little of his family's story, Clegg's Liberalism looks less an aberration, more an inevitability. How could this European possibly have become a Little Englander?

"Only in England," ventured his great, great aunt.

"Only in Europe," the great, great nephew has replied.

Clegg's family could be accused of much, no doubt, but scarcely of being dull.

2

AN ABUSE OF POWER?

"Come friendly bombs, and fall on Slough." Betjeman's entreaty might well have been chanted by the more literate pupils of nearby Caldicott, where Clegg arrived in 1975. Superficially, life for boys at this most privileged of preps could scarcely have been more gilded. Other old boys include Andrew Strauss, captain of the England cricket team, Ernest Saunders, one of the "Guinness Four", Ed Stoppard, actor, Adrian Jarvis, England rugby player, and Sir Alistair Buchanan, CEO of Ofgem.

It was and remains a feeder to Eton, where Clegg's contemporaries went on to find Cameron and much of the future Conservative front bench. Caldicott's headmaster Simon Doggart is a former Eton beak. Sports days are described as "Ascot-esque" with smart cars, elegant mothers and lavish picnics. While just 20 miles from London the school enjoys 40 acres and facilities to leave state school kids wondering if they had landed on Mars. It was convenient for the Cleggs, being a short drive from their house, and so Nick became a dayboy until boarding became compulsory in the final year. It was renowned for its sporting prowess, and Clegg excelled in school teams for tennis and rugby, even turning out in a match at Twickenham as flanker.

But some old boys insist all that gilt hid a very guilty secret. In 2008 a More4 documentary, *Chosen*, claimed the school had been in the grip of a paedophile ring that ran from the late 1960s through the1970s. It is one of the most harrowing pieces of television I've seen, and it described the school to which Clegg was entrusted aged seven. Few have made the link between the school and the Deputy Prime Minister, and there is no suggestion Clegg was abused.

Still, if these historic allegations were not black-mark enough against the school, the *Guardian* further alleged that Doggart and Lord Justice Scott Baker, former chairman of governors, did too little to deal with later allegations of sexual abuse in the early 2000s.

Not that you would gain any sense of this from Caldicott's website, chirruping with glowing write-ups in *Tatler* and good school guides. It announces: "Our philosophy... is to provide a warm and supportive environment in which a boy can flourish and grow academically and personally, and where everybody feels they are fully valued." Prospective parents are told who won the long jump and how Oriental cuisine has found its way onto the menu, but not, strangely, that the boarding school to which they might send their precious young had for long periods been the centre of allegations of sickening sexual and emotional abuse—abuse described to me as "ritualised and institutionalised".

During the film, five former pupils, by then middle aged, alleged staff subjected them to a curriculum of harm, including rape. The accused included Peter Wright, who not only owned the school but was head teacher from 1968 until retirement in 1993. In 2003 Wright was charged with 13 counts of sexual abuse and three of gross indecency. However, a judge ruled he could not assure Wright of a fair trial due to the passage of time. Some alleged abuse was said to have been committed by Wright, a former pupil of the school, when boys brought him early morning tea. He was also accused of trawling dormitories at night and inviting to his study "favourites". These, it was claimed, tended to be successful sportsmen, given elaborate uniforms and singled out for "treats", such as rides in his stable of sports cars. One alleged victim spoke in emotional, tearful terms of how the alleged abuse had left deep psychological scars that have never healed. Other perpetrators were said to be a few teachers employed by Wright.

These serious allegations notwithstanding, Wright retired to live opposite the school, where he is thought to remain, and was apparently asked to refrain from walking the grounds through a gap in a fence.

John Clare, later distinguished education correspondent for the *Daily Telegraph* who taught briefly at the school, concluded: "Naturally [Wright] must be presumed innocent. But I believe there was a case to answer and—like the five claimants—regret the judge decided a jury should not be allowed to hear it."

Following the film, more former pupils came forward. After a three year investigation by Thames Valley Police the Crown Prosecution Service is deciding whether to lay fresh charges. However, it received the file in January 2011, and time ticks slowly like a grandfather clock in a study no one enters. "If we don't get justice through the courts we will track these people down ourselves," one former pupil has even ventured. "It's very easy in the internet age. Some abusers are still leading respectable lives with wives and careers. Their neighbours should know they are living next to a paedophile."

The fight of these troubled souls to challenge what they think happened has been tortuous and disturbing, the anguish visible on the face of each man interviewed in the film. Yet other former pupils have reacted angrily, insisting there was no abuse. Arguments have flared—on one occasion during a chance encounter in a supermarket; once between two mothers in the school car park. Claimed victims have said past pupils have "lived a lie, not even telling partners". In one case it apparently took two years of repeated requests from a former pupil before police consented to take a statement. Further, police are understood to view evidence of alleged victims who have discussed their situation with fellow "Caldicottians" as "tainted". Yet it is difficult to see how, if campaigners had not actively sought other pupils, the CPS would have had a police investigation to ponder.

The testimony of former pupils could form a separate large volume, though none will be named for fear of prejudicing a possible trial. If they could speak, their testimony would include claims of crushed lives but also of fragile hope as some apparent victims have worked manfully towards recovery. Among them is a school friend of Clegg's. One alleged victim became a heroin addict who was passed, unrecognised, by his own mother as he sat begging in the street.

The fall-out has also set off emotional avalanches within families as old boys face ("confront" they now say) what happened. Despite growing awareness—some would say hysteria—about paedophilia, one parent told by her son years later that he believed he was abused immediately asked: "you aren't going to do anything with this information, are you?" If the allegations are found to be true the boys could never have been anything but victims, but there lingers, it seems, a stigma; a stigma alleged culprits apparently shifted to the innocent. If so, perhaps this would be the greatest abuse of all.

A now grown-man has said: "It was not just the children who were groomed, but parents." Wright, it has been claimed, would lavish attention and hospitality on parents, which some former pupils have insisted was part of his plan to win trust. He, no doubt, would say he was being a conscientious headmaster. One boy who did apparently complain of inappropriate behaviour was allegedly punched by his father for telling lies.

To triple underline, nobody I have identified has reason to believe Clegg was a victim, but the merest association of this sort renders his upbringing less picturesque than it might have appeared.

"Anyone who escaped abuse was lucky," one former pupil has said. "This was the environment in which Clegg was a pretty pupil who was good at tennis." The pupil had left the school by the time Clegg arrived, so this can only be taken as a general comment. As well as conceding he has no information to suggest Clegg was among them, his case against Wright and other teachers has never been proved, or even heard.

The rugby team was, according to some old boys, one of Wright's great passions. He would throw lavish dinners, where players' names were artfully worked into the menu. "It was all part of making boys feel special," one reports.

Wright, it is alleged, was not the only master to follow the progress of the rugby team closely, on and off the field of play. According to another who declines to be named, a master—no longer alive—would, during Clegg's time, make boys line up naked after rugby. They would then be told to enter a "plunge" pool. Yet the boys, supposedly, were made to feel this was "normal". One claims that certain boys were, according to a rota, taken by the master to be bathed in his private quarters. "I was rotated to be raped," one has insisted, almost matter-of-factly.

But, the old boy has contended, no one knew if others were abused because it was—allegedly—done in secret, one on one: each victim made to feel "chosen" and sworn to secrecy.

One, who describes himself as both a "good friend" of Clegg's at the school and a victim of sexual abuse, has made the important point that Clegg's silence in adulthood is entirely understandable: "If Nick wasn't abused himself he wouldn't know about abuse of others." This well-placed source has also confirmed he has no reason to believe Clegg was abused, and that the future leader never spoke of it.

Those allegedly less fortunate have finally spoken. The question now is whether the authorities have chosen to hear them.

Clegg's only public comment on the school is that it was "stiflingly conventional". This is not thought to have hindered his progress to becoming Head Prefect. However, Clegg had a reputation for cheekiness and questioning authority. Regardless of the allegations it was an authority that certainly needed questioning, with one master lapsing into parody, announcing the world would end by Christmas due to the Soviet peril.

Having written of such disturbing matters in preceding pages it seems trite to skate on to other aspects of Clegg's school career. The following will sound necessarily trivial.

"He might have been privileged but he was also very aware socially, both inside and outside the school," recalls Ian McFadyen, who works in a shelter in Edinburgh. "He was very thoughtful and creative. He was involved in the debating society. Nick was very sociable, being a member of the rugby team yet also theatrical." Among the plays he performed in, I'm told, was that Russian masterpiece about political intrigue, *The Government Inspector*.

"He was certainly very popular, I really liked him," says

McFadyen, who lost touch when the boys were sent to different public schools. This popularity might have been enhanced by "Dutch liquorice" from Clegg's mother. McFadyen concludes: "He was very quick, far too academic for Caldicott really. Westminster was more his speed."

And so, aged 13, Master Clegg was packed off to an enclave of London that would define his adult life. His parents had moved further afield to an exquisite house in rural Oxfordshire, so Clegg was sent as a weekly border. He found it a profound change and felt something of an *ingénue*, never having spent a night in London before.

Westminster School is as arcane, and thus expensive, as Eton. Fees nudge £30,000 a year, way above the average national salary. It was founded in the 11th century but has grown adept at navigating our more vulgar world. In 2005 *The Times* revealed it to be operating a price-fixing cartel, and even now it boasts the second highest acceptance rate to Oxbridge, while it frequently tops the *Financial Times* chart as Britain's best school.

However, among the monied children it selects, it values brain power over blood lines, further explaining subtle cultural differences with Old Etonian Cameron. As well as a veritable flotilla of Whig prime ministers, Westminster launched two philosophers: John Locke, that giant of the Enlightenment, and Jeremy Bentham, who gave us Utilitarianism. They are, simply, the two intellectual pillars of Liberalism.

Not that this legacy was the principle concern of young Clegg. Contemporaries report no sign of trauma from Caldicott. Indeed, the only prep school legacy appears to have been a passion for tennis, displaying a "stylish forehand" topped with a dangerous and cleverly disguised spin.

However, his team captain dropped him from a crucial match. "When it came to gritty competitive sport, Nick lacked the killer instinct," insists Edward Roussel, digital editor at the *Telegraph*. "He was the nice guy of the team and no match for a fiercely competitive group that included Michael Sherwood, now co-CEO of Goldman Sachs Europe, Gavin Rossdale, lead singer of rock band Bush, and Alex Michaelis, one of our top architects."

Academically, it was different. Roussel says Clegg declined to play the popular Westminster game of pretending it came easy: "He was overtly academic: a disciplined teenager, fluent seemingly in all known languages, who completed his homework on time. What Nick lacked in grit on the tennis court, he made up for in the classroom."

Yet he was not quite a model pupil. It was on a 1983 exchange to Germany aged 16—by when he could speak five languages—that Clegg grew drunk and burnt to a prickly cinder Germany's premier collection of cacti. The outrage apparently made front page local news, and he has said he was forced to undergo community service, digging gardens. He has since recounted the story at meetings amid considerable tittering, while insisting it's "not something I'm proud of". He tells the story with panache, down to how the cacti "began to glow rather beautifully" and his mother making him traipse round garden centres in search of obscure cacti to replenish the depleted stock of one very distraught German professor. However, the *Daily Mail* suggested after an exhaustive investigation that Clegg might have embellished the story. Richard Stokes, who taught Clegg German and was on the trip to Munich, says Clegg simply "singed four or five" cacti and that it was no great deal.

Whatever, Clegg is hardly guilty of a widespread re-writing of his history. This is not on a par with the fictional genius Jeffrey Archer exhibited, at least when writing his CV. Nor can it match the entirely un-corroborated story from Tony Blair that as a youth he snuck on an aeroplane bound for the Caribbean.

But like Blair, Clegg learned an invaluable lesson young, that if you are sufficiently confident to send yourself up, you will find an appreciative audience. Clegg will ruefully recall a youthful TV appearance on which two panellists fell asleep on him.

As well as tennis and languages, Clegg was steered towards acting to help overcome shyness. It became "a great love", rendered more exciting by Westminster's acceptance in the sixth form of a curious breed, provisionally classified as "girls".

For Clegg performed opposite a young woman of such porcelain beauty she might have been from a Victorian portrait. Helena Bonham-Carter, product of one of the great Liberal families, can be seen in a school photo standing yards from Clegg. She was to grow even more intimate with the future Deputy Prime Minister in *The Changeling*, when she was required to boot him between the legs, prompting him to collapse in feigned agony. "We got it down to a fairly fine art of her missing the crown jewels, so to speak," Clegg has recalled. "But once, she got it spot-on, and no acting was required."

While in Clegg's house, Liddell's, the future *Room with a View* actress was already gracing the London stage. Not that this seemed as glamorous to young Nick as it might, for also in his house were the sons of Ridley Scott and Sam Spiegel.

If acting was a "great love", it was not his greatest. He has admitted to me that one of his most embarrassing memories that still makes him squirm was publishing, aged 17, a poem of "infatuation" in his school magazine, *The Elizabethan*. I reprint it below, with apologies:

> *My love blasted you from my mind*
> >*Your skin too silken to be seen*
> *Your voice slipping through my brain*
> >*Your movements fluttering from within.*
> *But now. Yes, I can see you now,*
> >*Too dumb, squatted in my eyes,*
> *Poisoned like a dying pearl,*
> >*A killer's vengeance—twisted.*

With its bitter last lines, one hopes its object was not Corisande Albert, Clegg's first serious girlfriend who continued to date Clegg in an on/off way through university, and who remains a close friend.

"She has been an important figure in Nick's life," a mutual friend tells me "and over a number of years. She has always been very sympathetic to him." As for the poem, the friend says: "Nick would undoubtedly have had the piss ripped out of him."

The source recalls that Clegg loitered in "yard", a quad at the school's heart, in hope of *faux* casually bumping into her. Other objects of attention—for this was how teenage boys saw girls—included Imogen Stubbs. Clearly standards were high as "Helena [Bonham-Carter] was considered too eccentric to be really desirable."

After a gruelling campaign, Clegg apparently triumphed with Corisande. By happy coincidence she was also sister of Justin Albert, chosen in place of Clegg for that crucial tennis fixture against Ashburnham.

"She was probably more attractive than Nick," says one contemporary, a little unkindly. "Corisande was considered a real catch."

The Alberts gained a reputation for throwing the "wildest" and "biggest and best" parties of all Westminster's sixth-formers, and it was "quite a surprise" when Nick suddenly started showing up. Other guests were "very well heeled", often with familiar last names.

These gatherings were held at weekends, either at the family's massive house on Holland Park, later bought by Richard Branson, or the Albert's rambling Victorian farmhouse near Hay, where the family farm. Corisande's American father was a hugely successful international lawyer, while her mother, Revel Guest, is a distinguished documentary maker and major figure at the Hay Festival. She also owns the film rights to *War Horse*, the acclaimed book and West End play being turned into a film by Steven Spielberg. Guest's father was Oscar Guest, once a Liberal MP who was colleague and cousin of Winston Churchill. Another twist: Revel Guest's first job was secretary to then-Liberal leader, Jo Grimond, before she later stood for the Conservatives. Her values clearly remained sympathetic to the internationalism so beloved of Liberals, working for the European Movement before making documentaries about major political figures of the day.

Little wonder Clegg gravitated to the house. However, his behaviour was tame compared to contemporaries.

"These well-behaved children would suddenly go wild," one recalls. "Yet while some would be in the studio in the basement snogging, Nick would be in the living room being very civil. His conversation didn't have much gossip, more about the Shakespeare play he was in. I don't remember him doing drugs at school. Corisande was a day girl, but at the Albert's house there was no shortage of rooms to elope to..."

Amid all these well connected kids it was, a friend reports, noticeable "Nick wasn't snobbish. I think snobbery passed him by. Because of his cultural background he just didn't get that. It's probably not coincidental that he chose a girlfriend who was half American, half Welsh."

Clegg was entrusted by Dave Brown, Liddell's house master who has been described as "laissez faire", to help with house discipline. Clegg would patrol what was known as "billionaire's dorm", whose valuable cargo included Toby Rowland, son of "Tiny", Garth Weston of the Fortnum and Mason dynasty, and Mark Sainsbury, from another superior breed of grocer.

Displaying handy qualities for a future Liberal Democrat leader, Clegg was tricky to pigeon-hole, yet popular. To the question "what was he like?" even eloquent contemporaries murmur "I couldn't say, exactly." Sainsbury, for instance, tells me: "He was my head of house and a really decent and kind one at that. [But] I really don't have anything amusing or interesting on Nick. For whatever reason, he wasn't that memorable as a school chum."

Clegg was not considered cool, but was accepted by those who were. His friend Marcel Theroux recalls him being "quite proud he wasn't a follower of fashion, which took some doing because it was a trendy, knowing school. He wore cords and Kickers, but all the hard lads liked Nick and didn't care that he wore these silly shoes.

"And he was quite cheeky to teachers. He'd just look them in the eye, make jokes to them — and teachers love that."

Others, betraying the suspicion of intellectualism that can mark the public school man, talk of Clegg as a "kind of swat" and "slightly bland". Says one: "He was the guy who spoke Dutch and the suspicion was that he actually was a bit Dutch in a school that was very glamorous, where it was viewed as more important to be in a rock band than to get, as Nick had, As in all his subjects. But he was very thoughtful in the way he expressed himself."

One schoolmate who doesn't share these reminiscences of cloudy rosiness is, Clegg has told me, the character who claimed to have been bullied by him. These allegations were, to Clegg's fury, posted online, though they went unnoticed. Clegg insists he was traduced, and has no recollection of the individual. For a while it even made him wary of the internet, that flowering of liberal, free expression first championed by Ashdown. Certainly in adult life Clegg has made a point of campaigning against bullying. Clegg would also have been aware that public school bullies rarely win popularity contests. Cameron was damaged when Martin Ivens of the *Sunday Times* compared the Tory leader to Flashman, who liked to roast his fag in a spit over an inglenook fire.

As a footnote to this curious story, I understand the *Daily Telegraph*, looking for "interesting" material on Clegg, was contacted by a "fabulously rich" individual claiming to have been bullied by Clegg at school, but after sending a reporter to interview him, the editor decided the story "didn't stack up", and declined to run it.

"The claims seemed quite flaky," says an executive on the newspaper. "And it didn't square with memories of contemporaries."

Which leads to another awkward claim about Clegg's schooldays, made during the election: "I was Liberal leader's fag," was the headline, a potentially ruinous claim in Liberal circles. In fact, the suggestion was mooted by Louis Theroux, documentary maker and brother of Marcel, that at Westminster (school, not parliament) he was forced to wake Clegg with the morning papers: "People sleep in different ways," said Theroux, "and with Nick Clegg, the thing was he was a very deep sleeper. I would bend over him and kind of push him." Clegg, perhaps conveniently, has no recollection of these mornings. Certainly such draconian practices were reaching their, well, fag end. But this is the school which once had a ritual, "Light and Fire", whereby juniors had to rouse their senior every half hour from 3.30 am until he deigned to rise. Until recently boys were required to bring toast to elders, doff mortarboards to teachers and hold flaming torches to mark the route from school to Abbey.

Certainly in earlier years it was an austere, ecclesiastical place. One headmaster, a Dr Busby, was as noted for his belief in the birch as the classics, and was the inspiration, if that it be, for Pope's *Dunciad*. Still, he is said to have been scrupulously fair, thrashing royalist and puritan boy with impressive impartiality. Tellingly, Matthew Arnold's Victorian notions of team building in place of individual endeavour never caught on at Westminster. It had, then, a competitive ethos undimmed by the mildly modernising reforms of Dr John Rae, the school's renowned headmaster in the time of Clegg.

Despite Theroux's helpful reminiscences, Clegg was more thespian than disciplinarian, and found the necessary freedom at Westminster. Dominic Lawson has written of his relief arriving at Westminster after Eton: "Both are ancient foundations that began as charitable institutions for poor scholars but which, while still selecting on the basis of an entrance exam, now charge fees far beyond most families. Both have a private language that seems designed to create a sense of otherness. Yet they are a world apart from each other, as well. Eton is a country boarding school; the majority of Westminster's pupils are London commuters. Eton is for boys only; Westminster takes girls from the sixth form... At Eton boys wear tails; at Westminster... they don't. Social acceptability at Eton is won most easily by... 'old money'; at Westminster the only aristocracy is of the intellect. Above all, Eton teaches pupils how to conform to a particular notion of the civilised English gentleman; Westminster treasures the rebarbative individualist who challenges consensus."

No wonder it suited the singular Clegg, who stood out against the herd. He was pale, often angst-ridden over a romantic adventure or forthcoming play, and exhausted from staying up late working. Also, he was already addicted to cigarettes, contrary to school rules.

Yet there was nothing which suggested Clegg's career. "I don't recall any particular interest in politics," says an old boy. "With Helena it was blindingly obvious she was to be an actress. It wasn't so clear with Nick."

Thanks to natural intelligence, a privileged education and hard work he won a place at Robinson College, Cambridge, to read social anthropology. His choice was telling. Already he had encountered enough characters—some touched with greatness, others possibly by wickedness—to make him realise the enormity of his subject. And here at least was a clue to his future, for Clegg's interest in people has been central to his success.

Cartoonists have picked up on Clegg's habit of shoving a hand in pocket: a nonchalant gesture left from the too-clever-for-school teenager, indicative of a still youthful politician not fussed by form. Natural or studied, it was a look that would win him rave notices.

3

THIRTY LOVE

No Deputy Prime Minister had ever described himself as a former "ski bum", but that is how Clegg once characterised his gap-year self to me. Actually, from little remarks I sensed he had been quite diligent as an instructor in Hochfügen, in Austria's Tyrolean Zillertal. When I laughed at the unsuitability of such a first job, Clegg pointed out that it could scarcely have been more dutiful as he was confined to the nursery slopes "by a little hut decorated with pictures of Disney characters. Every time a child wanted to go to the loo, which was often, I couldn't leave anyone so I had to trudge the entire class across this snow field. It was a nightmare."

But greater torture was to come. One evening he was involved in a race with fellow instructors and took off over a treacherous gully. To his horror he saw a line of children below, so in avoiding them was hurled towards a tree. He ended in a mangled heap, unconscious and with a leg wrenched from its hip socket. A helicopter couldn't land so after a couple of freezing hours on ice he was bundled onto a snow plough, his leg dangling uselessly, and sped to hospital. He spent three months in plaster, feeling depressed and nursing himself through one of his break-ups with Corisande. It was during the miserable convalescence he took up transcendental meditation and attempted to write a novel, which he told me he discovered year later and found "embarrassing and unreadable".

Due to the accident he will need a hip replaced, and in winter complains of "gyp". But, after recovering, he took a brief internship in a Helsinki bank, helped by paternal connections—which came back to embarrass him in 2011 when he criticised the culture of work experience on the back of the old boy network. Helpfully, a Labour MP rose to ask if Clegg's conversion owed anything to his youthful experiences. Actually, this stint achieved little bar improving his coffee making technique, though a weekend in a log cabin left him with a lasting love of the Nordic landscape.

When he did finally arrive by the Cam he continued as at school, playing tennis, captaining his college team and larking about rather than embarking on feverish political activity. He appeared in a "cheerful" play about Aids, *The Normal Heart,* in which he played a gay lover who dies on stage. It was directed by his friend Sam Mendes and nearly won the National Student Drama Festival. He also appeared in another Mendes production, *Cyrano de Bergerac.*

For a politician who likes to stress that he is a Liberal "with every fibre of my being", those fibres were under fairly discreet wraps at Cambridge. There is circumstantial evidence he was a Conservative, though it is conceivable this is black propaganda from the blue corner. According to Tory membership records—kindly produced by Greg Clark, Tory MP, an "N Clegg" from Robinson College was member of the Conservative Club between 1986-7. There were no other Cleggs at the college. It is a story Clegg has denied, sort of ("no recollection", in his favoured construction).

Undeniably, though, he was not a member of the Liberals. "No Nick Clegg," says Martin Pierce, who chaired the club at the time and who stood in West Ham at the last general election. "Certainly it's odd if he had the slightest inclination towards Liberal politics as the Liberal Club had getting on for 200 members, had regular speaker meetings, a weekly social and controlled the Students Union for several years.

"That said, even if you could get a copy of his CUCA membership card, it wouldn't be a smoking gun—lots in those days still joined the political parties for the speaker meetings and social events. CUCA's were rather more fun than organic lentil burgers and cider at University Left."

However, there is a sting to Pierce's analysis: "I think an interesting thing about Nick—and maybe partly explains his willingness to go off *piste*—is that unlike just about every other Lib Dem, he's never really done the slog of retail politics to get his positions. His only difficult elections have been internal party ones.

He hasn't done the councillor thing, was elected on a PR list system as an MEP, and then inherited a Westminster seat we had already won. His lack of involvement at Cambridge was the start of a pattern that hasn't changed to this day." Pierce, incidentally, resigned from the party in disgust at the coalition, claiming that Clegg isn't a true Liberal. There might be some truth in Pierce's analysis of the Clegg rise, though could a little of Clegg's popularity be precisely because he doesn't resemble a stereo-typical activist?

Whatever, unlike with the Bullingdon crowd, there are no racy tales from Clegg's Oxbridge days of trashing restaurants or rolling fellow toffs down hills in Porta-loos. Instead Clegg did campaign for Survival International, though his suggestion that he was "so left wing I was virtually a communist" is harder to corroborate.

His one trip to the Union was not a success, as explained with customary colour: "It completely put me off," he has said. "It was full of all these red-faced girls with pearls and boys who were braying, completely sure of everything they knew. I think a more natural teenage state is confusion."

He has always refused to answer the "did you inhale?" question, offering the sharp retort: "next you will ask me if I threw sand in the sandpit". And this is not the only aspect of student days to excite debate. Clegg has ventured, under pressure from Piers Morgan— with the former *Mirror* editor's unswerving focus on questions of the deepest profundity—that during his well-spent youth he enjoyed the company of "no more than 30" girlfriends. For months, "Cleggover-gate" remained one of the few associations, positive or negative, most voters retained about the newly elected leader of Britain's third party, leaving in tatters the Alan Clark principle: "I do not under any circumstances discuss my relations with the ladies. I am a gentleman, not a hairdresser."

But with Clegg declaring open season on his personal life, hacks dug up university friends. Pippa Harris, who produced *Revolutionary Road* and owns a production company with Mendes, loyally declared Clegg "no swordsman. He already had a girlfriend from school. We all just laughed and said 'in your dreams, Nick.'" Whatever, Clegg confided in me after the rumpus erupted that

Miriam had exiled him (temporarily) to the spare bedroom.

Through university Clegg re-united periodically with Corisande, at Oxford reading classics. After a law conversion course she qualified as a barrister but deserted the High Court to follow her mother into documentaries. Later she moved to the Welsh Marches and had three small children, one of whom has tragically died. Her debut novel, *Falling Apart*, features a "successful and charming" MP. The heroine flees a "disastrous love affair in London", yet moving to the countryside is forced to confront "the darkest recesses of her childhood" as well as "the betrayal of those she believed were closest to her."

Clegg and Corisande gradually went separate ways. "It was on again, off again," I am told. "I don't think there was any dramatic break up."

Having also parted with Cambridge—with a 2:1—Clegg embarked on a road trip round America with the Theroux brothers, driving from Boston to California in a borrowed Ford. This long and painful journey was hindered by Clegg's demands to stop, not for what natives call "comfort breaks", but to meditate. Like smoking, transcendental meditation was by now an addiction, though in the case of TM Clegg could quit after five years. He admits he meditated to keep emotions in check, and ultimately realised this left him disengaged. According to Marcel Theroux, the Clegg of this time was "neurotic", though hardly a unique description of a student. The Theroux brothers sound demanding friends and took to calling Clegg (behind his back) "Grizzly Fish".

At a hard rock gig in Austin, Texas, the trio narrowly avoided being beaten up by bikers. The trip included a pilgrimage of rock stadia to see the artist then still known as Prince, about whom Clegg grew fanatical. According to Marcel, rather than politics, acting seemed a more likely career at this time, though he suggests Clegg was too "arrogant" to accept the vicissitudes of that profession.

In 1989 Clegg undertook a second masters, following the one given him by Cambridge, at the University of Minnesota, on the Political Philosophy of the Deep Green Movement. This has stood him in good stead with Liberal activists, though he found extreme ecologists unappealingly obsessive. Certainly Clegg started to think more deeply about politics. Slowly he began to articulate what was already fairly clear, namely that his instincts were liberal, though still with a small "l".

He moved to New York City and dabbled in radical politics, working as an intern checking facts for the then flamboyantly left-wing Christopher Hitchens at the *The Nation* magazine. For Clegg the time was marked as much by the excitement of finding himself an Englishman in New York, enjoying nightlife and attending a "fashionista" gathering with Marcel Theroux in drag: "We jumped into this party to find that, of course, the last thing fashionable people in New York are going to do is make a fool of themselves. All they did was put a little beauty spot on or something. We were these two English idiots. It was immensely embarrassing."

Two seemingly rather contrary aspects were developing in Clegg's character, producing an ambiguity which would serve him well later. Sloaney girls of the time report finding him attractive and carefree. But he also had an earnest side, endlessly reading Beckett's *Waiting for Godot,* and while in Minnesota performing in Beckett's one-man *Krapp's Last Tape*, about an old man who realises the youthful "fire in me" now amounts to a mere "burning to be gone". Years later he spoke to the *Guardian* of his continuing obsession with Beckett, finding the playwright ever more subversive: "The unsettling idea, most explicit in *Waiting for Godot,* is that life is habit, a series of motions devoid of meaning. It never gets any easier."

No wonder when I put to Clegg during the party leadership election a suggestion of the Huhne camp that he might be too fluffy and glossy to be taken entirely seriously, he bridled. "I do find this laughable," he said, not laughing. "I've spent much of my life trying to come across as not so serious. When I decided to stand for parliament and went to see various MPs, they all told me to lighten up."

As Clegg grew slowly more political he returned to Europe in 1990 and became a trainee for the G24 co-ordination unit in Brussels, but this lasted scarcely six month before he moved down the track to Bruges, where he studied politics for yet another masters at the grandly named College of Europe. This was founded by the EU to inculcate the continent's young elite with the European mission.

It certainly worked for Clegg, yet the ski chalet would still call with the insistency of a cuckoo clock and our subject was happiest, as he has admitted to me, skiing.

Clegg returned to the UK where he gained a job as a lobbyist for GJW, whose clients included Libya—a little awkwardly, as it would turn out. He has painted his role as purely backroom, though a colleague has been quoted saying he would represent the company at client meetings.

Clegg at this time was exceptionally well qualified, it just wasn't entirely clear what it was he was qualified for. Then in 1993 he won the *Financial Times* David Thomas Prize, named after a journalist killed in the first Iraq war. As reward the *Financial Times* sent him to Hungary to report on the privatisation of its industries, and he wrote a series of impressive articles. Would this finally be his break? The fire was in him, but more as a burning frustration.

4

A MARRIAGE OF INCONVENIENCE

Bruges is an impossibly beautiful Belgium town of totemic importance to anti-Federalists, following a speech on its banks by Margaret Thatcher. And with its romantic canals and priestly cloisters, it proved equally important a few years later for this passionate pro-European.

For it was here while studying at the European College that Clegg, wandering casually to a lecture, was hit by a "thunderbolt": he met Miriam González Durántez, a darkly seductive, serious-minded lawyer who was daughter of a Spanish senator. She didn't know it then, but she was also destined to be wife of a British Deputy Prime Minister.

There was nothing convenient about falling in love with this fellow student. True, Clegg had finally split with Corisande. But Clegg has told me that upon meeting the fabulously strong-minded Miriam he was not merely tongue-tied with nerves but, unusually for him, an inability to speak her tongue. Spanish was one of the few languages not in Clegg's firmament, while he found her English "entirely incomprehensible", so they communicated in broken French and private smiles.

While some men would have swooned then shuffled off in miserable defeat after ineffectual attempts at sign language, Clegg taught himself Spanish, and was soon fluent. But was she bowled over by his chivalry? Miriam's Shania Twain response (*That Don't Impress Me Much*) was evident when she later awarded Nick 8/10 for his accent. Far from finding this unappreciative, he loved her directness and "authenticity".

"I had to work really hard to get her interest over all those Frenchmen," he has told me. He found her "incredible" and was hooked, instantly and irredeemably. Miriam is less given to sentiment: "I was trying to help a friend to get close to Nick, and in the process fell for him. We knew very quickly we belonged together." And so the self-styled "Dutch Calvininist" fell for a Spanish catholic.

Their cross-cultural alliance was not easy, but that was part of the appeal. Miriam, even then, could be challenging. "I remember Nick saying how tough it can be going out with a woman of Latin temperament," claims a friend from this time. "And he found Miriam very temperamental. In contrast Corisande is quite gentle, and very warm: confident, good sense of humour. That could be a reason Nick and Corisande are still friends. I don't think Corisande is massively ambitious. She is a sympathetic figure in the background but doesn't have a relationship with Miriam."

However, Nick and Miriam shared a fierce intelligence and enjoyed conversational jousts, often about politics, with him telling me she has always been a notch to the right of him politically, a legacy of her conservative father. More challengingly, Clegg joined her in Flamenco classes. Alas it was not the machismo of his strutting moves that wowed her. Indeed, he was such murder on the dance floor Miriam's friends reasoned he must be mad about her to even try, when nature had bestowed upon him such modest dancing dexterity. Even Miriam saw the sweetness of the gesture and relented.

She had grown up in the somnolent village of Olmedo, 90 minutes drive north west of Madrid, which makes it sound like a sunny, Spanish version of Morton-on-the-Marsh. Yet she has said: "It might be just a short drive over the mountains, but it is worlds apart. It's very dry, very austere," she smiled. "Like the people."

Which she doesn't necessarily offer as criticism; indeed, she speaks of her childhood fondly. Both parents were teachers and papa, José Antonio, was village mayor. In 1977 he was elected a senator to the Spanish parliament for the right-ish Central Democratic Union. Its leader, Adolfo Suárez, became the first democratically elected Prime Minister after General Franco. British newspapers tried to establish a link between the father and Franco but were disappointed. He was actually of that noble generation that established Spanish democracy.

Miriam had read law at the University of Valladolid before winning a scholarship to Bruges. But her relationship with Nick was on/off as they worked in different countries. Then in 1994 Nick, 27, landed his first really proper job for the European Commission. The Brussels post was given to him by Brittan, former Conservative Trade and Industry Secretary who went on to serve as the EU's Vice President. It followed a letter from the Clegg neighbour Carrington to his old cabinet colleague. Which stinks, particularly as Clegg went to work in Brittan's department of external trade. However, Clegg did have to pass a highly competitive entrance exam in Wembley Arena, beating literally thousands of rivals. Miriam, meanwhile, secured a similarly high-powered job for Britain's other Commissioner, Chris Patten.

Over the next two years Clegg, with little economic experience, distributed wodges of aid to former Soviet countries in preparation for the single market, travelling the 'Stans where he was occasionally confronted by Kalashnikov wielding natives. He then became involved in some technical and rather dry stuff, including air travel negotiations with Moscow.

After two years Brittan plucked Clegg from this back-water and placed him in his *cabinet,* a private office of otherwise highly senior Eurocrats, where Clegg wrote speeches and advised on policy. Suddenly the young man who hadn't quite found his calling was being spoken to as a grown up. He became a huge Brittan favourite, who pushed him forward at every opportunity. Clegg was in charge of negotiating the EU's position in accession talks to the World Trade Organisation with Russia and China, a phenomenally important task which gave him a taste for high politics.

Clegg referred to this key role in the televised debates. It cast him in impressive contrast to Cameron, whose weightiest role prior to parliament was as one of those "I'll have to get back to you on that" press officers for Carlton.

Nick and Miriam, meanwhile, weren't merely a "power couple", they were jet-propelled (by now Miriam was advising Patten on

Middle East policy). Yet friends report that more evident at this time than Clegg's earnestness was a light charm. As well as being at the heart of Brussels life he still enjoyed tennis and a beer. It was, says a friend of long standing, "a golden period."

"He had become a lot more confident," the friend recalls. "Running Brittan's office was a big thing. He was a major figure in the Commission and there were lots of trade disputes with America and to a lesser extend Asia. This was heavyweight stuff and it was very impressive he was handling it all so young, and all while remaining very breezy. He laughed a lot then. And all his skills, such as speaking lots of languages that were sniggered about in England, were suddenly hugely valuable.

"He was going out with Miriam who was very pretty, quite glam. He had this great job. And they were the centre of this web of 20,000 functionaries, as well as all the lawyers and journalists round the Commission."

Clegg would take holidays with Miriam's family in Spain and find himself drawn into political arguments with José Antonio who, in contrast to Clegg, was a staunch admirer of Margaret Thatcher.

Miriam was working in Patten's office when she received a call announcing her father had been killed in a car crash. While driving to a meeting his Mercedes crashed head on with a lorry, it is thought after he suffered a heart-attack. He was 58. Miriam was, understandably, devastated and Brittan sent home an ashen-faced Clegg to comfort her.

Meanwhile, Clegg's career was finally ablaze. Brittan suggested to him that he had a strong set of views and should consider a political career. It hit Clegg like a revelation. To Brittan the only surprise was the nature of Clegg's beliefs.

For bafflingly, as Brittan was to report to Ashdown, Clegg "thinks he is one of you lot, a Liberal". Ashdown tells me: "Leon said to me 'He is the brightest young man I've met in politics. I've done everything I possibly can to persuade him to be a Tory but for some inexplicable reason he wants to be a Liberal. I think you should help him'. Leon didn't understand the Liberal Democrats and I told him I couldn't parachute him into a safe seat."

Still, Ashdown agreed to a meeting and tells me he "instantly identified Nick as a future leader. It's the old charisma factor. He could speak extremely well. And I'm always impressed when someone is fluent in so many languages. I was so struck by his intelligence, and an ability to write like a dream." The admiration was reciprocated. It had been Ashdown's campaign to grant British citizenship to the people of Hong Kong that made Clegg realise politics could be more elevated than the Con-Lab daily squabble.

Ashdown gave Clegg a moral lift, but it left him much to do. The Liberal Democrats are considered a political party, but from the inside can feel more like a loose association of individuals. Any candidate who goes off into the wilds in the hope of gaining election is essentially on their own—there is no slick machine, no cheque from Lord Ashcroft.

Clegg soon set to work, gaining advice from key Liberal Democrats including Alison Suttie, later rewarded with a job in his leader's office. He also rang the party's HQ and startled an official by announcing he would like to "join the party and become an MP." Stodgier hopefuls might have joined before making the call. With his clipped tones, Thomas Pink demeanour and connection to Brittan some wondered if he was a dissatisfied Tory. Others, including Lord Rennard, party chief executive, saw him as perfectly placed to stand for the European parliament.

If Ashdown told Clegg "about the political facts of life", these were not the only facts with which Clegg wrestled. For it was on his way to a selection meeting that he found himself the subject of an even more important judgement.

"I proposed to Miriam on the platform at Rauceby station," Clegg has said. "We were waiting for the train to Sleaford. Every relationship," he added with a twinkle "has its magical moments." Clegg was seeking to gain election to the European parliament for the East Midlands, and it was here he dragged this glamorous figure. They continued the train journey in silence, as they absorbed the magnitude of their decision. They married in Spain in 2000, her entire village turning out and underlying to British guests how Miriam's family was of the soil.

At the reception she grabbed a microphone and weaved between tables making an eloquent, clever, speech poking gentle fun at her new husband. Among the domestic secrets blown that afternoon were that Clegg would insist on luxuriating in bed each morning reading the *Financial Times,* a homely anecdote for Louis Theroux. In the Spanish style they celebrated till dawn, when Miriam made survivors hot chocolate.

Anyway, back to Sleaford. There aren't many safe seats for the Liberal Democrats but the East Midlands division Clegg fought in 1999 could scarcely have been more dangerous. Indeed, the constituency was expected to fight back pretty tenaciously. The party there, if not dead, was looking a little peaky. And so this smooth Eurocrat found himself driving around a vast area, as alien to him as any remote Chinese town he had visited for the EU. He was undoubtedly green, never having canvassed, and frequently found himself lost. Yet he had *something,* as Brittan identified. A meeting Clegg organised addressed by Ashdown and Shirley Williams even passed for a bit of glamour in the contest.

Standing for election hardened Clegg. I'm told he stormed from a meeting and slammed the door after a party official declined to back him for the nomination. He also developed a combustible relationship with Paul Holmes, local left winger who became chairman of the parliamentary party. Clegg detected a lack of gratitude for help getting Holmes elected to Chesterfield in 2001. They were also divided by sharply different dispositions and backgrounds. After one lively discussion in a pub Clegg again stomped off. He later vowed that if he were elected leader he would expel Holmes, declaring him "a socialist, not a Liberal." It's a threat that became redundant when the voters of Chesterfield relieved Holmes of his duties in 2010. However, even Holmes acknowledged it was to the credit of Clegg and other privileged "Orange Bookers" they had not chosen the easier path of becoming Conservatives.

Despite the vicissitudes, Clegg, 32, won, largely through charm and hard work, becoming the first Liberal to represent the region since an Ernest Pickering's sadly now neglected triumph of 1931.

Clegg had a particularly startling effect on Tory-leaning women, some of whom were said to keep his election leaflets because they liked his visage. Certainly local Lib Dem poll ratings were boosted, prompting Ashdown to tip Clegg publicly as a politician to watch, which Ashdown has done closely since, mainly with pride and just occasionally irritation.

This ushered in a happy period for Clegg, living in Brussels once more, now as an MEP. Clegg will talk wistfully of Miriam playing Chopin's *Waltz in A Minor* at the piano—while pregnant, with the couple's first child, Antonio.

While in Brussels he persuaded Bill Newton Dunn, Conservative MEP, to defect to the Lib Dems. Cosily, Newton Dunn later succeeded him as MEP for the East Midlands.

Clegg co-founded the Campaign for Parliamentary Reform, and was ahead of his time in campaigning against expenses abuse in the European Parliament. Soon he was made Trade and Industry spokesman for the ELDR, the umbrella group of European liberal parties. In 2000 Clegg drafted an EU law, described in all earnestness as "local loop unbundling". The measure was highly significant, opening telephone systems across the EU to competition, but unlike more earnest Liberals Clegg could laugh at the absurdity of the name and by extension the occasional bureaucratic boredom of Brussels life.

Clegg was a European to the core but he did not share the obsession of colleagues for the institutions of the EU. He found procedures dull and would not always hide his contempt. This prompted Andrew Duff, fellow Lib Dem MEP, to wonder if Clegg was a "Conservative sleeper." If he had been Tory, Clegg would have found it much easier to win election for that party. The truth was simply that Clegg thought remote EU institutions had to justify themselves to voters, whereas some MEPs were so immersed in EU process they could forget about its purpose.

Clegg campaigned for devolution of EU activity, but newspapers have trawled this period for evidence of a desire to "sell out" national interests. One, stoically, waded through every fortnightly column he wrote while an MEP for *Guardian*

Unlimited. It believed it had struck gold with an article from 2002. In it Clegg accused Brown of encouraging "condescension" towards Germany, which was mild enough, but the piece then seemed to suggest the legacy of Britain's history was somehow more burdensome than Germany's: "all nations have a cross to bear, and none more so than Germany with its memories of Nazism. But the British cross is more insidious still. A misplaced sense of superiority, sustained by delusions of grandeur and a tenacious obsession with the last war, is much harder to shake off."

Oh dear. One can see what Clegg meant. He would hardly be the first to suggest Britain's Second World War "victory" encouraged a refusal to tackle social and economic ills, hence the oft quoted line about our losing the peace. And Germany has indeed dealt with its wartime ghosts remarkably. But for someone who writes as smoothly as Clegg it sacrificed proportion for rhetorical flourish, for it implied some parity between the 20th century histories of Britain and Germany. And that is a no-go area.

While Clegg was an MEP, what passed for the Lib Dem machine did finally put its back behind him, and the gilded circle including high-powered businessmen Ian Wright and Sherlock worked their tricks. Sherlock recalls: "Ian rang from his car phone and said 'Paddy has asked me to see Nick Clegg'. I replied 'Who is Nick Clegg?' To which Ian said: 'He is going to lead the party. I've been to see him in Nottingham.' I replied 'Have you had a few drinks?'"

But Wright was adamant: "Paddy has asked me to raise some money and I want your help." Sherlock's unusually brusque reply (which he tells against himself) was "why should I?" By now Wright was growing impatient: "Neil, just believe me. One day he will be leader of our party."

In 2002 Clegg decided he would not seek re-election to Brussels, arguing publicly that the battle to sell Europe was in Britain, not Belgium. Privately, he has admitted to exhaustion spending his life on planes between Brussels, Strasbourg, the East Midlands and London when he had a young family. But it was primarily because he spied a bigger prize: a return to his old stomping ground of Westminster. Still, it was a bold move as being elected to anything is hard enough as a Liberal Democrat and politicians very rarely give up seats voluntarily.

Clegg looked at a few constituencies and Rennard now had his well-trained ear to the ground. After a couple of false starts, news emerged that Richard Allan was to stand down in Sheffield Hallam, where Clegg had campaigned while representing the nearby East Midlands.

It was certainly appealing: a couple of hours by train from London and the wealthiest constituency in the north containing more graduates than any seat in England. In atmosphere, it could have been a million miles from bracing, post-industrial Sheffield sentimentalised in *The Full Monty*. And it was that rare commodity, a relatively safe Lib Dem seat.

But a general election was still three or four years distant, and Clegg knew there would be a gap from his standing down in 2004 to a British general election one or two years later. But the prize was too big to ignore and he announced his resignation. Hallam took to Clegg instantly, his charm and intelligence propelling the young southerner to the nomination.

But relinquishing his European seat he found himself out of work and out of pocket. Miriam was working in Brussels and he needed a house in his putative constituency, and also somewhere in London, which would be the family base if and when elected. And so he took a part time job as a lobbyist. This was offered by Andrew Gifford, Liberal fixer of old with house in Knightsbridge and estate in Scotland. In his statement upon joining GPlus Clegg suggested a willingness to lobby on behalf of private companies those public bodies he had been working with as an elected politician.

"It's especially exciting to be joining GPlus at a time when Brussels is moving more and more to the centre of business concerns," his statement gushed. "With the EU taking in ten more countries and adopting a new Constitution, organisations need more than ever intelligent professional help in engaging with the EU." Clegg represented clients including Hertz and British Gas.

Compare this to his election promise to "clean up lobbying...[when] you will once again be able to look at our

Parliament with pride, not contempt." There is no suggestion he did anything that needed cleaning up, but for a party that takes the high-ground it wasn't the happiest interlude.

He also gained a part time teaching post lecturing in the politics department of Sheffield University, as well as giving seminars at his old University of Cambridge, on International Relations. Meanwhile, he was throwing himself into canvassing.

But it was a testing time. He was alone in Sheffield, often holding Antonio while Miriam worked for Patten. A Tory MP has referred to his (now ex) wife as being kept "hostage" in the constituency. Miriam, a cynic might suggest, would probably not be taken dead or alive in Sheffield. Clegg was also a little lonely. Other than a fellow lecturer, he had few local friends. So he had plenty to worry about, not least whether he would win the constituency in the following year's general election.

Then the really bad stuff happened. Antonio grew ill, but a succession of hospitals just offered more antibiotics. Fears grew so intense that the extended family came to visit, as Antonio apparently began slipping away. Finally, in the nick of time, a specialist correctly diagnosed the illness as pleurisy. Antonio's lung was hastily drained and he slowly recovered.

Through all this Miriam was with child number two, and before Antonio was out of danger Miriam suffered severe complications with her pregnancy. Indeed, at one stage it looked as if Clegg might lose her. Meanwhile, he was spending nights in hospital comforting Antonio. Thankfully Miriam pulled through and gave birth to a second son, Alberto. But still Clegg described this as "the worst year of my life".

And it left its mark. David Laws has told me that a year later after Clegg entered parliament and Laws was urging him to be the leadership candidate for the modernising Orange Book movement, Clegg replied that he was uncertain as Antonio was still recovering: "Nick said 'I'll have to ask Miriam.'"

Anyway, Clegg threw himself into his Hallam campaign. Astutely, Clegg stuck to the popular outgoing MP. This culminated, thanks to a tradition of the local party, in an appearance in *Jack and* the *Beanstalk* with a mock swordfight between Clegg and Allen. The new man placed a foot on the latter's throat and declared with a flourish: "I'm in charge now."

Clegg won with over 50 per cent of the vote, bagging a majority of 8,682. By Lib Dem standards this was a resounding victory, representing one of the smallest swings away from a party in a seat where the incumbent was standing down (4.3 per cent). It is an unusually sprawling constituency, starting almost in Sheffield's city centre yet spreading vastly out into the Peak District National Park, which has provided Clegg with numerous photo ops and much loved weekend walks. It had once been a safe Conservative seat but is now the only stretch of South Yorkshire you won't find on political maps painted an angry red.

The nonchalant hand in pocket, the easy smile, the well timed intervention helped by all those acting classes: Westminster School had given him valuable lessons for Westminster parliament. Suddenly he looked a formidable politician in the making. Had that school tennis captain misjudged its man?

5

THE ORANGE MARCH

The most desperate, soul-sapping signs in any work place proclaim: "You don't have to be mad to work here—but it helps." Normally these are followed by a Maoist army of exclamation marks, just in case you haven't quite got the point that, despite appearances to the contrary, the guys at this filling station/ odour repellent factory/BBC Diversity Unit want you to believe they are the zaniest fun-seekers you could ever have the pleasure of working with.

But if such a sign appeared above the desk of a Liberal Democrat operative it could, more legitimately, be taken as a simple statement of fact. For why would anyone sane go into politics as a Lib Dem? It leads to years of lost deposits, slammed doors and defeat—or worse, sympathy. Not only do Liberal Democrats fare particularly badly owing to the iniquities of the electoral system, most of the few seats they have been allowed to win are a very long way away from London, where the political class of all parties is based. Just listen to Ashdown, who sacrificed a thrilling career throttling enemy insurgents in the jungles of Borneo and the like to take on the initially even less hospitable natives of Yeovil. He will rattle off the names of the fallen, a generation of aspiring young politician that marched bravely from London to fight some rural outpost far from home, never to be seen again; they are probably still there, several elections later, wading through the swamps of Humberside or Bognor, unaware that peace—for now at least—has been declared.

Working in newspapers I've seen countless colleagues chat up the appropriate honcho in Conservative HQ to win a place on the "A" List, inveigle their way onto the shortlist of a seat convenient for "town", and before you know it one is expected to call them "Honourable". No doubt it isn't really so simple, but that is how it can appear to Lib Dems. Potential candidates for the party's nomination in a particular seat are banned from seeking the endorsement of the party hierarchy, and in any case such praise might backfire in this most cussed, contrary and localised of parties. Oh, and if they succeed and become Lib Dem candidates, their real problems begin.

Because much of the Liberal revival since Grimond has been based on community politics—beavering away to mend bus shelters and bottle banks—candidates are expected to be "of" the area. Indeed, Lib Dems have made hay lambasting Tory and Labour opponents for treating constituencies like rotten boroughs, to be visited only during elections, so most candidates live in the place they hope to represent. Other parties regard this as deeply eccentric. Often Lib Dems have to sacrifice careers and uproot families on the slim chance local hard work and national earthquakes might hurl them in the general direction of Westminster. If by some miracle they triumph, they enter a two party parliament for a third party—and realise that all the obstacles they have faced until that point have been mere trifles.

Most Liberal Democrat MPs have had to work harder than a Cameron or Miliband. And Clegg's crowd, having considerable opportunities in the outside world, made greater sacrifices than an earlier generation of Lib Dem.

If much of politics is timing and luck Clegg was fortunate to arrive in parliament when the party found its most promising performers in a generation. Many were called Orange Book Liberal Democrats, who reacted against the state-driven policies of the then party leader, Charles Kennedy, campaigning to return the Lib Dems to their more individualistic, liberal roots.

The indulgence of readers does not allow chapters on all key players, but several must be highlighted. Danny Alexander is probably the least well-known politician in the country, relative to his importance. Clegg calls the man he met years before in the Britain in Europe group his best friend in politics. "If there is a kitchen cabinet," remarks Laws "it probably isn't William Hague so much; it's more David and George, and Nick and Danny."

After leading the successful Lib Dem coalition negotiating team Alexander was made Secretary of State for Scotland, a hugely satisfying appointment for one who learned his Liberalism on his grandfather's Highland knee. With Edinburgh's devolved administration he had a relatively light departmental workload, enabling him to moonlight for Clegg, scrutinising other departments. This was especially vital in ministries where there wasn't a Lib Dem in charge, which was most. But after the resignation of Laws, Alexander had to slot into the key Chief Secretary role to keep an eye on the money. Quite a promotion, this, for one that political commentator Andrew Rawnsley described, with majesterial condescension, as "a former press officer for a national park". It is no coincidence that for the following few months Clegg looked exhausted, prompting snide articles suggesting he lacked stamina.

Though un-showy, Alexander has a skill for twisting arms without his opponent entirely realising they are in pain, as demonstrated by his skilful leading of coalition negotiations. Like Clegg he is on the party's right but is instinctively consensual, to the frustration of Orange Book ultras such as Jeremy Browne. Another major player says: "He doesn't see things that ideologically. He probably would have been quite comfortable in a coalition with Labour."

When I shared a platform with Alexander at a Lib Dem fringe meeting I argued the party should shout more loudly about its belief in letting individuals and communities make more decisions about their own lives. Alexander called instead for greater "fairness", and it was his softer-edged message that was most warmly received. Alexander, like Clegg, appreciates that without the old-guard's occasionally batty devotion to the Liberal cause over many unrewarding decades there would have been no party to revive—and if a bit of political fuzz keeps them happy, then a little clarity should be sacrificed.

Certain senior figures affect not to understand Clegg's attachment to Alexander, but while they are prone to cause Clegg trouble, Alexander sublimates his ego to support Clegg. It is a loyalty on which Clegg relies.

Yet key players warn against mistaking loyalty for lack of ambition. Many see him as the most plausible successor from the Orange Book wing. "Shortly after he was elected I asked him what he saw himself becoming," one recalls. "He replied 'party leader'."

Two other key figures in the Clegg revolution have been Browne, formerly a financial consultant and public relations executive, and Norman Lamb, an employment lawyer. Both are on the party's dry, economically literate wing, and both have displayed considerable flair. Lamb acts as gatekeeper for Clegg at Number 10. He is a savvy media operator who gained positive publicity for shifting Lib Dem health policy towards the needs of patients away from bureaucrats.

As minister of state at the Foreign Office Browne has grown so used to presidential fawnings his bedroom is probably decorated with a red carpet. A Laws protégé and MP for nearby Taunton, Browne is arguably the party's most right-wing MP. Tall, ram-rod straight and voluble, the ambassador's son could be mistaken for the brighter kind of army officer. But the fanatical QPR supporter was actually born in Islington and spent much of his childhood abroad. Any apparent stiffness is tempered by a keen laugh, and he has been known to take the *Daily Telegraph* into meetings largely to gain a rise from fellow Lib Dems. No wonder he has won over Hague at the Foreign Office. Indeed, Tories report he has even been known to take more robust positions than them in certain discussions. When the subject is negotiations with the EU, this proves particularly delicious. His joviality obscures a more reflective side and a sharp political mind which examines any party decision for signs of selling out the Orange creed.

He, too, has made major sacrifices, his marriage ending under the strain of juggling work in different places. Yet his yo-yoing between Taunton and Westminster on the late night train has paid off, enabling him to first win and then hold a seat the Tories still believe theirs by right. Modestly he does not include himself in this description, but says: "The great quality that no one ever mentions about top flight politicians is endurance."

These few individuals, in partnership with Laws, Chris Huhne and Vince Cable, were the small parliamentary team that brought about the Clegg revolution. For the transformation they wrought, as radical as the Blair and Cameron coups, was achieved by such a small band of fighters they slipped virtually unnoticed under the media radar.

There have certainly been rows. As Laws says: "Nick, Chris and Vince are the three most senior parliamentarians in the party and they all have their egos and personalities, but I think they work well together. None would be the others first choice to go on holiday or have dinner with but they work together without problem in government."

Strip away the white tie and tails from the Cameroons, and the Clegg circle is scarcely less silver spooned, or tongued; but there are differences. If the Cameroons enjoy aristocratic connections, most Lib Dems hail from professional backgrounds. If bugles and horses hooves provided the soundtrack to the Conservative childhood, the Liberal is normally weaned on good argument and bad table manners. Tories tend to hail from pony-paddock country, Liberals from towns and the Celtic fringes. No Liberal should be remotely snobbish, but if they are it will be intellectual rather than social. And they are resolutely uninterested in keeping up appearances. Ronnie Fearn, then a Lib Dem MP, once told me out canvassing: "you can always spot if a household is going to be one of ours: the garden will be overgrown. Liberals have more interesting things to do." They are also, invariably, a little more serious of purpose, believing there are injustices to be righted. If to some Cameroons politics can be a game about politicians, to Cleggites it is a war of thought—to be waged in the interests of those less privileged than themselves.

Still there were, during Clegg's smooth rise, a few murmurs. Activists often regard giving a leg up to promising talents, not as sensible politics, but as cheating. So among more puritanical Lib Dems there is a suspicion the party's "magic circle" fixed it for Clegg.

Even an admirer has told me: "Nick has never had to struggle in his life. It has all come too easy." The success of others has a tendency to look simple, of course. Perhaps Clegg has made it look effortless because he is damn good at what he does. Besides, for the careerist there are smoother avenues to tread to Downing Street than via Cowley Street.

Yet Clegg has undeniably benefited from rich and powerful benefactors. For one that campaigns for "a new politics", his back-story does have the faintest whiff of the old boy network. However, no one should be pilloried for their birth, be it silver-spooned or hand to mouth. The question is whether a politician has sought to cement those privileges or worked towards a more meritocratic future.

If Clegg was helped early on through a parental connection by Lords Carrington and Brittan, today he draws on his own nexus of powerful, well connected friends. Among those who have helped include a triumvirate of powerful lobbyists: Sherlock, director and head of public affairs at KPMG who is known in senior Lib Dem circles as "Mr Fix-it", Wright, head of corporate affairs at Diageo; and Michael Young, former lobbyist for gold mining interests. If the Lib Dems have a golden circle, these guys are 24 carat. And they don't conform to Liberal stereotype, being suited, sober and shaven. When Sherlock was out canvassing and told by an unresponsive voter "you politicians are only after one thing", he grew so exasperated he wrote his existing salary on a piece of paper and demanded the by-now cowering voter read the amount: "Do you still think," Sherlock demanded "I want to get into parliament to get rich?"

These are influential figures that flit effortlessly around establish-ment circles. While recent leaders have come and gone, these have remained, helping with everything from firing off letters to the newspapers to hiring staff. It was these three who the *Telegraph* was to reveal during the campaign had been paying money into Clegg's bank account—to pay staff as it turned out.

Clegg is also assisted by his chief strategic adviser, an old friend he described to me as "brilliant", former joint managing director of Saatchi & Saatchi UK, John Sharkey. Clegg might have considered him less brilliant when Sharkey left in a taxi a secret assessment of Clegg's performance in the first TV debate, including the view that one of his boss's answers was "offensive". Unusually for a senior Lib Dem he had worked, in a professional capacity at Saatchi, for the

1987 Conservative election campaign. This saw posters featuring a British soldier with his arms raised in surrender with the slogan: "Labour's approach to arms". A party political broadcast ended with the hymn *I Vow to Thee, My Country*, complete with fluttering Union flag. However, the Saatchi-Norman Tebbit campaign was considered not quite bracing enough for Tory tastes. On "wobbly Thursday", David Young grabbed Tebbit by the lapels and shouted: "Norman, listen to me, we are about to lose this fucking election."

As well as senior business figures, Clegg is at home with media players and old thespian friends. I recall asking him one afternoon what he was doing later. Going to a film premiere, it turned out. Oh, and Halle Berry was to be there.

As well as to the Theroux brothers, Clegg remains close to Mendes. Colin Firth, introduced by Mendes, became a firm supporter and hugged Miriam at parties, though he has not shown the resolution of King George in his off-screen role, recently renouncing his former friend. Bonham-Carter remains supportive, telling a reporter while lending her backing to the AV campaign that her old-schoolmate was doing a good job in impossible circumstances. Others to come out as Cleggites have included Martin Amis and Richard Dawkins. If intellectuals have often backed Labour, there are signs that the clarity of Clegg's thought has attracted bright people. Oh, and celebrities. Kate Winslet, Daniel Radcliffe, The Kooks and Razorlight all pledged support. There is even an indie band called The Strange Death of Liberal England.

And while the party would like to say this new found acceptability is due to bright, successful people seeing the virtue of Liberalism, we should acknowledge the role of something more nebulous, namely charm. That Clegg has it was evident when he stood triumphantly outside parliament with Joanna Lumley cooing in his ear.

And to think Liberal stardust once stretched no further than Clement Freud advertising tinned dog food. To call the Lib Dems cool might be an exaggeration, but thanks to Clegg they have perhaps ceased to be embarrassing.

If his views are those of an outsider, socially Clegg is pure insider. And this is reflected in how he lives. Along with his flower-draped £1 million plus house in Putney, he bought a constituency home. Clegg described this as "modest, semi-detached, pebble-dashed," which was slightly condescending to the constituents next door.

During the campaign Clegg was questioned about his claiming more than £80,000 in the last four years in expenses for this "modest" home, not to mention an Ikea cake tin (it's always the details). According to the council, his Ecclesall ward with its wide tree-lined avenues is "ranked within the 10 per cent least deprived wards nationally."

Recently, semi-detached houses on Clegg's street have sold from £325,000 to £420,000. However, when Clegg sold the house in the summer of 2011 he returned the capital gain to the Exchequer, without public announcement.

Clegg's world, then, is not one of painful deprivation. It's one of success, surrounded by successful people. It has more in common with the worlds of Miliband or Cameron than with many voters. And this, critics would say, is reflected in how he has transformed his party just as Tory and Labour modernisers changed theirs. He is of the political class. But the Liberal Democrats have long been awash with real life stories. Political class is precisely what they needed, and this is what Clegg and his circle have delivered.

It is hard to exaggerate how much Clegg's circle, which Ashdown so inspired, has improved the gene pool of the Liberal Democratic family. And it is to the credit of Ashdown's political offspring that they have forged careers in Liberal Democratic politics. There can, then, only be two possible motivations for their perseverance with Liberalism: either they really are mad, or they believe in it.

6

DAVID LAWS

A TORY JUST LONGING TO COME OUT?

If David Laws turned up just as he was to a fancy dress party, fellow guests would probably hazard he had come as a Tory MP. Royal blue suit, hair cut more neatly than a croquet lawn, and the avuncular air of one who apparently hasn't spent as much time as he might have wished north of about Buckinghamshire: all would win praise for being a devilishly convincing disguise. If party-goers lured him into talking about the dazzling City career that enabled him to "retire" at 28, his move into politics and his dry economic opinions, they might wonder if he was taking this party game a little far.

But actually the only party this key architect both of the Lib Dem revival and of the coalition agreement has ever shown passion for is the Liberal Democrats. He even gave up a telephone number salary to become a backroom researcher for the party on £14,000 a year. It is precisely because he is so sure of his Liberalism that he won't pander to party prejudices. Indeed, he has long enjoyed teasing fellow Libs by mentioning his love of playing rugby ("on the right wing, of course"), or even his curious affection for Michael Winner's restaurant reviews.

You can understand George Osborne's confusion when, in the last parliament, he asked this son of a Surrey-dwelling City banker and Tory voting housewife if he would defect to the Conservatives in return for a seat in the Shadow Cabinet. Well, didn't the Laws CV suggest an MP straight out of Tory central casting? Independent school in Weybridge, *Observer* Schools Mace Debating Champion, double first in economics from Cambridge, vice president of JP Morgan aged 24, and millionaire aged 28 when he became a managing director of BZW running two departments with an annual profit of $100 million. After all, Paddy Ashdown has said that when

Laws canvassed with the outgoing Liberal Democrat leader in the hope of inheriting Yeovil, Laws would, to meld with his boss, wear "mufti"; but from the day he was elected Laws only ever appeared suited. Wasn't it obvious he was harbouring a secret, namely that he was a Conservative just waiting to come out?

And this, remember, was even before he became Chief Secretary to the Treasury and introduced such a thorough, well thought-out round of cuts that he was hailed as the coalition's early star and even—by the *Wall Street Journal*—a future Prime Minister.

All of which fitted snugly with the substance of a dry political career. Not only did he create *The Orange Book* (with Paul Marshall), he wrote its most controversial—and probably "right wing"—chapter, advocating French style private medical insurance, which earned him a two hour dressing down at the Liberal Democrat shadow cabinet. As Education Spokesman he developed Ashdown's idea of free schools, long before Conservatives embraced the policy. For at least six months in the run up to the election he advocated privately, against Cable's party policy, spending cuts. He had also been among leading agitators for Kennedy to stand down, ostensibly out of exasperation at his leader's "health problems" (in Laws' coy words), but, fundamentally, at what he saw as Kennedy's intellectual somnolence.

But it is no surprise Laws rebuffed Osborne. He is a Liberal to his core, of a rigorous, unbending persuasion the party hasn't known since Grimond. When Laws was appointed Chief Secretary and announced £6 billion cuts, even some Tories baulked at this Gladstonian correction of government overspend. Osborne had boasted to journalists he had pulled off a masterstroke in manoeuvring a Liberal Democrat into the Chief Secretary role, ensuring the Lib Dems shared the political pain of cuts. But Laws insists he was lined up to be Transport Secretary and it was *he* who pushed Clegg to let him loose on the Treasury, forfeiting the chance to run his own department. Liberal Democrat support took the kind of hit Kevin Pietersen gives an old cricket ball, just as Osborne foresaw, but Laws does not regret investing some of the party's capital to mine political gold. He argues that by demonstrating toughness the party will, eventually, be rewarded with the prize of economic credibility. Laws actually enjoyed shedding the cuddly cardie image. Malcolm Bruce, former Lib Dem Treasury spokesman, has said: "Laws is an unreconstructed 19th-century Liberal. He believes in free trade and small government. Government should do the job only government can do. There's no point having a large public sector if the users of public services are getting poorer." This is probably why Ashdown describes it as "a liberalism of the mind, not the heart".

Yet the above picture only captures one side of Laws. If the spiky little dig that he is a "crypto Tory" is unfair, so too is the label "economic Liberal". Just as he believes government should interfere as little as possible economically, so he believes it should be hands-off socially. And this is the only consistent Liberal position. The fundamental contradiction of Thatcherism was that it expected people to be economically self-sufficient yet socially subservient to a state that could peer and snoop into every crevice of the citizen's personal life. Laws did not fall into that trap, which is acknowledged by Dr Evan Harris, former MP on the party's left who considers Laws a "social liberal" on a range of subjects including "abortion, faith schools, religion and the state. He is also very sensible on discrimination issues and sex education." Bruce accepts the point: "His economic liberalism is tempered by his social liberalism."

The interesting speculation is whether this "social Liberalism" has been fed by fear of bigotry had he come out as gay. An anonymous Tory MP has been quoted saying Laws confided he would be Conservative but for Section 28, a notorious measure of the Thatcher government which banned "positive promotion of homosexuality in schools". Laws denies this, telling me he was just as put-off by the Tory stance on "foreigners" and on the victims of their own economic policies in the eighties.

Still, Section 28 did spread disapproval of any life that wavered from a 1950s sense of "normal", creating a climate in which Laws felt unable to tell many colleagues or even relations he was gay. When I ventured to ask recently if it was this that stopped him standing for the leadership, he looked thoughtfully out of a window and replied:

"I don't know. It's something that's been with me so long I don't know how I would feel about that if I did have a family..." The first time I sat down to lunch with him I asked, as a crass conversational gambit, whether he had children. He said "no, I don't", staring at his plate. I got the message but felt profoundly sorry that someone so un-censorious should live in dread of censure.

Liberalism is often described as "tolerant" but it is no such thing, certainly in the bedroom. It is better cast as non-judgmental. It simply does not accept that agents of the state, church or even *Daily Telegraph* have the right to an opinion over actions that have no effect on anyone else. Laws had been close for several years to Jamie Lundie, a lobbyist whom he met while both worked for the party. And it was this relationship—the revelation of which he so feared—that cost him his ministerial job.

What the case did not reveal in Laws was some spivvy, Tory Boy greed. Laws had made a decent amount of money before entering parliament. He had a house in the South of France and a thatched cottage near Yeovil. He may have joked to friends that he couldn't wait for the day he was out of politics when he could trade his old Audi for an Aston Martin, but wealth isn't what makes him tick. If it did, would he have quit the City for the Lib Dems? Indeed, officials were so suspicious after his interview they checked out his story—why, they wondered, would anyone this good possibly want to give up huge riches to toil for *us*?

Ashdown puts the later scandal down to a desire for privacy, and hopes others will not judge him harshly, though says: "he was a very foolish boy. His election leaflets were about how he was whiter than white."

"This is a tragedy," says a friend. "Anybody who knows David knows he is so obsessed with politics he doesn't notice things like decent furniture or art. His house has no decorations other than a few photos of him meeting various politicians. When I stayed, there was no food in the cupboards and the fridge was empty bar a single bottle of champagne and, strangely, a packet of crisps."

Scarcely can a minister have been hounded from office with such warmth, and it is a sign of his stellar abilities that Laws had scarcely resigned before many were calling for his return, so "to the ministry-born" did Laws seem.

In his Treasury office under a portrait of the great Liberal Chancellor Lloyd George, Laws had landed the job for which he had been born. "What I so loved was I thought I could really get on with the substance of decision making, yet it would be behind the scenes," he tells me wistfully. "How little I knew." If you had to choose one quality the role required and he possessed it would be "rigour".

He cut vigorously—even laying siege to the ministerial car pool—yet found money for personally cherished policies such as the pupil premium. Even in the unlikely event he never holds office again, his ensuring that the least privileged will have significantly more spent on their education, and often in substantially improved schools, would be some legacy.

And this throws up the other key facet of the Liberalism of Laws that Osborne and even some with Orange rosettes don't always appreciate. Laws is a Liberal, but not a Libertarian. He recognises that with a Briton's success or failure still largely determined by the time they reach the worldly age of two, there must be massively more help for the young disadvantaged. The only moral basis for a free, capitalist race to the finishing line is if we all start at the same point, yet equality of opportunity can sometimes seem as far off as ever. It is no coincidence Laws was adamant that for the coalition to go ahead, Osborne would have to forget about reducing inheritance tax for the already relatively well-off, and instead take the low paid out of tax.

As well as being an important thinker about British politics, Laws was also proving an effective fighter, evidenced by the entertaining spat he instigated by revealing that his Labour predecessor Liam Byrne had left him a note reading: "Dear Chief Secretary, I'm afraid there is no money. Kind regards—and good luck! Liam."

Byrne's flippancy appalled Laws. Everything about Laws fizzes efficiency. On a recent visit to his Commons office I found his curtain rail had collapsed and he was agitated that the authorities were being vague about when they might mend it—not because he needed the curtains drawn, but because he likes things working.

While Liberals tend to love little better than homemade wine and yellowing pamphlets, Laws prides himself on owning no filing cabinets. Instead he stores important stuff in his brain and unimportant stuff in his shredder. Documents are returned to colleagues with ticks against paragraphs he agrees with, crosses against those he takes issue with, and a bank of exclamation marks against those he considers ridiculous. He is not given to existential flourishes, still less to talk about feelings or life away from Westminster. What he enjoys is highly detailed debate about policy, interspersed with light and usually good natured political gossip. Yet despite that apparently closed personality he commands great affection in the friends he has forged during his political career.

Partly that must spring from an innate decency combined with a (controlled) playfulness. But I suspect it's mainly because he puts so much into a career he admits to loving. Even as a researcher, aged 29, he marched into a packed press room with hacks on deadline, climbed on a chair and explained precisely how the then Conservative Chancellor was wrong to accuse the Lib Dems of getting their numbers in a twist. The Institute of Fiscal Studies then vindicated Laws. Later Laws spent endless long, seemingly dull hours, pouring over Treasury papers and spotted a £5 billion "black hole" in Brown's finances.

For all his high-mindedness he is not short of low cunning. Browne, beaten by Laws to the Yeovil nomination before landing Taunton, says he was dismayed during that contest when canvassing to find members all seemed to have received a charming, ink-written letter from Laws, invariably placed in a prominent position above their mantelpiece, thanking them for their hospitality when he had visited the day before. It seemed a common courtesy, except it broke the rules which rigorously control what literature prospective candidates can send members. Browne has long forgiven Laws and after the campaign became a huge admirer. Laws, in turn, argued for Browne's promotion. Browne has the grace to admit that even his then girlfriend told him that at the Yeovil selection meeting Laws made one of the best speeches she had ever heard.

Laws will never be to Clegg what Brown was to Blair because Laws has never had ambition for the top job, be it due to personal circumstance or refusal to trim his message. But perhaps he will be regarded as Clegg's Alan Milburn or Keith Joseph; Joseph was never the most important minister to *Thatcher*, but was the most important minister to *Thatcherism*. If anything the importance of Laws increased after his resignation. He would send Clegg a stream of emails, invariably acted upon. One who attended a brainstorming session at Chevening remarks: "it was noticeable that not only was David in attendance, many of the positional papers had been written by him. He was forcing the intellectual agenda." He could also be found closeted in London with Michael Gove, formulating education policy.

But did Laws ever crave to be centre stage, or was he happy tinkling the ivories in the shadows? "I thought fairly early on Nick was the right one to lead the party, with a small 'l' liberal background, better able to build alliances and a formidable communicator—whereas to the party I was the unacceptable face of *The Orange Book*.

"It's always been policy that has interested me. Plus my City background taught me to be direct. It was a quality that was admired there, but in politics it can cause difficulty. When confronting things in the party, my natural tendency was to take them on in an aggressive way. The leader needs to be more patient. Nick is better at that."

Any politician's protestations about lack of ambition come with health warnings, but from the first time I met Laws he made clear he would be happy as a junior education minister, if he could implement his ideas. His fantasy job would be Chancellor, but realizes that is difficult as a Liberal Democrat. There was talk of him running Clegg's office, though Laws would be better deployed in a department rich in policy possibilities such as Education. Meanwhile, he was left serving his unofficial sentence in the prison of inactivity. Even opponents acknowledged privately that if he doesn't find his way back it would be a huge waste.

What Laws wanted to avoid was being a perpetual backbencher, which would prompt him to leave politics. Indeed, I understand the first draft of his resignation letter also stated that he would stand down as an MP. Only Ashdown and his constituency chair talked him round. "I promised to give time to thinking about stepping down," he told me.

Because unlike a lot of intellectual politicians—Joseph being a notorious example—Laws has only ever been interested in ideas that make a very practical difference, reflected in an ability to empathise with different types of people: "Not only is he brilliant at all the stuff at Westminster," Browne remarked "he is surprisingly good on a human level, and can talk to an elderly lady about her garden with as much ease as to an economist about GDP figures."

I recall his rage following a visit to a town where there were two secondary schools, one popular and one unpopular; the education authority regarded the successful one as the problem as it was drawing pupils from the failing one. And that captured everything that infuriates Laws. Why, he demanded, deny children places at the best schools? Why had the education authority lost sight of its primary role, improving life chances of children, and instead taken to defending failing institutions of state? What, in short, was "progressive" about blocking a child's progression?

Laws join the Tories? Theirs, I predict, is a party he could never revel in.

7

PAUL "MONEYBAGS" MARSHALL

A WEALTH OF IDEAS

From his lair high above the Thames surveying a city over which he holds much sway, there is a touch of Goldfinger to Paul Marshall. The comically wealthy hedge-fund manager has no white cat but his paws do reach as far as those of a medium-sized tiger economy. He is quiet, floppy-haired and friendly, but not much escapes his eyes, or fidgety brain. As sushi is served for lunch in his vast boardroom he toys with the dead fish, but doesn't eat.

Marshall is one of the most significant—and secret—forces behind the Liberal Democrat revival. In partnership with another City talent, Laws, this financier and philanthropist who founded one of Europe's most powerful hedge-funds set about transforming Britain's third party. But he did so in a very Liberal way. Charles Kennedy, for whom Marshall worked as a young researcher, has privately dubbed him "Moneybags Marshall", and he has indeed hosted City dinners to raise funds for the party. But it would hardly have been the financier's style to "do a Lord Ashcroft" (the Belize-loving businessman accused of liking Conservatism so much he bought the party). While Ashcroft's deposits in Conservative vaults have allowed him to strut around Central Office deciding on election strategy with all the self-deprecating charm of PG Wodehouse's Roderick Spode, Marshall's contribution to Liberalism has been as much intellectual as fiscal. He has re-launched a think tank and co-edited a rather technical book on policy. So far, so dry? So not.

These were arguably two of the most significant landmarks on Britain's journey to coalition. The think tank was CentreForum and the publication *The Orange Book*. Driving these two apparently rather ponderous vehicles, Marshall, hair flying wildly in the wind, transported the party to a new intellectual vantage point. For a movement that would once have thundered across any battlefield to attack tariffs and monopolies it had, in recent years, retreated to the last trench defending special interests of state. The masterstroke of Marshall and his key ally Laws was to demonstrate how market mechanisms could be exploited to achieve socially desirable ends.

CentreForum, under the enquiring leadership of Julian Astle, questioned the entire Liberal Democrat approach to domestic politics. "Until then Liberal Democrat policy had been about out-bidding Labour to add more to the public shopping list," ventures Astle. "That was OK under Conservative governments and the first two years of Blair when he kept to Tory spending commitments, but then it became a binge. The high water mark was the 2005 manifesto. By then the party seemed to think every single social problem could be solved by chucking a billion or two more at it than Labour." Even Kennedy later admitted the manifesto's flaws, and critics included left-ish figures such as Duncan Brack, who told me it was "incoherent".

What alarmed Astle, Marshall, Laws and co was not merely the amount of these spending commitments but their style: "We challenged the assumption that the state should supply all public services. We pushed academies and free schools." Crucially, as the liberals of CentreForum were nudging their way down this unfamiliar street, they bumped into conservatives of Policy Exchange, journeying the same way. "Everything we were writing and everything they were writing," says Astle "could have been put together and it would have been perfectly coherent."

From 2006, CentreForum argued that to allow meaningful choice there had to be an increase in the range of supply of good schools, and that meant looking beyond those provided by church and state: "Businesses, philanthropists, livery companies, charities, universities—anyone who could deliver good education should be allowed to supply it."

A similar, non-statist picture emerged on welfare. If the existing Lib Dem position was to measure compassion by how much government spent, CentreForum focused on how to lift people off benefit and into work. "One by one," says Astle "we challenged the shibboleths of the Kennedy era."

Perhaps the quirkiest idea to emerge, which typified CentreForum's approach, was on prisons. Why, it asked, hand blank cheques to companies that run prisons? Prisons have become Britain's most expensive seats of learning, just about the last British institutions to offer free higher education, but where the only course on the syllabus is crime. Why not incentivise these companies to transform their universities of criminality into schools of humanity, capable of reforming offenders? With half Britain's prisoners functionally illiterate and addicted to drugs, is it surprising many are back behind bars in time for next morning's porridge? Under the CentreForum alternative, prisons with low re-offending rates would be paid more: suddenly operators would have reason to teach guests about the evils of drugs and the goodness of books. The benefits to society—and to prisoners—would be immeasurable. But while Liberals have long campaigned for prison reform, believing that incarceration should be about changing rather than merely punishing criminals, few before *The Orange Book* or CentreForum would have countenanced such market solutions.

If you measure the value of a thought by its utility then unquestionably the Orange Book/CentreForum idea that will have the profoundest effect on Britain is the pupil premium, a cornerstone of the coalition agreement. Not only is this pushing vast sums towards the education of the least advantaged, it has potential to empower parents to decide where to send their child to school. This stemmed from a paper written by Clegg—based on his experiences in Holland—in *The Orange Book.*

There has been great intellectual energy around CentreForum, a point recognised by Gove, Conservative Education Secretary, who has paid tribute to the flow of ideas between those Liberal Democrats not wedded to uniform state provision and those Conservatives genuinely troubled by the inequality of life chances.

Unlike Ashcroft's political spending, Marshall has said the money he has sunk into CentreForum is about "trying to get good

ideas implemented... it's up to the party whether it accepts them."
Ingeniously, he once ventured "money is a major disadvantage in
British politics, both having it and giving it. It's what people then
associate you with. I just want to participate in a political process, a
battle of ideas, in a one-member, one-vote party. I have one vote,
like everybody else, and also want my ideas to be influential. I don't
want them to be devalued by the fact I've got money." Marshall has
insisted that if he were to bankroll the party on a lavish scale
"people will say, 'well, he's trying to buy policy'. If I don't, people
think I'm stingy.

"I've a lifelong passion for politics. I'm a lifelong liberal. I'm
trying to contribute to better ideas and help us get into government.
Funnily enough, money doesn't really help."

While Kennedy's circle liked Marshall's money, it appeared less
keen on his ideas. Oddly for a party that probably values education
more highly than any other, there was concern, even fear, over where
too much free thought might lead. Or so it seemed to those around
Marshall. The leadership wanted a think tank and the resulting
gravitas, but perhaps only if it would confirm opinions they already
held. *The Orange Book* had changed the party's intellectual
landscape. Now CentreForum worked hard to hang policy flesh on
those philosophical bones. Heavyweights such as Adair Turner were
commissioned to write challenging pamphlets, egged on by Marshall
and Astle.

Marshall read history at Oxford, focusing on the Liberal Party's high
Victorian and Edwardian pomp, and it imbued him with a love of
Liberalism. Tellingly, his favourite speech is Churchill's oration in
Dundee because "it defined the difference between socialism and
Liberalism":

"Socialism seeks to pull down wealth; Liberalism seeks to raise
up poverty. Socialism would destroy private interests; Liberalism
would preserve private interests in the only way in which they can be
safely and justly preserved, namely, by reconciling them with public
right. Socialism would kill enterprise; Liberalism would rescue
enterprise from the trammels of privilege and preference. Socialism

assails the pre-eminence of the individual; Liberalism seeks, and shall seek more in the future, to build up a minimum standard for the mass. Socialism exalts the rule; Liberalism exalts the man. Socialism attacks capital; Liberalism attacks monopoly."

Marshall joined the SDP as a "political virgin" and flew back from Germany, where he was living, to campaign in the 1983 election. Before going to INSEAD Business School in 1985, he wrote to all six SDP MPs asking for work experience. Kennedy was the only one to offer the chance. "Vehemently I was not a socialist," he says "but the appeal was that the party brought together social justice and markets, and looked as if it could achieve power." In 1987 he stood for the unwinnable West London seat of Fulham, but was baffled by the following "merger" that left centre politics less rather than more united. Disillusioned, he dipped out of politics to swim in those City waters of free-flowing money.

His career took off at Mercury Asset Management where by 1989 he was chief investment officer for European equities, managing funds worth $12 billion. He co-founded Marshall Wace in 1997 and within a few years this was ranked among Europe's top ten hedge funds, controlling a portfolio of an estimated £10 billion. On rare appearances on programmes such as BBC's *Any Questions* he would be introduced as "one of the most powerful men in the City".

But in 2003 Marshall began to think more seriously about politics, and approached Laws at the Brighton conference. This has not gone down in history like the meeting in the Willis' Tea Room of 1859 between Lords Palmerston and Russell that led to the formation of the Liberal Party, but the encounter on the terrace of the Grand Hotel was hardly without significance. Marshall asked, in exasperation, "what are we going to do about this party? Can you help me?" A precocious question, perhaps, for one without a senior role, but Laws didn't need to be asked twice: "He said 'let's do a book.'" Its purpose? To reclaim the party's liberal heritage.

But this might have been seen as a challenge to Kennedy and his social democratic assumptions. "We didn't tell Charles for six months," Marshall smiles mischievously. But with the 2005 election approaching, Marshall came clean, and to win Kennedy over invited him to write the foreword. One suggestion is Marshall drafted a version for Kennedy, and that the Liberal Democrat leader accepted it without changing a word. Marshall is tight lipped, but says: "I don't think he was engaged with policy." It wasn't, says Marshall, that Kennedy was opposed to new thought so much as he simply didn't see politics as primarily a battle of ideas: "He would make a former teacher education spokesman or a former doctor health spokesman. For Charles it wasn't about ideology but ability." The problem was these MPs started to sound suspiciously like spokesmen for the NHS or NUT rather than for their party, let alone for citizens who rely on these services—ironic, really, when Liberals had long criticised the class-based arguments of the Conservative and Labour parties for defending special interests.

Gradually the differences grew more intense between Kennedy and the new generation. Orange Book Liberals DID see things ideologically.

"I was concerned the party was adopting too many statist positions," recalls Marshall. "There is a cycle in politics. The state becomes bigger, then smaller. It was right to say the state had grown too small under the Conservatives, so I agreed with the Lib Dem policy of putting a penny on income tax to improve education." But then, when state spending as a proportion of GDP shot up, "we didn't shift back." On Health there was "absolutely no interest in a pluralist approach," that is, allowing a variety of providers, private and voluntary as well as public.

Indeed, Marshall is also scathing about the Lib Dems 2005 manifesto, "offering goodies, a tick box of bribes," including the party's promise on tuition fees. Tellingly he says: "We could never have had a coalition with the Tories after that manifesto." Kennedy's strategy was to offer a pledge card bearing five promises. "There was absolutely no intellectual coherence," says Marshall. "It would have been impossible to form a government on that basis. There is a sharp contrast to that and the programme on which Nick fought the last election."

Marshall met Clegg when the latter was a young MEP: "I thought he was telegenic, bright and pragmatic." With Marshall the word "pragmatic" is a double-edged compliment. Though he identified Clegg as the future leader most likely to push an Orange Book agenda, he was also aware Clegg, like most top-flight politicians, will sometimes sacrifice clarity for consensus.

No criticism of Clegg will cross Marshall's lips, but a friend says: "Paul is very aware that while Nick is associated with Orange Book Liberalism, he has kept open a much wider set of channels. It explains people like Danny Alexander and Neil Sherlock. It shows he isn't really a radical. Nick works with trimmers. He is a bit suspicious of people like Paul and even David. Their ideas on education, for instance, were very watered down." Clegg (and Alexander and Sherlock) would respond that a party will only take so much change, and that a healthy dose of pragmatism isn't a bad quality in a politician of the centre in coalition. And they would probably be right, for in government they have implemented the Orange Book agenda, but thanks to the emollience of Alexander and co they avoided a massive bust up with the party.

Still, some around Marshall looked in concern at Clegg's first hundred days, even wondering if they should have backed Huhne. "Nick was just very cautious," says Marshall, who found Martin Narey's social mobility commission that Clegg set up "a damp squib". Other's would counter that the report from the Bernardo chief executive did at least reiterate how two babies born in adjoining hospital beds will have entirely different life chances thanks to our class system—and that, in 2010, cannot be banged on about enough.

Fundamentally, CentreForum types will say that, far from being right wingers, it is they who are driven by revulsion for social injustice, and are looking for radical ways to improve the lives of those who have been handed few chances. They claim Clegg has less interest in these meat and bone issues than in traditional Liberal pre-occupations such as civil rights, internationalism and constitutional reform.

Yet Marshall acknowledges that in government Clegg has championed social mobility and made it a core element of Liberal Democrat identity. "Nick's commitment to social mobility may turn out to be our most important contribution to this Coalition," he says. "It is fundamentally different from Labour, which primarily seeks to equalise outcomes through fiscal transfers. The Liberal approach to social justice is about enabling all people to achieve their potential. It is about opportunity, not dependency."

And this ties in with Marshall's big political interest, the need for fundamental public service reform. Throughout Labour's reign he made a robust critique of Gordon Brown's refusal to re-structure the antiquated, unresponsive services he was virtually force feeding billions of pounds. While some Liberals pulled their punches when attacking Labour's top down spending—reasoning Conservatives had so badly underfunded schools and hospitals any "investment" was hard to criticise—Marshall warned that spending would be "up to the European average on health and [yet we] will have far worse results, and up to the European average on education and we have far worse results. Labour has blown it".

Yet he remained cynical of Conservative re-branding, considering it superficial. And for all his apparent ease with the right, Marshall's primary political interest is actually how to give the deprived his advantages. Not that he seems to enjoy the trappings especially. He has lived in the same house in SW London for years. He even acquired his office, not for its high panorama but its low rent. He is a major figure in Ark, a charity which helps children of abuse, illness, disability and poverty. Even in his leisure—his passion is Manchester United—he is interested in how fans and communities could be given more power over increasingly remote clubs.

As for his own chances of power, he toyed before the election with standing in Holborn and St Pancras. However, commitment to his job remained paramount and he decided to remain in his preferred position, the shadows. They are shadows from which he continues to pull many strings.

I ask whether, when he looks back to the misery of that conference by the seaside, he believed Liberal Democrats would be transformed so soon into a party of government. He ponders, then says: "No, but I did believe there were half a dozen Liberal Democrat MPs coming through of genuine ability. Part of my motivation was to provide a shop window for their talents." Marshall designed some very fetching window displays. And the public, it transpired, liked Marshall's wares.

What's that noise: surely not the purrs of a large, white cat...?

8

VINCE CABLE

A BOSSA NOVA NOT YET OVER

It is a rare achievement, to become a major politician in what was for over half a century dismissed as also-ran political party. Even the profile of a Liberal Democrat leader hovered often somewhere between that of Mullah Omah and a figure of fun on *Extras,* which might explain why the party's MPs of more discreet reputation can be driven into such indiscreet scandals; gaining a high profile by simply being a good politician has proved mighty elusive for Lib Dems.

Sir Menzies Campbell was a rare exception, becoming a *Newsnight* habitué long before he took on the party leadership, but he could opine from the high moral ground of international affairs. Vince Cable is remarkable for becoming arguably the country's most trusted authority in the hard fought and morally grubby ground of money.

From the moment in 2003 when the former Shell chief economist was appointed Shadow Chancellor, the media warmed to him, finding a gravitas that wasn't immediately evident in the man destined to become his Conservative counterpart, George Osborne. In significant part it was about tone. If the Tory appeared a little shrill, Cable's serious, honest manner reassured.

This was invaluable for a party long considered strong on "soft" questions but weak on "hard" answers. Suddenly the Lib Dem voice was heard not only on polar bears and gender equality but on deficit reduction and banking regulation.

Soon Cable was effectively being asked to adjudicate as a trusted wise head well above the childish political fray, an *éminence grise* on the small screen. Crucially he predicted the economic meltdown while government and official opposition alike were essentially humming "crisis? What crisis?" As early as 2003 he demanded of Brown: "Is not the brutal truth that... the growth of the British economy is sustained by consumer spending pinned against record levels of personal debt, which is secured, if at all, against house prices that the Bank of England describes as well above equilibrium?" Cable has played down his prescience, saying he didn't see the cold front blowing from America which would gather into the global storm. Critics carped that he had been predicting gloom for too long before the doom, but if an architect says a building lacks foundations, his findings are hardly rendered wrong by the building taking time to collapse. Huhne has remarked: "Right the way up to 2008 we were being pooh-poohed by the Labour Treasury front bench, accused of being sandwich-board men in Oxford Street, warning doom is nigh. The arrogance with which they dismissed concerns is breathtaking."

As well as mastering national economics, Cable proved a dexterous politician. His idea to reduce income tax for the low paid was a masterstroke, a political triangulation Osborne has had the grace to admit he wished he'd come up with. Was it, a confused political class wondered, right or left wing? It was a tax cut (right), but weighted to help the poor (so left). Either way the proposal was popular, consistent with the party's Radical tradition of helping the vulnerable to help themselves. It boosted low incomes, not with more deadening benefit, but with higher take home pay, incentivising work. This came to epitomise the Orange Book approach, using market solutions to achieve socially desirable ends. It frustrated Cable that Campbell did not promote the policy, prompting the Shadow Chancellor to complain privately at a party conference that Sir Ming was not even planning to mention it in his oration.

"Vince's approach is to tax bad things first," says Marshall. "So first consumption, then assets, and only then income. Income is what you tax least. Vince, in framing it that way, was so much cleverer than any rival politician. The Tories had never seen it like that." If Marshall has a criticism it is that the redistributive element went too far, and wouldn't raise enough to justify it.

Another rare Cable achievement was to gain respect from both wings of the party. He had been a Labour parliamentary candidate who knew Brown from Glasgow University days, so could hardly be dismissed as a "closet Tory". Yet he had come to see, more clearly than many Liberal Democrats, that the post-war settlement hadn't worked, and to improve living standards and public services of the disadvantaged, government would have to empower them as individuals. Advisers from the party's right such as Julian Astle have called him one of the few really big political figures of the age. And impressively for a senior politician, he was open to new thought, likely to suggest over dinner "yes, we should look into that..." As the coalition was formed, even a Tory commentator swooned: "How we need him as our Prime Minister!"

Critics attributed his rise to an ambiguity, deliberate or accidental, which made him hard to pigeon-hole. In the lead-up to the last election when Jeremy Browne was Cable's *de facto* deputy, Browne would complain that conducting media interviews was a nightmare as he wasn't always sure whether Cable's line was that the government was cutting too little or too much. "Jeremy used to say 'I don't mind which one but I do wish it was one or the other,'" a minister recalls. "Everyone loved Vince's tone but the words were all over the place."

Tory papers cast Cable as a left-wing firebrand, a scourge of fat cats and monstrous media moguls. But rivals on the left have a strikingly different take: "His contribution to *The Orange Book* was so right wing it had to be watered down," says a policy wonk. "Nick has told me he often has to rein Vince in, such as when he suggested any civil servant earning over £100,000 a year should be made to re-apply for his job."

A minister recalls an earlier discussion when Lib Dems were thrashing out policy on local income tax. "Someone asked whether the tax would be higher for top earners the way income tax is, and Vince said 'Well I don't agree with that. I don't think people should pay more than 50 per cent tax.'"

Meanwhile the wonk also points to decidedly old fashioned moral positions which don't always fit with the social Liberalism of activists. If one of the key divisions in British politics cutting across left and right is between roundheads and cavaliers, Cable is a roundhead.

Winning over the cantankerous rank and file was challenge enough, but few could have predicted Cable would grow into such a national treasure, gracing the floor as a contestant on *Strictly Come Dancing*. Yet for a man who has attained the highest level in ballroom dancing—an "International Supreme Award"—he doesn't always move comfortably in his own skin.

He is diffident, even a little awkward, with none of the easy loquaciousness of Charlie "Chat Show" Kennedy. He has a tendency to screw up his eyes and look down at an interlocutor, not from self-importance, but to see them better. One senior admirer, wishing Cable might have become party leader, remarked: "If only he didn't have ear hair."

But in a frivolous age it might have been precisely because Cable wasn't blow-dried and moisturised that people took to him so. More than this, if charm is a political weapon, how much deadlier is niceness? Cable is a man who has endured a difficult life while making few complaints. He and his three children were devastated by the death in 2001 of wife and mother, Olympia Rebelo, a Goan Roman Catholic who Cable married in the teeth of opposition from his disapproving father. A working class Tory, Vince's father declared mixed marriages "don't work", a prejudice reciprocated by Olympia's father.

Cable met Olympia "in the unromantic setting of a York mental hospital where we happened to be working as nurses during a summer vacation." His ardour was sufficiently powerful for him to take a job in Kenya, where she went to live, and wooed her further.

After the couple's marriage in Nairobi in 1968 they didn't speak to either family for five years. It was a strong union, later captured by their daughter Aida as "incredibly close and affectionate", with Cable sharing the school run and ironing with his volcanic but affectionate music-teacher wife. Their children—barrister, opera singer and scientist—are all Cambridge graduates, like papa. They recall a cheerful childhood scored by classical music. This was interspersed with embarrassing interludes of dad practicing ballroom dancing steps on Saturday mornings, down supermarket aisles.

But as the 1997 election approached, Olympia's breast cancer—which the couple believed cured—returned. At Olympia's insistence, Cable fought the election, while holding down his job at Shell. He continued to look after his ailing wife until her death in 2001, from when Cable cut a lonely figure. It is a lasting sadness she experienced the years of wilderness but none of the dizziness.

Whenever a spouse dies, journalists play up a couple's closeness to accentuate the tragedy of the rupture, but in Cable's case the reported pain seems, if anything, understated. Despite the spring that has returned to his step since a second marriage to Rachel, he wears old and new wedding rings, one gold, one silver—letting off a dazzling light. Cable's three children, now grown, opposed the second marriage but are now reconciled.

Cable was born in York in 1943 and attended a local grammar, commenting that "my upbringing wasn't so happy". Indeed, the cosiness kindled in his family could be seen as a response to the coldness of childhood. There was, he says, "no emotional warmth and quite a lot of tension". Papa banned Vince, who wanted to be a writer, from studying anything "arty", while Vince's mother was hospitalised for depression. His class-obsessed father started in a factory aged 15, rose to be a teacher at a technical college, and died delivering leaflets for the Conservatives in a snowstorm. If Cable rejected his father's politics he accepted a little of his Puritanism, or what Cable calls his "workaholism". He says his mother gave him a "self-effacing modesty", which he confesses he has now lost—indeed, one rival has detected a growing vanity.

At Cambridge Cable read natural sciences and economics while rising to become president of the Union. He was a Liberal but later, studying for a PhD at Glasgow, became a Labour councillor. He contested Glasgow Hillhead for Labour in 1970 and became special adviser to John Smith, later Labour leader. But disenchanted by Labour's leftward lurch, Cable joined the newly formed SDP in 1982. In 1997 he finally defeated Tory Toby Jessel in Twickenham, where he has increased his majority at three subsequent elections.

As economics spokesman he said the party should stand for "fairer taxes, not higher taxes". As far back as 2005, Cable was floating the possibility of a Conservative coalition, earning a rebuke from Kennedy. Within months Cable was deputed to hand his leader a letter from MPs demanding his resignation, a dagger blow for Kennedy and a case of "Et tu, Vince?"

With Sir Ming elected leader as the unity candidate, Cable became deputy and his reputation rose further. The one occasion his political antennae might have deserted him was in proposing a "mansion tax", with its invigorating historical resonances with Lloyd George's land tax and crusade against aristocracy. But one man's "mansion" is another's maisonette and in the expensive South East, relatively ordinary abodes would be caught—not least, as the London *Standard* reported gleefully, sundry semis in his Twickenham backyard. It was not a policy that made it into the coalition agreement with the Conservatives.

With Sir Ming harried from office in 2007, Cable stood in, and soon won acclaim, even from sketch writers, particularly for his deadly attack on Brown at Prime Minister's Questions, telling his old acquaintance he had undergone a "remarkable transformation in the last few weeks from Stalin to Mr Bean, creating chaos out of order rather than order out of chaos". Ouch. The *Economist* hailed it "the single best line of Gordon Brown's premiership".

Meanwhile, Cable kept up his more sober critique, warning against indebtedness. This built on his reputation for probity, after his early call to nationalise the ailing Northern Rock, and his coruscating attack on ministers for losing data on 25 million child benefit claims. His stance suited the suddenly sombre age, a rather Victorian figure standing out against a Labour Party as bewitched by fast money as the Conservatives. Cable, voters realised, would never be caught with Mandelson or Osborne on a plutocrat's floating gin palace.

If timing is all then Cable's biggest mistake might have been to enter the national stage late. After Sir Ming was pilloried for being "decrepit", the party could hardly replace one mature gent with another—especially with the luxuriantly coiffed Clegg and Huhne waiting expectantly in grease paint. After taking soundings, Cable did not stand.

But in 2010 he became Business Secretary, the most senior Lib Dem in government save Clegg, and evidence that if Cable hadn't been prepared to tango with Tories there would have been no coalition. But his reputation was damaged by a sting operation involving undercover *Telegraph* reporters. During a secretly taped conversation with a couple Cable believed to be constituents, he declared his intention to wage "war" on Rupert Murdoch. Perhaps a similar sting on Liam Fox might have revealed the Defence Secretary's determination to wage war on Liberal Democrats or poor people, but alas *Telegraph* subterfuge didn't extend to Conservatives. It made Cable unpopular, briefly, with colleagues, and he was stripped of responsibility for regulating media, thus denying Cable (and indeed the *Telegraph*) the spectre of a humbled Murdoch.

Since then, Cable has cranked up the pressure, attacking what he sees as Cameron's illiberal position on immigration, on moral as well as practical grounds. As Business Secretary he acknowledges the massive contribution of foreign workers to our economy. Little by little his language grew less temperate.

However, Tory ministers speak with respect for the hard decisions Cable has made, not least pushing through rises in tuition fees, despite long standing Lib Dem opposition. They realise that if they can keep Cable inside the tent the coalition might survive; if he takes the air outside, the tent may blow after him.

Besides, as we've seen, political success is not determined by commentators. If Cable has pandered to the gallery, it will not have harmed his standing. And since his appearance on *Strictly*—which Clegg apparently felt a *pas de deux* too close with our celebrity culture—the ballroom dancer's popularity can only have increased among the populace to a "10".

His standing and humour were hit by the difficulty of a Conservative coalition, of reeling with reaction. He started to emit the discreet melancholy of a character in a late Saul Bellow or John

Updike novel. But Cable has overcome much, not least grief and anonymity. Tories who revelled in his humbling over Murdoch suddenly looked foolish with the explosion of the phone hacking scandal. Once again Cable was revealed to have been the voice in the wilderness.

He is unlikely to go gentle into that good night. Cable is strictly business.

9

CHRIS HUHNE

FROM LSD VIA SLD TO CID

Some politicians have easy charm; Chris Huhne's is a little more difficult. Colleagues variously describe him as "ruthless", "ambitious" and "arrogant". Even one of his closest allies tells me "Chris isn't very warm". He is rarely one for small talk, so interviewers don't ask him those banal, popular culture questions from the *Smash Hits* canon of political journalism such as "what's your favourite band?" (I've even seen "what's your favourite colour?"). Fools, you see, are not suffered by the Secretary of State for Climate Change, gladly or otherwise.

But I've never met a colleague who doesn't respect Huhne. And when a politician complains that a fellow MP is ruthless, ambitious or arrogant, isn't he actually saying: "he's better than me"? There was at least a hint of that in the grumble of some around Clegg when they said Huhne broke an undertaking not to stand against Campbell for the party's leadership. Huhne had been in parliament for just a year and many colleagues, including a furious Clegg, viewed Huhne's bid as not merely precocious but treacherous: the party was in crisis after Kennedy's enforced resignation and all likely candidates, Huhne included, had agreed to rally round Campbell in a public display of unity.

When I've questioned Huhne about his *volte face* he has said variously that he had never given a guarantee not to stand and that he was considerably older than Clegg, so while Nick would have other opportunities, this might have been his one shot. But another explanation is that Huhne simply saw his chance and went for it. One very senior figure complains: "He's always got his eye on the main chance." But for a senior politician, is that a heinous crime—or a job reference? Neither Brown nor Cameron was likely to say to a Liberal

Democrat leader "my dear fellow—after you". The qualities that can make Huhne a challenging colleague render him a formidable opponent.

But many of Huhne's former allies in the Orange Book camp felt bruised, and never forgave him. I witnessed the Huhne machine's tactics during his second leadership campaign, and it certainly couldn't be accused of diffidence.

Huhne was bold—arguably outperforming the telegenic Clegg in their live leadership debate—even if Orange Bookers doubted his sincerity. "He has been highly cynical pandering to the left," one colleague, now a minister, told me.

However, Huhne insisted to me subsequently that he has always been at the "centre" of the party, and was expressing honestly-held opinions. Indeed, he claims any duplicity was on the other side. He points to *The Orange Book* itself: he only agreed to contribute, he said, on condition he could read everyone else's essay as he didn't want to rock Kennedy's already shaky boat. But mysteriously the controversial Laws chapter was never sent him. An issue with the printer was blamed but Huhne was angry, saying he would never have grown involved. Certainly his intellectual powers are prodigious and he is largely responsible for the party's environmental and green tax policies which have given the Lib Dems such a lead on this key issue.

Huhne's flaw is a refusal to humour those of meaner intelligence. A populist touch might be faintly despicable, but also indispensible to be party leader in an age when you have to come across as affable on a TV studio's squidgy sofa as well as rapier sharp on the floor of the House.

In his televised debate with Clegg when an amusing anecdote was required, he launched in with an "I remember when I was in the European parliament…", at which point he would have lost 90 per cent of his audience. Laws claims that as the coalition negotiations dragged on, Huhne suggested the party should brief the press that such talks on the continent typically last for weeks. As Laws surmised, such an argument—however cogently constructed—was unlikely to satisfy the hounds of Fleet Street. However, any pomposity is, as a former colleague says, "a simple inability to see himself as others see him. He is actually a very nice guy."

If Huhne was desperately unlucky to lose the leadership to Clegg, he was luckier in birth. He was born in West London in 1954 to a successful businessman, Peter Paul-Huhne, and fifties screen and stage actress Ann Murray.

At Westminster School—where Clegg would follow—he was considered bright, bordering on brilliant. By 17 he possessed a positively unnatural grasp of economics. But that was far from his only passion.

"He was a huge lothario," I'm told by Patrick Wintour, political editor of the *Guardian* and friend through Westminster and Oxford who became Huhne's best man. "There was a different conquest every weekend, while I stayed in listening to my James Taylor LPs." Huhne's personality, then, was already firmly established even before his exposure to Paris during a stint at the Sorbonne.

At Oxford he bagged a first in PPE and a reputation for agitation. A photo resurfaced during a leadership bid of a long-haired radical joyously leading a student protest. Huhne appeared to be brandishing a park bench. But while the press subsequently built Huhne into a revolutionary, Wintour points out that at Oxford in 1973 to be a supporter of the soft-left *Tribune* Group marked him as almost reactionary when most students "were either members of one Trot group or another or were professional hippies". When Huhne and co were attempting to batter down a door it was to establish a central Student Union, not destroy capitalism.

"He always seemed a little older than contemporaries," recalls Wintour "and determined to make a success of himself far more than most. He was never short of an opinion and always better read." He was rarely seen out of a beret, reflecting a Europeanism fed by summers at the family's "lovely though very run down" holiday cottage in the Languedoc.

As editor of *Isis*, the Oxford student paper, he bossed many future big names of British journalism, including Tina Brown. When Huhne was 19 an article appeared under his name extolling the charms of LSD experimentation, though when newspapers later dug this up they must surely have known that it would have made a more startling story if a student of the era had penned a coruscating condemnation of mind-altering substances. Huhne has confessed to being a "revolting" student, which is surely preferable to being an unquestioning one.

He dropped a barrel from his name and travelled to India as an undercover stringer, defying a ban on western journalists. He then landed a job on the *Economist* and later the *Guardian*, rising to be economics editor and writing a thoughtful, balanced column, free of milky socialist pieties. After a stint at the *Independent on Sunday* he hung up his pen in 1994 and skipped to more lucrative pastures in the Square Mile, later founding a credit ratings agency which tried to calculate "scientifically" the risk of investing in different countries. This trousered £3.5 million, providing what he has called a "cushion". This decidedly plump posterior-rest enabled him to buy seven or nine houses (estimates vary), which in an American politician might be regarded as an achievement, but in Britain was exposed as a dirty secret.

Throughout his journalistic career Huhne had remained politically active, though gradually lost faith with Labour. "He was always very political, and despite talk of being a careerist, became obsessed with voting reform and so joined the SDP, poor man," says Wintour. "He was not as calculating as some think. If he had not done so he would have been a Labour cabinet minister in the Blair years."

After various tilts at Westminster he was, in 1999, elected to the European Parliament, where he mastered the technocratic intricacies of that most process-driven institution. His profile grew. In a joint interview with Clegg, the duo were billed by Rachel Sylvester as the "Lennon and McCartney of the Lib Dems"—but though they were equals there was always the suspicion Clegg would be first among them.

Still, the two old boys of Westminster School entered Westminster parliament together in 2005, where Huhne wasted little time before launching his first leadership bid.

There was gleeful press interest when claims surfaced he owned a share of an Egyptian goldmine. So interesting did some newspapers start finding him they promoted him from being "Chris Whom?" to "Nine Homes Huhne", making more of his wealth than his wealth of experience. He was particularly irked when *Observer* hack Nick Cohen made repeated reference to Huhne's private number plate, H11HNE.

He had been married, since 1984, to Vicky Pryce, who had left her husband and taken her two children to live with Huhne. Subsequently the Huhnes had three children together.

"There are two sides to Chris," Wintour reflects. "One is very authoritative and demanding, the other funny, self aware and vulnerable. The great thing about Vicky was that she punctured his pomposity."

Pryce became a senior civil servant who in the miniscule world of the British establishment came to work in the private office of Cable at the point Huhne's affair with Carina Trimingham was exposed. Pryce quickly left for a job in the private sector. According to a tabloid source familiar with the story Huhne was given virtually no notice that his affair was to be revealed, an echo of the Robin Cook *cause celeb* when the Foreign Secretary was forced to make an instant decision whether to stick with his wife or twist with his mistress. I saw Huhne shortly afterwards and he looked exhausted, shattered.

One friend remarks: "He managed his break up hopelessly, but I don't think they [Chris and Vicky] had been happy for a long time, and she can be relentless. It is horrible what has happened and however angry she is, she has not been well advised. But that is not much use now."

Trimingham was a former party worker and Sky reporter who tabloids labelled "bisexual". A bizarre spat erupted when newspapers suggested she wore Dr Martens (she pleaded innocent of the charge). However she was shod, coverage was shoddy, with Trimingham and Pryce both subjected to intrusion. Trimingham had worked on Huhne's leadership bid against Clegg and a relationship developed, apparently later. Certainly she was very committed, booing loudly when it was announced victory was Clegg's.

Pryce, meanwhile, appears to regard Huhne's desertion as less a request for a divorce than a declaration of war. She is even rumoured to be following in the gold-trodden path of Margaret Cook, who wrote a robust account of Robin's record as a husband, and then a further study on "the demented world of men in power". Pryce's book is reportedly entitled *Thirty Minutes to Kill the Story*, a reference to Huhne's alleged reaction when he discovered the press had rumbled his affair.

As well as fighting over the couple's property portfolio, Pryce is rumoured to have leaked to a newspaper claims that Huhne tried to pass on a speeding offence to avoid a driving ban. Huhne denied the allegations. After police said they would interview Huhne, any credit rating agency tracking his career would have marked it down sharply. Indeed, he found himself in the unusual position of being simultaneously the bookies favourite to be the next cabinet minister sacked and also to be Clegg's replacement. Such has been the turbulence at 20,000 feet aboard Air Clegg.

As the crisis deepened even Conservative ministers marvelled at Huhne's focus, as he remained relentless in pursuit of an argument even while fitting in interviews with CID. But any half-human, half-politician was bound to feel profoundly wounded by this savage fight. I'm told all his children bar his eldest daughter turned against him, with one apparently willing to testify it was him driving the speeding car. Pryce even rang to discuss the case in a call that was taped, and not at Huhne's end. The cabinet minister realised half way through and protested his innocence. A transcript found its way into print.

While privately acknowledging his failings, Huhne was understood to feel bitter at the low skulduggery and raw hate he apparently faced. All his private papers remained in the family home in his Eastleigh constituency, including the diary that would establish his whereabouts at the crucial time, yet Pryce apparently refused him access. And then there was the presence of a friend of Pryce's, whom friends of Huhne claimed was "poison" and "stoking it up".

Huhne was also furious that even a Lib Dem appeared to be briefing against him after stories emerged making clear that this incident was different to an earlier allegation for which Huhne did possess an alibi. According to one friend the blame lay either with Norman Baker (highly unlikely) "or else Chris thinks the paper simply made it up".

Yet Huhne has remarkable powers of recovery and within days was telling friends he was confident there would be no charges. "Vicky has finally woken up to what she is letting herself in for," said a friend. "She could be charged with perverting the course of justice too. She has run away and just wants to drop the whole thing." Meanwhile newspapers dispatched reporters to Brussels in the hope of uncovering any further colourful details about his time as an MEP. They returned empty handed.

The trial by newspaper should not overshadow Huhne's contributions, which provide more points in his favour than might or might not end up on his driving license.

Huhne was the main cheerleader for the coalition, forcing the party to see that its instinctive opposition was based primarily on tribal dislike of Conservatives. He emphasized repeatedly that with an economy in freefall, stable majority government was essential. He was also sanguine about the political cost, telling me he thought the party's poll rating could fall to as low as 5 per cent, as voters punished the party for dealing with the Tories and delivering cuts. However, he argued that after three hard years the economy would recover and the administration would gain political room to introduce measures that would lead to political recovery.

And as Climate Change secretary Huhne faced full on the difficult question of nuclear power. Traditionally Liberals regarded the atomic option as radioactive, politically as well as environmentally. But even before the election Huhne went some way towards persuading his party that in the battle against global warming it might be a necessary evil. Indeed, with coal-fired power stations ruled out due to their emissions, and Huhne committed to highly ambitious targets on greenhouse gases, he was relying on nuclear to cover our energy needs. If anyone could pull the party behind this difficult measure it was Huhne.

In government Huhne was not shy about drawing on a CV far

more extensive than most cabinet colleagues. He said: "I spent five years in the City heading a team which eyeballed finance ministers and central bank governors when they were facing massive problems. I never want a British Chancellor to be in the position these guys were in. Therefore it's essential we tackle this deficit." Privately, however, he was thought to harbour significant doubts about the scale of cuts and engaged in cabinet rows on the subject.

He is a deft operator, Huhne, and was unavoidably detained at a UN climate-change conference which, no doubt to his chagrin, forced him to miss the controversial Commons vote on raising tuition fees.

With Clegg's popularity slipping there was press speculation Huhne would replace him as leader, which Huhne's friends did little to discourage. But suddenly his priority was to hold what he had. Besides, fighting climate change is challenge enough. Indeed, the environment is a cause he identified back in the early eighties, before it was fashionable. He was not about to give up the chance to make vital decisions in this critical area without a struggle.

Whatever Clegg and Huhne felt for each other privately, they knew they needed each other against the Tory tiger. Huhne was badly wounded, but the swordsman had yet to relinquish his spear.

10

LAST ORDERS

From the moment the bong of Big Ben bade him back to Westminster, Clegg looked a future leader: thoughtful, articulate and personable. And a "family man". He was also candidate of the party's bright, modernising wing that coalesced under the informal title "Orange Book Liberals", arguing that the party's belief in freedom should extend to our economic settlement.

Laws had been in parliament longer and, with the serious hedge fund player Marshall, was the driving force behind *The Orange Book*. But Clegg had scarcely found a desk in parliament before Laws and other Orange Book Lib Dems identified Clegg as the one to wear the rather rusty crown. Clegg and Laws became dining companions between evening votes, though they abandoned Shepherds, the stuffy Westminster restaurant, after Clegg apparently spotted a cockroach on the other's otherwise finished plate.

"I remember talking to Nick in 2005, not long after he was elected and telling him I thought he should be next leader," Laws tells me. "He was flattered, but had endured a difficult year. One of his sons had been ill. Family is very central to him. In fact I don't know how people with families manage to do politics. He said 'if I stand I will have to talk this through with Miriam and get her agreement.'"

It didn't take Clegg long, however, to square any domestic circles. And here we come to this story's second "Granita moment", Granita being the now defunct Islington restaurant where Tony Blair munched on rabbit and polenta while persuading Gordon Brown not to run against him—as Brown glowered, sipped water and felt his ambitions being eaten alive.

The Lib Dem equivalent was a happier meeting, in the sunny

garden of the Dinnington Docks pub near Hinton St George, South Somerset. Clegg had come down the night before to speak to Yeovil Lib Dems. "I introduced him by saying not only is Nick a friend, he is a future leader of the party," recalls Laws. Next day, after a couple of engagements, Laws was driving Clegg across that beautiful old Roman Road, the Fosse Way, deep in the Somerset countryside on their way to lunch when Clegg said: "I have spoken to Miriam and she has given the green light."

Over lunch Clegg pushed Laws: "Are you sure you won't want to stand?"

"No," Laws replied. "You are the best person for the job." Unlike Brown with Blair, Laws has not claimed subsequently that Clegg promised to stand aside in his second term—which might, in any case, sound a little presumptuous in a party that hadn't seen active service in the front line of British politics for eight decades.

If colleagues took to Clegg, journalists scooped him up with greater alacrity, unusual for a Lib Dem. They saw in him the same modernising ambition they had admired in Blair and Cameron, a willingness to run against the party. The old guard would also argue that Clegg was a little too similar to Blair and Cameron, being smooth, metropolitan and pro-market—a familiar figure at journalistic lunches in Christopher's American Bar and Grill in Covent Garden, and in the evening on the dinner party circuit.

For as well as being identified early on as the Lib Dem to watch, he was also good company. His easy manner won admirers, and he was comfortable with the teasing and gossip of a media lunch. So he would tell Andrew Rawnsley how cushy the columnist had it for taking skiing holidays and being able to collect his kids from school. When he visited my house in the country he burst through to my study declaring "I've got to see this" before exploding in mirth: "you lucky bugger!"

All of which would count for little except he had brain and ambition to go with the winning manner. But from the outset of his parliamentary career Clegg had a less easy relationship with Kennedy. The leader appointed him Europe spokesman under Sir Menzies Campbell, with whom Clegg formed a close, almost father-son friendship. But Kennedy suspected Clegg harboured ambition, and ambition is not always a quality admired by leaders in subordinates. "Nick has a great future," a close Kennedy aide growled at me "but he has only just entered parliament. He needs to be patient."

But Clegg was impatient with the drift. He shared the frustration of Laws with Kennedy's "health problems", which they found shambolic. This was despite a sharp team Kennedy had around him, including Lord Razzall (known as "Razzall-Dazzle"), a former head of a major City law firm whose partner is a fellow peer, Baroness Bonham-Carter.

Kennedy tended to see politics as the slow march of historical forces, whereas Clegg and Laws wanted to actively engage the enemy. They also feared the party had meandered too left, sometimes outflanking Labour in defence of producer interests. They would be driven to despair when Kennedy roused Lib Dem audiences by declaring that people didn't want choice in hospitals, they just wanted a good one near where they lived. To which Orange Book Liberals would retort under their breath: "you may as well say you want honey for tea," for it entirely begged the question how you delivered a good local hospital.

Clegg's position could scarcely have jarred more with his leader's. In a controversial interview that won Clegg pats on the back (external) and hatchets in the back (internal), he told Marie Woolf, then of the *Independent*: "I think breaking up the NHS is exactly what you do need to do to make it a more responsive service." And Woolf lured him into further rumination, about the insurance-based systems of mainland Europe and Canada, a suggestion which was to land Laws in such trouble: "I think it would be really, really daft to rule out any other model from Europe or elsewhere," Clegg said. "I do think they deserve to be looked at because frankly the faults of the British health service compared to others still leave much to be desired." Later he grew sceptical of the workability of insurance schemes, but his willingness to think afresh challenged the leadership.

So Clegg was one who signed a letter circulated by Cable calling for Kennedy to resign. It was brutal. I liked Kennedy and had made very minor contributions to a few of his speeches. I was also the last journalist to conduct an interview with him in his leader's office, and my jaw remained on the floor for much of it. Even before he resigned Kennedy looked a man mauled half to death, and his close pack of loyal staff snarled of betrayal. With the door shut and his gatekeepers outside fending off the hounds howling for political meat, Kennedy spoke more softly of wanting to get better for his child. I felt terribly sorry, reflecting how happy he had seemed when I'd interviewed him a few years before on the eve of his wedding.

But it also wasn't hard to see why his MPs were revolting, particularly talented young ones who had little time for the late night indulgences of Commons clubmen. They were aghast at stories of their party leader setting off for far-flung towns to make a speech, only to arrive at the station in no state to deliver it. For while Kennedy insisted he had his drinking under control, he told me he had not received professional help other than a brief chat with his doctor, and nor would he. Anyone who has tried to help an alcoholic knows well the denial process, and how radical the change in behaviour must be to tackle dependency. His MPs had confronted Kennedy twice before and he had promised to quit. Alas I didn't leave his study with huge confidence that this time would be so different.

For a party sometimes characterised as squeamish, it betrayed little sentimentality in deposing Kennedy. In a touching show of loyalty, an ITN reporter who had worked for Kennedy revealed his alcoholism. At a press conference, extraordinary as it was emotional, Kennedy admitted his problem. But lingering hopes that he could cling on were washed away in a torrent of insincere sympathy. "Charles needs to go away and get help", his MPs intoned.

But none of this caused Clegg to crack open the Champers. The widely-held assumption was that Kennedy would struggle on for another couple of years, giving Clegg time to develop his political brand. But across the parliamentary party there was an acceptance Kennedy would have to go immediately.

Clegg declared himself unready, having only entered parliament the year before. Moreover, the party was in turmoil. Clegg reasoned that the Lib Dems needed a reassuring, unity candidate. Very swiftly most alighted upon the impeccably sober Sir Menzies Campbell QC.

After all, it was hard to imagine anyone more consensual or deserving of loyalty than the former Olympic sprinter. But journalists, being naturally generous spirits, interpreted Clegg's reluctance as cowardice. Why, they demanded, would Clegg not seize the moment as Cameron had with such verve, rather than electing a stop-gap years too late out of the starting blocks? However, Clegg responded that for all Cameron's apparent freshness, he had served a full term before standing. What could not be so easily dismissed was the suggestion that the "Ming" team—effectively run by Clegg, Laws and Browne—was about young cardinals voting for old popes.

Campbell had, in his courteous way, been lobbying for the job even before Kennedy announced his resignation. At a dinner when Campbell was asked if he wanted the top job, he demurred as a gentleman must; but across the table, through a fog of cigarette smoke, the gravely tones of Lady Campbell settled the matter: "Of course you want it Ming. Don't be ridiculous."

As soon as Kennedy announced his resignation, Laws took it upon himself to rally support for Campbell, but he encountered an early obstacle in the formidable form of Ashdown. Campbell had taken Ashdown to dinner at the Reform Club in the hope of persuading him to endorse him, and while Ashdown had said he would back his old friend if he must, he felt it time for the next generation. Ashdown told Laws in stronger terms he wanted Clegg.

Ashdown eventually did back Campbell, but first urged Clegg to throw his sombrero into the ring: "I told Nick this is the one time you can fight an election and afford to lose. And looking at how close Chris Huhne fought Ming, I think Nick could have won."

Laws disagrees. "I think it would have been a bad idea for Nick to stand," he tells me now. "Having asked Ming to, it would have made the result very uncertain as then everyone would have thrown hats into the ring. I never felt there was a moment he felt seriously he might. He would have asked those of us who had been involved in asking Ming to stand. I think what gave him cause to think was Paddy pushing him so hard."

However, Clegg was furious when Huhne apparently broke an agreement not to fight. Huhne had been the only Liberal Democrat parliamentarian at Clegg's wedding but a mutual antipathy grew, and lingered.

When Campbell declared himself a candidate, he was introduced by Clegg. It was central to the Campbell strategy to show that even though he was the oldster, he had support of bright young things. However, Clegg's speech was perhaps a little too good. Laws smiles: "though I'm sure this wasn't his intention, everyone must have thought 'Nick should be the next leader of the party'."

When I interviewed Campbell during his campaign I feared an unseemly bout of mud-wrestling could damage his hitherto impeccable record. In his office in Portcullis House I found him tired, unsurprisingly in a tough political contest after a battle with cancer. Nor was he in the best mood. Even without the affliction of a honking cough, he would still have been spluttering, so irritated was he that two female journalists had dared ask why he and Lady Elspeth had never had children: "Bloody impertinent!" he told me. Which it was, but I had to restrain myself from replying that if he really wanted to be leader he had better grow used to worse impertinences. Later his more natural congeniality returned, but I wondered if he might have fared better in a less vulgar era, the Edwardian age of the Liberal Prime Minister Campbell Bannerman rather than the second Elizabethan age of Campbell.

For the Orange Book movement there was little sign Campbell would embrace market-orientated policies. Even Browne, acting as Campbell's press officer and sitting in on our interview, remarked afterwards (off the record): "I'm sorry. That was pretty awful."

To Clegg's intense relief Campbell won, despite strong showing from Huhne, whose vigorous campaign made even some of Sir Ming's staunchest supporters wonder if they had backed the right thoroughbred. Privately, Clegg found Campbell's rather old-fashioned economic policies scarcely more illuminating than Kennedy's, but he recognised in Campbell a professional who would bring discipline. There was also secret satisfaction that Campbell had not lost to such an able man of 51 who could have gone on and on.

Style is also an underrated factor. Though of different generations, Clegg felt comfortable with the chalk-striped, serious-minded Campbell, who could both move with ease from high minded political debate to social conversation. The pair liked each other, and it showed. Clegg was less taken by the Kennedy way, with its boisterous and faintly crumpled late night ruminations over whisky about the tide and drift of political waters.

Clegg had scarcely been in parliament a year, was not yet in the shadow cabinet and since becoming an MP had not stood for election among colleagues. Yet he had a style and a stance that appealed to pretty well all he met. Before he'd campaigned and before even Campbell had creased those long chalk-striped trousers under the leader's desk, Clegg was seen as heir apparent. It was an assumption neither Huhne nor Campbell would manage to shift.

11

ON MING AND MERCY

Campbell rewarded Clegg for his crucial support with the plum Home Affairs brief. And Clegg took advantage, demonstrating in winning ways how old Liberal values could be recast to tackle new social problems.

So he dissected the government's anti-terrorism legislation, but also recognised liberals had to show they could answer the demand of the granny on the 19th floor: "what are you going to do about the thugs ruining my life?" So Clegg would argue that not only were ID cards wrong in themselves, their scraping would fund 10,000 officers on the beat.

By assuring the public that the party understood its fears, Clegg earned the space to advocate liberal solutions. Politically, this meant Liberal Democrats could no longer be dismissed as "soft". So while Clegg argued, powerfully, that criminals were in part driven to re-offend by poor prisons that did nothing to reform behaviour, he also suggested that psychotic criminals who were beyond change might have to be banged up longer.

But it was the Liberalism that shone through. When asked for his political torchbearer, he mentioned Martin Luther for his "anger and courage" as the hero of the Enlightenment, but settled for Trevor Wilcox: "The chap who single handedly defeated ID cards in 1953. He is a classic example of British Liberalism. He was a drycleaner from north London at a time when everyone had to carry ID cards, and when asked for his by police he refused 'because I'm a Liberal.' From that single, dignified act of defiance one person defeated a system."

Similarly on the hot subject of Britishness, which long made Liberals queasy (one Liberal Democrat MP in my hearing expressed horror upon spying a pair of Union Flag cufflinks), Clegg argued: "Let's re-appropriate Britishness: it's not just great men—Locke, Newton—it's the Suffragettes, the Peasants' Revolt, individuals putting two fingers up to London. It's a rich tradition of dissent, a profound objection to arbitrary power." It was a classic Clegg construction, patriotic and progressive in one breath.

And this hardly went unnoticed, even by the media, which was not so much urging him to stand as grumbling he wasn't already leader.

For the bitchers and stitchers had scarcely stopped sniggering about Kennedy's alcohol intake before they started on Campbell, claiming he took naps in the afternoon and even—bafflingly—that he wore sock garters. More seriously, Laws and Clegg drew up an action plan for Campbell's first Hundred Days, but this dynamism dissipated. Party media advisers started asking me after a month how they should "launch" Campbell. They didn't grasp that as far as the media was concerned Campbell was already in mothballs waiting to be scrapped. Indeed, the press gang had greatly enjoyed, in their predictable words, calling last orders on Kennedy; they weren't going to hang about in sounding "time, gentleman, please" on Campbell.

Clegg was caught in a minor rumpus at the 2006 conference when Kevin Maguire in the *New Statesman* claimed to have overheard Clegg on Bournemouth station loudly denigrating Campbell. The "Minger", as Maguire dubbed Clegg, apparently shouted into his mobile "about an aged Olympic sprinter off to a slow start". The article said Clegg, "between sips of Red Bull", characterised "Ming the Mediocre" as "hesitant and disorganised, commits avoidable errors and lacks momentum but—this was the loyal bit—is capable of recovering." Maguire, a reliable but avowedly Labour journalist, claimed Campbell's reputation was only saved from further assassination by the loud arrival of a Virgin Express. Maguire concluded: "With friends like Clegg, who needs Simon Hughes?"

Criticism of Campbell intensified but he inherited a party machine that needed a thorough service. Campbell's re-organisation was essential though it was frustrating so much of the front man's energy was frittered away on backroom tasks.

The public was instinctively more impressed than the media. At one point the party's poll rating hit 20 per cent, while Campbell's approval level briefly overtook Cameron's.

And Campbell did give freedom to Clegg, Laws and co to explore new thought, even if he was not always comfortable with the result. Cable for instance pipped Osborne to the policy of closing tax loopholes on non-doms, calculated to save enough to reduce income tax to 16p in the pound—the lowest rate since Lloyd George was wrestling the Kaiser.

Remarkably, given Campbell's attachment to the post-war political settlement, the party began to develop its most credible policies since Grimond. Yet frustratingly, Lib Dems seemed reluctant to flaunt their wares.

Blaming the media convinces only partly. The press has long been pathologically anti Lib Dem, and cartoons depicting a proud dandy like Ming as some Zimmer-shuffling geriatric must have hurt intensely. But the Lib Dems weren't pushing the positive policies they were developing. Being such a moral man, Ming could, on occasion, seem happier talking about how a Liberal Democrat government would make you poorer and sadder, not richer and happier. Perhaps it also reflected subtle cultural differences between Scotland and England. If Scotland can sometimes seem quite comfortable in hair shirts, England has always expected silk. Emphasising green taxes might have played well with high-minded, wealthy, progressives, but what of far larger numbers struggling with Brown's high tax and low quality public services?

Liberal Democrats did now have policies for the struggling middle, but not a salesman who truly believed in the new range. If Campbell could have talked with a little more candour about his humble origins in Glasgow, his message might have resonated, but Sir Ming must have sounded decidedly patrician to an electrician.

Ultimately, polls don't lie. The party's rating dipped to 13 per cent, or lower. As one loyalist MP told me mournfully: "You can't go on saying the public is wrong if it's not buying your product."

Liberal Democrats found themselves in a frighteningly similar position to the one that had driven them to regicide with Kennedy: that is, being an object of ridicule over their leader. Huhne tried to look loyal but was struggling. How he must have muttered: "I told you".

Gradually the pressure grew on Clegg to challenge, from the media more than from within the party, which was all too comfortable with unpopularity. This period grew hugely fraught for Clegg, who could hardy assassinate the man who had given him political life. Yet he also feared privately the party was withering. Ashdown was among those who have admitted to me they were urging Clegg to ask the men in grey sandals to depose yet another leader. Publicly Clegg still insisted he wasn't ready, and besides Sir Ming was doing a splendid job. But in an echo of the notorious rumpus over Michael Portillo ordering telephone lines in preparation for a tilt at the Conservative leadership, there are some suggestions he thought about severing his connections.

In the most damaging story to hit Clegg during the later general election, the *Daily Telegraph* alleged that at around the time of Campbell's difficulties, a cabal of wealthy businessmen paid money into his private bank account. The insinuation was they were doing so to enrich Clegg. The editor's strong—unpublished—suspicion was different: that while professing public loyalty to "Ming", Clegg was using the money to hire a researcher to prepare a leadership bid.

Meanwhile, supporters were expressing private frustration that Clegg was prevaricating, arguing that Campbell was offering no critique of Brown's statist record. While cartoonists were merciless with Ming, sketching him being helped onto platforms by his carer, Clegg was trekking across the tundra, even sharing a tent with Conservative MP Eddie Vaizey. Ostensibly they were looking at the melting ice caps, but really they were looking cool, like Cameron.

"That was my first intimate moment with Nick, and he didn't even call me afterwards," chortles Ed Vaizey, now Tory minister of Culture. "I hope he doesn't behave like that with David." A farcical moment occurred when "amid all this snow we suddenly got signals and all our BlackBerrys started going with news from our offices. It turned out a Sky poll had made Nick the most fancied MP. I was number nine. Even to this day Nick insists on calling me 'Number Nine.'"

Clegg also worked hard at cultivating the party beyond his Orange Book comfort zone. He even contributed a suitably non-controversial essay to *Reinventing the State,* edited by two leading thinkers of the left, Duncan Brack and Richard Grayson. This was an attempt by the party's radicals to win back intellectual high ground from the right.

And as Home Affairs spokesman Clegg continued to propound strongly liberal policies which won praise from both wings. A particular focus was prisons. How, he argued, could we be surprised we had so much crime when over half our prisoners were functionally illiterate, and an even higher proportion addicts?

He spoke with compassion and pragmatism, influenced by a remarkable ex-con, Bobby Cummines, who campaigns for the rehabilitation of offenders. Cummines is suited now, but otherwise makes an unlikely political adviser. A former bank robber, he has been put inside for every crime from possession of a sawn-off shotgun to manslaughter, and been dubbed by then Home Office minister David Mellor "one of Britain's most dangerous men".

Cummines talks glowingly of Clegg. He recalls how Clegg had been so engrossed in one conversation he stayed for extra hours, arriving late for an obligatory appearance at a Liberal Democrat fundraising ball.

For what Cummines was doing was very Clegg, foreshadowing an aspect of Cameron's Big Society. "Unlock" had, when Cummines arrived, been a lose association of ex-prisoners, but he persuaded members that talking about problems was of limited value. Within months he turned it into a registered charity and lobbied banks on behalf of prisoners. Until then "re-habilitated" offenders were routinely denied basic tools of economic life such as chequebooks. "Of course they couldn't integrate," Cummines says. "They were pushed back into the black economy." Rather than moaning, though, Cummines persuaded banks—and mortgage and insurance companies and landlord associations—that they were neglecting a large market. They didn't have to study the numbers long. All this, of course, fitted with Clegg's political outlook of letting individuals lead worthwhile lives, including those British "untouchables", former guests of Her Majesty.

But it was the regal displeasure of another grand dame whose punishment Clegg found most fearsome. At the 2007 annual conference, Sir Ming's wife, Lady Elspeth, collared him in the lobby of the Grand and asked if he was trying to undermine her husband. Or rather she drawled, with the withering authority only a major general's daughter can muster, "I don't know if you are being helpful or not". To the glee of press men who rarely find much to scintillate them at such gatherings, this "hand-bagging" was captured by a loitering TV crew—complete with Clegg's stumbling assurance that "I'm trying to be". To compound the image of Campbell's hopelessness, he was caught on camera pointing down an eco-lavatory. The press scarcely needed to fashion a headline, but they did anyway, just to make sure.

Lampoon levels were rising. Other Lib Dem conferences "moments" were recalled. These included the 1992 debate which apparently banned the fairground sale of goldfish (or so the press claimed. Some averred that goldfish had won an important exemption); the 1978 arrival of Jeremy Thorpe while facing a charge of conspiracy to murder; and the delegate who declared herself a witch who could see evil spirits lurking around Simon Hughes, even though saner heads assured her these were only Rosie Barnes and David Owen. Clegg, however, would struggle to top the Liberal Assembly moment when Sir Alan Comyns Carr, during a classic debate about a pair of obscure islands in the Taiwan straights, declared: "Fellow Liberals. The eyes of the world are on us — I do not want to say anything which might exacerbate the situation in Quemoy and Matsu."

Clegg's problem had arisen, closer to home, at a fringe meeting the previous evening. Perhaps the first rule of Lib Dem events this broke was that it was packed. It was also slickly organized, by the *Observer*, and featured Clegg in rather grand wing back being interviewed by the equally avuncular Rawnsley. The *coup de grace* was a film of the young Clegg. Not only did it seem self-promoting (vulgar, obviously) it was "presidential".

Rawnsley quizzed Clegg about his ambitions and life, a line of question that could only be interesting if Clegg ever intended to become important. Rawnsley wheedled out of Clegg the quite scandalous admission that he did hope, one day, to be more than just an obscure Liberal Democrat MP. Clegg admitted he did harbour leadership ambitions for the future, but that he wouldn't stand against Ming.

Clegg felt bruised by the furious reaction. What, he asked privately, was he meant to say? That he had no ambition? As one who was there I can report the remark seemed innocuous. I doubt Rawnsley felt he had reeled in a prize scoop. Besides, Clegg's appeal rested on his frankness and refusal to peddle banalities ("Ming is our leader; I will follow...").

Still, the rumpus probably did Clegg more good than harm. The question of standing was now purely one of "when", not "if". Clegg was cultivating powerful allies, in press and party. And there were more handclaps than handbags. After one lunch for editors and columnists I organised on his behalf, a well-known journalist remarked: "He speaks five languages. Six if you count 'human'."

But rather than Clegg, it was Campbell's old friend Brown who did for the then Liberal Democrat leader. The prime minister's first attempt at political assassination took place shortly after he moved into Downing Street in the summer of 2007. He invited Campbell to Number 10 and offered government jobs to a few grand old men and women of Liberalism. Brown had already gone over Campbell's head and offered Ashdown Northern Ireland. Campbell told Brown he would mull over his proposals for 24 hours, when he told Brown the gulf was too great. Labour, inevitably, leaked news of the meeting, focusing on Campbell's prevarication. Campbell was criticised for vacillating. What, activists demanded, could have been in this for the Lib Dems—they would have been used merely as bullet-proof vests by Brown. It might have served to make Brown appear less friendless but if he were serious, why hadn't he approached Campbell first and proposed a coalition?

If Campbell narrowly survived that attempt, he was taken out, less by a clean Brown bullet than a stray one from Brown's by-now smoky revolver. As Brown's early promise of inclusiveness and change was quickly revealed to be the sham sceptics always took it to be, his poll rating slid in the autumn of 2007, and he cancelled plans for an early election. It gave him a longer rent on his beloved Number 10, but at the expense of near-certain rather than merely likely repossession later on.

And if the rot set in for Labour, it was curtains for Campbell. With no election imminent, Lib Dems realised, a little excitedly, that they just about had time to squeeze in one more leadership election before the country next went to the polls.

Whether deliberately or mistakenly, Cable was lured into a frank answer on the Today Programme. Indeed, so brutally frank was his answer that poor Ming never recovered. Cable agreed that Campbell's leadership was "certainly under discussion", which was embarrassing seeing as he was meant to be Campbell's deputy. He added "I don't think it's under threat", which is rather like throttling someone to death and then expressing the hope they will feel better in the morning. A party stalwart, Sir Chris Clarke, used the same medium to advise Campbell to "go with dignity back to being foreign affairs spokesman, where the world listens to you." Later that day Simon Hughes, party president, announced that Campbell would step down and join Kennedy in the now thronging ex-leaders' retirement home.

As Cable became a—brilliant—acting leader, Clegg declared that Campbell had been treated "appallingly", a victim of "barely disguised ageism". All true, but Clegg was the barely disguised beneficiary.

12

CLEGG'S TRIUMPH

Even for the steel city, the day seemed to be painted a particularly dark shade of gunmetal grey. But adherents to Liberalism were in sunny mood that Sheffield morning as Clegg fired the starting gun on his leadership bid. His chosen venue was a revamped arts centre. Admittedly, it felt more like a parish council venue trying to look cool than the launch-pad for the leadership of a major party. I recognised only one other national newspaper journalist, a sketch writer intending to tell as many jokes at the party's expense as possible. Clegg didn't even have a stage to speak from, and looked awkward as the grand-eloquent words jarred in a room of scarcely fifty. But it passed without slip and most present saw enough to think they were looking at a future leader.

Clegg, facing a single but formidable challenge from a battle-hardened Huhne, was torn over how to fight. Initially he wanted to run "against his party". And there was certainly much to challenge. But this was a dangerous strategy in a party a little too comfortable with failure.

When Clegg announced his candidacy through an interview with me in the *Observer*, he was tempted to agree that individuals as well as communities should be given choice in hospitals and schools. "We have a bewildering array of choice when we walk into a supermarket, but feel passive recipients of state largesse," he said. "I want a sense of empowerment on a daily basis for people accessing health care and good education." He saw this as working with the grain of modern society, where an increasingly educated, wealthy, consumerist and independently-minded population wanted to shape their own lives. And this desire to make decisions should be a freedom enjoyed by all, not just the rich. Clegg's argument sounded compelling. If this be the age of Liberalism, he suggested, shouldn't it be the Liberal Democrats shaping it?

But I pushed him on the specifics of how choice should be introduced into public services. His replies were nuanced, and afterwards Clegg berated me for nudging him further than he intended in public. Filing my interview I didn't think I'd picked up much of a scoop, but someone in the Huhne camp felt differently, and a peculiarly Liberal wrath descended.

A Huhne aide sent a dossier to the producer of a TV show on which Clegg and Huhne were to appear, titled "Calamity Clegg". This damaging tag was to re-surface later on (Conservative funded) literature in the AV referendum campaign, which ironically perhaps Huhne took as proof of Conservative treachery.

The TV presenter brandished at Clegg the dossier, which claimed that—among other crimes—the young pretender wanted to let the market rip in the public sector, a bombshell he had apparently confided to his "close personal friend Jasper Gerard", an exaggeration on both counts.

The dossier also picked up on remarks by Clegg to another journalist, Rachel Sylvester, which seemed to imply support for school vouchers. Actually Clegg had not wandered too far from the path of party policy for a "pupil premium", though he hadn't ruled out that money parents would receive from the state to educate their child could be "cashed" at private schools.

Under fire on TV, Huhne distanced himself from the dossier, saying he hadn't approved it and the title was dreamed up by a "young researcher". Clegg attacked Huhne for poisoning an internal party election.

Afterwards Sherlock rang, urging me to enter the blogosphere and "clarify" what Clegg had said. Clegg also made a formal complaint to the party supremo, Lord Rennard, and I was among those asked for their version. Sensibly, Rennard presided in judicial seriousness over a thorough investigation—then waited till the row had blown over to do nothing

On the substance my sympathy lay with Clegg. Empowering individuals in schools and hospitals is essential to drive up standards, difficult though it is. Huhne's solution, to devolve decisions from Whitehall to councils, would surely only transfer power from one bunch of bureaucrats to another. And to try to paint Clegg as a "crypto Tory" was a travesty, because Clegg was fundamentally opposed to any system allowing the rich to buy a better education or treatment through the public sector, and rightly so.

Yet I did understand Huhne's desire for clarity: he was justified in fleshing out the one substantive difference between candidates in an election to decide the party's future. How he went about it, however, was vicious.

Incidentally, in a triffling postscript to the "Calamity Clegg" rumpus, two newspapers alleged much later, while exposing Huhne's affair, that the author of the now-forgotten dossier was Trimingham, his new lover. For Huhne to have characterised her as a "young researcher" was certainly chivalrous, for at the time she was a senior aide of 41.

Clegg had told me earlier in his career that his leadership campaign would be bold and transformative, like Blair's and Cameron's. But as the campaign got underway he was advised that such boldness would backfire. So rather than sail into the wind, he tacked a mite to the left. In the main live set-piece TV debate, he was, some felt, tentative. He talked about "fairness", with its useful ambiguity.

Even I wasn't as impressed as I expected to be and texted Alexander. "What do you mean?" he replied. "Are you alright?" Clegg, he insisted, had done well. It wasn't entirely how it looked from my sofa, but you can't fault Alexander's loyalty. I received a call from a senior MP who once harboured his own leadership ambitions: "What did you think?" he asked. "Nick is meant to be the great communicator. Now I'm even less sure of voting for him."

Laws expressed occasional private frustrations during the campaign, such as when Clegg declined to deliver a radical speech about education reform, but says now: "Nick might have lost in 2007 by being too Orange Book. The Lib Dems weren't in the same place Labour had been with Tony Blair and thus open to accepting a really radical message. The Lib Dems had been out of power too long.

They had grown used to losing, whereas for Labour being out of office really hurt."

Another senior figure closely involved, who declines to be named, says: "The leadership election didn't have many sparkling moments. There wasn't enough of a 100 days plan. And the support team around Nick lacked strength."

Ashdown was blunter. "It was a lacklustre campaign," he told me. Urged on by some Orange Bookers, he invited Clegg to breakfast and left him feeling more scrambled than the scarcely touched eggs. Ashdown accused his protégé of fighting a weak campaign, and warned he would need to be bolder.

"It was very private at the time but I have to say many of his closest allies were worried," Ashdown tells me. "I thought he lacked the courage of his convictions. The campaign was also disorganised. And the result was bloody close." Clegg emerged visibly chastened, and admitted to me it had been humbling.

At the suitably modernist St Martin's Lane Hotel with its blank walls and Phillip Stark furniture (so Cameron), Clegg was declared leader. But he had ducked over the finishing line by just 500 votes, the smallest margin to settle the leadership of a major party since the advent of mass membership elections. As one who had been the bookies run-away favourite and darling of the media class, Clegg felt almost as if he'd lost. Huhne supporters hissed. Clegg followers gasped, like survivors of a car crash. Clegg just appeared drained. Indeed, the only one to manage a smile was Huhne. It emerged later a sizeable chunk of ballots had been delayed in the post, and they would have handed victory to the defeated candidate. Such are the narrow margins between career-defining success and life-haunting failure. Graciously, Huhne did not challenge the result.

But away from the cameras the kind of bitterness rarely expressed in a Liberal Democrat leadership election was souring friendships. We cannot include Clegg and Huhne's friendship in this, if only because there wasn't much to sour.

"Their working relationship was frosty after the leadership election," one senior shadow cabinet figure turned minister tells me. "The day after the leadership election was announced Nick rang

Chris and offered him the foreign affairs brief. Chris refused and said if that was all he was being offered he would resign, and that without him Nick's leadership wouldn't last five minutes. I think he swore and slammed the phone down."

In private Orange Book Liberals accused Huhne of fighting a dishonest campaign, pandering to the unrealistic leftist assumptions of some activists. The judgement was a little harsh. And besides, saying what he believed was not necessarily an allegation that could be levelled at Clegg. Either way it was clear Huhne had fought the more aggressive campaign, though as the outsider he had less to lose.

Campbell left the declaration quickly, assured the election had delivered the result he had secretly wished. He also seemed relieved to be free of the press interest in trivia.

Despite the kind words of Laws, Clegg admitted afterwards in private he had fought an uninspiring campaign. He claimed to have learned, but some had doubts. He decided not to hire a top media fixer. Talk of employing Tim Haimes, then a *Times* columnist, came to nothing. He overlooked Julian Astle to run his office, considering him too maverick and right wing. This annoyed Ashdown, who had relied heavily on Astle while running Bosnia-Herzegovina.

"The decisiveness about staff was not there," Ashdown tells me. "You need to be challenged. Julian was like the little man standing in front of the tank. He would keep on at me, and it's useful. At a final point I would just say 'fuck off'."

One chauvinist muttered Clegg was relying on the same "posh Scottish girls" that had run Sir Ming's office. Even parliamentary friends wondered how much he had learned, and whether they were the right lessons.

But just as Blair-Brown had pulled off a coup in taking over the Labour Party and Cameron-Osborne had declared their own form of Marshall Law in the Conservative Party, so Clegg-Laws had taken over their party with a panache that was every bit as audacious. If he had won more by virtue of what he didn't say as what he did, his statesmanlike pose ensured both wings of the party swung behind their new leader.

A poor campaign? If you like. But also one of the most successful coups Westminster had seen. For, like all the best coups, it was conducted when everyone else was sleeping.

The first call Clegg received when he arrived in his new leader's office was from Cameron. It was brief but warm, even inviting Clegg to dinner, an offer Clegg declined politely. Gordon Brown also telephoned but was, felt Clegg, "utterly graceless", to the point where the Liberal wondered why the PM had bothered. It was a chilly start to a relationship that would remain colder than the Clyde.

More importantly, he managed to bury a rather large hatchet *with* rather than *in* Huhne. Clegg offered him the Home Affairs brief, and while it wasn't the Treasury job Huhne wanted, it was good enough. "From then on they had a fairly good relationship," one of the party's main players tells me. "Chris accepted Nick would probably be leader for the rest of his career. He realised he had to be trusted to be in Nick's inner circle and have a cabinet job, as Chris was hopeful right back then there would be a coalition. He became part of the inner core."

While Huhne made successful guerrilla attacks on the government, Clegg struggled for definition. And understandably so. Across all parties there is private acknowledgement that leading the Liberal Democrats is one of the hardest jobs in politics, with the media operating a fiercely observed blackout, only broken when journalists shine a searchlight on something embarrassing. Until an election campaign when journalists suddenly remember that nearly a third of voters actually back a party with orange rosettes, Lord Lucan could quite easily lead the Liberal Democrats and scarcely anyone would notice.

The media, like the parliamentary amphitheatre, favours a simplistic, adversarial picture, so in one corner was Brown, in the other Cameron. And Clegg was nowhere. If he was regarded at all, it was as a pesky bantam-weight getting in the way. The thicket of newsprint could all be pruned back to one question: was Cameron ready to replace Brown?

The two issues which dominated Clegg's leadership in opposition were MPs expenses and the gathering economic storm. With expenses, no Liberal Democrat was caught with his hand quite so firmly wedged in the public till as with certain Tory and Labour politicians, yet there were too many petty, borderline claims for Clegg to moralise as enthusiastically as he might have liked. Consequently, the public's attitude was largely one of "a plague on all your houses".

The downturn, in contrast, did provide a modest upturn in Lib Dem fortunes. After all, well before collapse of Northern Rock the party had warned that the credit boom was unsustainable. But this was considered very much Cable's triumph, and indeed the media used the shadow Chancellor's obvious mastery of economics to belittle the new leader, saying Cable made Clegg look out of his depth. Cable played an impressively straight bat, refusing to use his burgeoning "national treasure" status to undermine Clegg. Nevertheless, to be so overshadowed by the previous acting leader was clearly worrying for Clegg. It was a sign of his maturity that rather than treating Cable as a threat he recognised that if the party was to be taken seriously it needed more than one voice, and ultimately a strong Cable would mean a stronger Clegg.

But Clegg is by nature sensitive and privately the criticism stung. As leader Campbell had been able to blame his failure to shove an elegantly shod toe into the daily political scuffle on the huge job he had behind the scenes knocking order into the party. But some began to mutter that Clegg had less excuse. Moreover, he didn't seem to be mastering the off-stage stuff. A powerful backer even says: "Why didn't he sack Rennard? I'm sure Huhne would have. He'd been there too long, yet Nick waited for him to resign. He took a year to appoint a fundraiser and didn't move to put his own people on committees. Can you imagine Chris making that mistake?"

Rennard, for his part, points out that every Lib Dem leader is ignored until his profile—and prospects—are transformed by a general election. This did not stop one implacable parliamentary opponent from arguing witheringly (though privately): "Clegg was elected as the great communicator, so who, precisely, is he communicating with?"

Even Ashdown tells me: "Many of us started to think 'oops, have we chosen the right man? Have we over-estimated him?' But you have to remember I became leader after one parliament. Nick didn't even have one. He also doesn't like the Commons. He finds it quite bruising. And finding yourself leader, there is so much to do. It is like entering a secret garden."

A former adviser was even more brutal around this time, telling me: "the problem with Nick is it has come too easy. He looks fat, like he's enjoyed too many lunches in Brussels with Leon Brittan. And he needs to cut his hair to lose that ridiculous, Cameron fop." Within weeks both Clegg and the equally luxuriantly coiffed Laws were both sporting short hair.

Some began to grumble Clegg lacked a common touch. He announced a commission to tackle political alienation among the young, chaired by Brian Eno. The Roxy Music synthesiser player (retired) is a great British iconoclast and expressed delight to me with Clegg's victory at a celebratory party, first, a little serenely, at Planet Hollywood, then at Millbank. But these days the David Bowie/ U2 producer who lives in a manor house in Oxfordshire was hardly getting down with the kids.

"Even Brian didn't understand why he was asked," Marshall tells me. "Pointless." Marshall was among those disappointed by Clegg's early "trimming".

Before his first day in the job Clegg went on Radio 1 and was asked his favourite record, which he should have been briefed to answer before appearing on a show about pop tunes. He offered *Changes* by Bowie, a compilation album. This was the main story about Clegg in next day's red tops and, predictably, he was ridiculed.

In contrast, when Michael Berkeley asked him to select his Radio 3 playlist for the unashamedly elitist *Private Passions* (a *Desert Island Discs* for those who read books) the selection had, unusually, the whiff of personal choice: Strauss's *Four Last Songs*, Schubert's *Impromptu* in E flat minor and Chopin's posthumous *Waltz* in A minor. To the question "when did you last cry?" he replied: "listening to music." Again there were snorts of derision, presumably from those who preferred the pugilism of Prescott to politics of sensitivity. Surely after the macho, dumbed-down Blair years it was refreshing for a British politician to engage in high culture. That said, if ever a politician proffers a handshake to the higher pleasures he also needs to be seen high-fiving a lower pleasure. Clegg, almost uniquely in British politics, doesn't pretend to support a football team, and even managed to look faintly bored as guest of honour when Barcelona obliterated Manchester United in the Champions League Final. When it was suggested it might be possible to snaffle Clegg a slot on Jeremy Clarkson's hugely popular *Top Gear*, he launched into an attack on Clarkson's apparently facile anti-green posturing and declared "you won't get me on with that idiot".

All this was trivial compared to Clegg's big decisions. For instance after the party's principled opposition to the Iraq war, Clegg felt it couldn't become the purely anti-war party. Cases had to be judged on merits, and he decided to visit Afghanistan and demonstrate his commitment to seeing through an invasion that virtually all serious figures had supported but which was now provoking flip-flopping.

A crunch issue which many say Clegg got wrong was tuition fees. Abolishing fees was one of the last major spending commitments left from the Kennedy era, and had proved hugely popular—not only among students, but parents, too. It was a policy Liberal Democrats held dear. For all the jokes about degree courses that hardly added to a Platonic search for truth (Applied Windsurfing, anyone?), the expansion of higher education had been one of the great advances of recent years. University had been a middle class club, as elitist in its way as Brooks or White's, but worse because it was heavily subsidised by those whose children would never be allowed to join. Now far greater numbers enjoyed the life-changing opportunities presented by higher education, though admittedly the main beneficiaries appeared to be the less bright middle class rather the bright working class. The fear about fees was that it would further keep the poorest out.

Yet there were strong counter arguments. Among Orange Book ultras was belief that universities should develop revenue streams beyond the state. And despite their expansion, they had admitted shamefully few under-privileged students, so why should the poor continue to subsidise them?

Clegg argued forcefully to scrap the commitment to abolish fees, cautiously in interviews, forcefully in private. Mainly this was due to cost. He had already ripped up an entire chequebook of promises, such as free care for the elderly, so why ring-fence students?

But in a classic Clegg triangulation he argued that in an era of cuts there was a progressive case to raise fees. To reduce inequality money would be better spent earlier in a child's development. If life journeys can largely be mapped when an infant still has a dummy in his or her mouth then the emphasis needs to be on pre-school provision. At the very least the pupil premium becomes massively more significant than abolishing fees.

But the arguments were difficult. In a meeting of the Federal Policy Committee, Clegg was outvoted 18-5, underlining the point of Orange Bookers that he should have pushed his people onto key committees. "Privately Nick continued to agree the policy should go," says one on the right. "But he also said he didn't think reversing the policy was do-able." By contrast a figure on the left says: "He would have lost the vote at conference. We saved him from embarrassing defeat."

Clegg did not give up, however. In a Q&A session at the 2009 autumn conference he refused to promise the policy would be in the manifesto. After a major row, left wingers led by Evan Harris MP wrote to the *Guardian* warning they would not allow Clegg to slaughter this holiest of holy cows. If Clegg had intended to challenge them, he backed down, a decision with huge reverberations.

But it was one of the very few old-style spending policies on which he did hold fire. Quietly, party policy was changing in accordance with the Orange Book/CentreForum revolution.

Despite the "calamity" tag, Clegg had dropped few clangers, but one he must regret from around this time took place on an aeroplane. He was talking to Danny Alexander about a possible shadow cabinet reshuffle. Unbeknown to the pair, a *Mirror* journalist was sitting in the seat in front. Realising he was earning column inches as well as air miles, the hack began to scribble furiously. When the conversation was plastered across the tabloid, Clegg claimed much of it was contrived.

He was reported saying he wanted to demote Huhne from home affairs for someone "more emotionally intelligent". About Steve Webb he was allegedly blunter: "He must go. He's a problem. I can't stand the man. We need someone with good ideas. At the moment, they just don't add up." Julia Goldsworthy, meanwhile, needed to be moved because she was being "patronised" as local government spokesman. Only Laws came out well, being described as "the best brain we have" though also as not enjoying his job at Education.

The froideur between Clegg and Huhne is no secret but Clegg has never been known to denigrate his old rival's abilities. Given the deal they struck after the leadership election it seems unlikely Clegg would have considered demoting him, and never did. And if Clegg had such a downer on Webb why would he later give him a job in government? Finally the suggestion that Laws was not happy with education came as news to him, and a move to Environment would have been odd—so odd it never happened. But Clegg, normally a defender of government whistle blowers, found himself with that rare commodity: unwanted publicity.

The incident that transformed Clegg's early leadership was about to arrive. Ironically, rather than letting him demonstrate a new Liberalism, it was a classic old-style Liberal crusade—albeit beefed up, like Clegg's pronouncements on Britishness, with populist patriotism.

Labour had denied Gurkhas British citizenship. It seemed a betrayal to expect people to die for a country they were not allowed to live in. This was a point Clegg made powerfully, putting him in a long line of Liberal leaders from Gladstone to Ashdown standing out against the hordes to defend a foreign people. A less elevated consideration was that Joanna Lumley had joined the fight with Clegg. Her father had been a Gurkha officer, and she slammed the decision with equal force. As Labour spin doctors should have realised early on—and if Alastair Campbell were more involved, they surely would have done—any row that leaves a party on the wrong side of an argument with a national treasure such as Ms Lumley will only end in hauling up the white flag.

Laws certainly saw this as the turning point: "Until the success of the Gurkha campaign it wasn't going that brilliantly. Then he suddenly looked transformed, like a winner that glittered."

Clegg also scored a direct hit when he called for the speaker, Michael Martin, to resign in the wake of the expenses scandal. It was a shrewd, populist move because for all the speaker's self-styled working class ways, he was actually using old style union tactics to defend extraordinary privileges.

Martin duly resigned after Clegg broke a convention that party leaders don't call for the head of the speaker, a tradition that had survived quite peacefully since 1695.

"I knew it wasn't done," Clegg grinned later "but I probably hadn't quite twigged there was this unwritten rule that you can't say things like that." He doesn't regret it. "The leader of the Liberal Democrats should be prepared to break a few unwritten rules."

Headline grabbing though these successes were, they were guerrilla responses to someone else's agenda. They didn't (terrible cliché alert), provide a "narrative" about what Lib Dem government could do for the typical voter.

However, just because that narrative wasn't being written about doesn't mean it wasn't being written. Clegg's biggest achievement during this period was the quiet re-shaping of Liberal Democrat policy. It is hard to underestimate the change in assumptions that went on, yet Clegg managed change with a tact that provoked remarkably little dissent.

So in January 2008 Clegg said that in schools and hospitals the "state must back off and allow the genius of grassroots innovation, diversity and experimentation." He challenged the shibboleths, not only of the left but of the party's powerful local government base, when he called for "a new liberal model of schools that are non-selective, under local government strategic oversight but not run by the council." Six months later he pushed his party again, this time on tax—publishing a policy document called *Make It Happen*, outlining plans for cuts in public spending and backing Cable's strategy for tax cuts for the low paid.

Inevitably some feathers of a red-ish tinge were ruffled. One on the left remarks: "I don't think Nick was managing the party well. The last conference before an election is normally inspiring. This wasn't. There were too many rows. And on an issue like tuition fees it was the leadership shown to be unrealistic theoreticians, not activists."

The same source also recalls a pre-manifesto meeting of the Federal Policy Committee in July 2009 which he says Clegg chaired badly, particularly when discussing local income tax: "He was stroppy. Paddy would have reached a compromise but Nick didn't see why he should, or even how he could. Vince was worse, saying things like 'I'm trying to be reasonable'. Before Vince stalked out he said that unless the committee agreed with him he would go to the papers tomorrow and say our policy was rubbish."

But Clegg was adroit at drawing the sting. Those who argued Clegg should have been bolder in facing down malcontents were, to a considerable extent, left to wonder what the fuss had been about. Rather than hectoring, Clegg had relied on a combination of calm intelligence and gentle persuasion. So while at that eve of election conference activists might have grumbled at the bar, they heard Clegg in the hall when he warned that after polling we would face "savage cuts". He didn't elaborate but this was the nearest any party leader came to telling the public what a dire economic position Britain faced. It is hard to image Kennedy or even Campbell delivering such a message.

The public wasn't listening, however. Entering the campaign it had no clear notion of what Liberal Democrats stood for. Despite Cable's prominence, few were aware of the popular policy of tax cuts for the low paid. However, Clegg was fashioning a coherent programme. He wanted to free people from Labour's authoritarian-ism—socially and economically.

Other Liberal Democrat programmes of recent years may have been progressive, centre left and well intentioned but none were avowedly Liberal. Indeed, David Steel had all but ceded the Liberal ground to the Conservatives when he said we had a Labour Party obsessed with equality and a Conservative Party obsessed with liberty, but "what about fraternity?" Admittedly the remark was made when the highly un-fraternal Thatcher was in Downing Street, but from that moment Liberal Democrats forfeited one of the most precious commodities in British politics to the Tories: Liberalism.

Now Clegg was reclaiming the creed. Once more the party's policies were grounded in that philosophy, perhaps for the first time since Grimond. And while Clegg hadn't exactly wowed, he had moved along quite nicely, with Lib Dems entering the election 5 per cent up on the start of the previous campaign.

Newspapers might have snoozed through this particular Orange revolution, but at last there was a Liberal standard to rally around. Liberals did believe in freedom, after all.

13

"I AGREE WITH NICK"

Clegg stole onto the theatre of war with the shock and awe of a stealth bomber. The Liberal Democrats were not on the radar of the media or of the other two parties, so Clegg's explosion on to the warzone was mesmeric.

Even Cameron didn't see Clegg coming, brushing aside with haughty self-confidence suggestions Clegg might shine in televised debates. It was quite a miscalculation, particularly as Cameron had long been intrigued by what he saw as a "mini-me" (not long after Clegg entered parliament, Cameron asked me about him). Brown was certainly fearful, but of Cameron not Clegg, believing he could dismiss the leader of the smallest party as another toffee-nosed public schoolboy unfit to wear a big man's boots.

But from the moment Cameron and Brown accepted they had to include Clegg—a condition of rules which guarantee at least a degree of impartial coverage at election time—the new boy saw his chance, when the third party could enjoy parity. Its support tends to rise during campaigns, blown along by the windstorm—OK, the gentle breeze—of publicity: "Oh yes, the Liberal Democrats," puzzle the public. "I'd forgotten them." And how much stronger the jolt with Clegg on prime time, treated as equal to the Prime Minister and Leader of the Opposition.

He spent months rehearsing, Laws playing Cameron, Huhne Brown; Clegg played himself. The jousts were far from jocular, sometimes ending in shouting matches with participants taking a couple of minutes to come out of their roles. The key lesson Clegg drew was that Cameron and Brown would veer between ignoring and patronising him. It would be hard to make an impression but his solution was to go, aggressively but extremely politely, on the offensive against both.

Ashdown, so critical of his protégé's early form, is generous about Clegg's later performance. "All the gifts we had seen flowered beautifully in the election," he says. "I was particularly struck by his ability to argue off the back foot, such as on Trident or immigration. He has fulfilled all my hopes."

As well as underestimating Clegg, rivals under-estimated his party. It had been scandal and split free. Its policy prospectus had been transformed into a serious programme. And researchers of rival parties scouring the manifesto for embarrassing promises—free pot for the under fives, that sort of thing—were disappointed.

Papers that had been so derisive talked only of "Clegg-mania". In an age of newness, Clegg was novelty. And nice. He looked right, being judged by women the most attractive leader. He also scored highly among men as the leader with whom they would most enjoy a pint. Even opponents felt obliged to pretend to like him. Brown and Cameron fell into the trap of agreeing with Clegg to diss the other, prompting Lib Dems to trail behind the leader during walkabouts with placards proclaiming "I agree with Nick".

Which the public did. Lib Dem ratings soared. According to some samples they were in the lead. Councillors fielded as parliamentary "paper" candidates suddenly fantasised: could I really park my posterior on those comfortable green benches? Could Cleggy do it?

Hacks on Clegg's battle bus were seized by a new sensation: interest. Japanese film crews and *Time* wanted a piece of the Cleggmeister. He also attracted the young. If the public was a little hazy on the actualité, so what? There was more than a whiff of the television reality contest in all this, but after years of playing the smaller clubs in unfashionable towns, Clegg was suddenly, in the inimitable words of Cheryl Cole, "looking like a little pop star".

Cameron had wanted to make it a personality contest—he just hadn't registered what was gleefully apparent to those who knew the Lib Dem leader, that in any contest of character, Clegg would certainly give him a fight and quite possibly a major fright.

There was intense infighting in Central Office. Who was the dummkopf, senior figures demanded, who felt TV debates would be a good idea, turning a two-way contest the Conservatives were narrowly winning into a three way contest they were drawing? Against Brown's scuffed DMs the Cameron brogue would look polished, but against the shiny new loafer of Clegg? Clegg not only shone by displaying the very qualities for which Cameron had been rightly praised—charm, reasonableness, humour—he showed substance, too. "Cameron-lite" suddenly felt "Cameron-heavy". A few months earlier commentators felt the Tories only needed to play out till the final whistle and hope to win on the own goals Brown had scored in the Downing Street leg. According to one Tory minister, Andy Coulson, Cameron's controversial media manipulator, came close to resigning long before that little misunderstanding about phone tapping—so bitter was the recrimination within Central Office. For the man who was meant to be served as the *amuse bouche* had actually eaten the other two for breakfast.

Suddenly the public realised there were genuine options with three very distinct parties, not some parody of democracy where voters choose between social kindness and economic competence.

A Lib Dem leader must be doing something right when he is subject of furious splashes in the *Telegraph*, *Mail* and *Express* on the same day. Fleet Street was in tumult. One paper revealed Clegg was passionately pro-European, which was not the greatest shock. Nobody was much bothered by the *Express*, though it probably suggested Clegg was a threat to the Magna Carta, roast beef and property prices. Another even accused him of making a "Nazi slur", which was more imaginative, and prompted a customarily laconic reaction from Clegg: "I've gone from being Churchill to a Nazi in less than a week."

Most damaging was the *Telegraph* story, under a massive headline, that businessmen had funnelled money into a Clegg private bank account. It was cautiously written but anyone glancing at a newsstand might have thought that a man who wanted to be Prime Minister was corrupt. In the wake of the expenses scandal this was horrific.

The party has long suffered a harsh press but it hasn't helped itself, contriving to be both dismissive and terrified. I'm told a Clegg aide failed to return the *Telegraph*'s calls till 8 pm. By then the editor, Tony Gallagher (who after dinners for party leaders had privately declared Clegg by far the most likeable) had decided to splash on the story. Ian Dale, Tory blogger, called the revelation "shameful"; Mandelson, a "Tory smear".

In fact the money had been raised by three businessmen to pay for a researcher in Clegg's office. All money—plus a bit more, supplemented by Clegg—could be traced going to the researcher as a modest wage.

One of the businessmen, Sherlock, can now laugh: "Lib Dem gives money to Lib Dem shocker. Next day the paper was massively downplaying it. I think it was reduced to asking whether the researcher's National Insurance was paid, and it was." It prompted the "I blame Nick Clegg" phenomenon, becoming one of the biggest stories on Twitter worldwide as people took to blaming him, ironically, for everything from tampering with the breaks on Princess Diana's car to failing to give a man he had never met a spare kidney.

Sherlock denies Gallagher's suggestion that the researcher was part of a planned leadership bid: "Nick had not long been elected and only had funds for one researcher and needed someone to keep on top of the constituency work. Now he was expected to shadow the Home Office and he needed someone full time." Sherlock, Wright et al were just doing as Ashdown demanded all those years before: looking after Nick. Certainly there was no scandal, but it showed the political weather changing. Twitterers may have jokingly blamed Clegg for rain, but Clegg could be forgiven for wondering what had happened to the sunshine.

Suddenly Clegg was being treated like just another politician, or worse: a threat. A large chunk of a Radio 1 phone-in was hijacked by debate over whether he should have claimed expenses for that Ikea cake tin (on balance "not" agreed the audience and a rather ragged Clegg).

Meanwhile there was a sense that the campaign looked like a banquet without a pudding. Clegg repeated lines that had worked well earlier. Where was the fresh angle to seize the agenda that a Campbell would have crafted? Rivals were now less "I agree with Nick", more "Nick, get real". Privately, some—notably Ashdown—argued he needed to say something fresh.

"It's always the final week with Lib Dem campaigns," Ashdown tells me. "Lib Dem campaigns are brilliant, but towards the end lack of resources always show. Perhaps we also relaxed on our laurels and then the Tories really stoked up the fear in the last week on immigration and crime. It was effective in a nation that already felt frightened."

But was it not also a failure of strategy? The party could, for instance, have briefed the Sunday papers before polling that Clegg had decided to rule out a coalition with Brown. This would have seized the agenda, stoked Labour in-fighting and assured Tory-waverers that a vote for Clegg wasn't a vote for Brown. This is endorsed by Martin Tod, Lib Dem candidate for Winchester, who tells me: "Certainly in this part of England, a big part of the election was the desire to get rid of Brown. Given that we so profoundly disagreed with him on so many issues and that he repeatedly showed himself to be unable to work collaboratively even with people in his party, it was a mistake to let the Tories appear to be the only ones who wanted to get rid of him."

More fundamentally, Andrew Russell, psephologist at Manchester University who studied the election closely, tells me he has identified two significant problems with the Lib Dem campaign: failure to convert the enthusiasm of young people into votes (of which more later) and over-confidence. In previous elections the master strategist Rennard had moved his meagre forces round the map during campaigns with the skill of Viscount Alanbrooke, but Russell says this time the Orange army foolishly believed its own propaganda—activists and candidates in hitherto fairly hopeless seats reported such positive feedback they insisted on staying to fight rather than moving, as in previous elections, to nearby seats still in the game.

And perhaps it was not merely local parties growing carried away. A Lib Dem organiser in Islington, a major target seat, was told there would be no leader's visit because the seat was considered won. "Instead Nick visited some seat in south London we were never going to win," I am told. "We knew from canvass returns we weren't winning in Islington, but were ignored."

Still, given the party's resources, Clegg fought massively better than his party had dared hope. So there was profound disappointment when results filtered in. Liberal Democrats ended with 57 seats, roughly the number Clegg expected before he stole the electoral show, but five down on election time before and nearly 50 less than looked in his grasp a week earlier. The nation even bade a tearful farewell to Lembit Opik. If the snap verdict was that Clegg had won the campaign but lost the war, all was not over. There was just a chance that Clegg might win the peace. All would depend on his skill to negotiate with his fellow war leaders a treaty to establish a new order.

14

SCHAUDENFREUDE AND CHAUFFEURS

As Clegg contemplated the plate of Digestives before his high command meeting in Cowley Street, his primary concern was that the Liberal Democrats would not be swallowed up by either of the other parties or by the hunger of the media for a decision.

Clegg started by announcing that Cameron's aide, Ed Llewellyn, had made contact. So too had Brown, through Vince Cable, suggesting a "rainbow coalition". The courting had begun, just as everyone present knew it would.

For in the run up to the election Clegg had instructed five of the party's nimblest minds to pump intellectual iron together for several months to work out the permutations. This secret cell, led by Alexander, probed and pummelled every scenario into submission. Policy papers were also prepared for dealing with both parties.

Alexander's secret report, based on these deliberations, concluded that outright coalition with the Conservatives would be extremely tricky due to policy, and coalition with Labour even harder thanks to the maths (Labour was always likely to win fewer seats than the Tories). While no options were ruled out, a limited agreement with the Conservatives seemed the least improbable outcome, which would see Lib Dems offering support from opposition benches on key measures to a minority Cameron government. One senior figure now admits the policy paper covering negotiations with Labour was a little half-hearted as no one could foresee circumstances in which this particular kite could grow airborne. Equally, few envisaged Cameron conceding anything on electoral reform, which made full Tory coalition virtually impossible.

The Churchillian voice in the wilderness belonged to Clegg's old party rival, Huhne. He had irritated colleagues by refusing to endorse Alexander's findings and submitted to Clegg a minority report ("a minority of one," he has joked to me). It argued all roads might lead to full Conservative coalition. Ever the *homme sereux*, he produced research showing that seven of the 10 biggest "fiscal consolidations" in the OECD since 1970 had been under coalition governments. With the Greek economy in flames and the conflagration threatening to blow north, markets would surely favour stable government with a clear majority. All agreed that with the economic temperature rising, voters would expect Liberal Democrats to work for the national interest. But no politician can ever entirely separate high principle from low cunning and even Laws was wary of growing too intimate with the Conservatives for party reasons. He didn't believe Cameron would compromise on fair votes, and without that Laws was convinced Clegg would be unable to gain endorsement from the party. Perhaps Laws also found the proposal harder to embrace because of its proponent. Laws had struggled to forgive Huhne for standing for the party leadership against Campbell.

Huhne was an unlikely advocate of a Tory tryst. After all, hadn't the former Guardianista run against Clegg for the party leadership on a platform of protecting public services from market mechanisms? But Huhne, like Clegg, had learned in the European parliament that you must sometimes jaw-jaw with those you would rather jab on the jaw. Having followed his successful journalistic career by making quite enough in the City to ensure that none of his millions would ever go lonely, he was highly ambitious and had no more time than Clegg for the amateurism of warm aspiration sometimes found in his party.

He thought it possible the Conservatives might concede a referendum on electoral reform, even if it ran counter to their long-term interests, because the prize valued by high Tories above all is power, immediately. Without power, no other policy matters. Indeed, more cynical Tories would dismiss mere policy as almost incidental to raw politics. I remember coming up against this private Conservative thought at lunch with the late Alan Clark when I used the phrase "obsessed with power for its own sake", rather disparagingly. The squire of Saltwood Castle shot me a quizzical look: "and what's wrong with that?"

Huhne tells me he invoked Disraeli. Hadn't the great Victorian Conservative, Huhne asked, outflanked his Liberal rival, Gladstone, granting votes to working men? So might not a Conservative cut from the same dashing, hand-stitched cloth be equally audacious, and go as far as Labour on a new plan to change the way we vote? Cameron, Huhne realised, was also likely to be under pressure to deal. Outright Conservative victory required a swing of historic proportions, yet this was what his party demanded. If Cameron didn't deliver—against an opponent as inviting as Brown—what would be the reaction of Tory right wingers yearning for a return to the un-pasturised Thatcherism of Simon Heffer? After all, Tories are not always the most forgiving breed. Cameron, Huhne saw, would be alive to such dangers and calculate that this might be his one chance to have his portrait hung on the canary yellow walls of the Number 10 staircase. Given that, a whole field of prized Tory cows might be herded off to the coalition abattoir. Accuse the Conservatives of much, but it would be unfair to ascribe to them an excessive sentimentality.

So what were Clegg's instincts on this day of days? Though strongly anti-Conservative, he never shared his colleagues' finger-jabbing loathing. Clegg preferred to judge on what he found, which was, in equal measure, a Conservative Party too hard-hearted and a Labour Party too soft-headed.

One of Clegg's qualities is an ability to look at problems dispassionately. Predecessors such as Kennedy and Campbell might struggle to make the emotional leap to government with Conservatives. Clegg was less handicapped by such historical antagonism. While the Scotsmen saw their task as re-uniting the centre left, Clegg, as far back as 2006, was telling me it would be wrong to prop up a "discredited" Labour government. And as he has admitted in an interview that closes this book his experiences in opposition had softened his opposition to a Tory deal.

Moreover, even if the media had scarcely noticed, Clegg and a tiny cadre had mounted an audacious and highly successful coup.

Clegg's takeover of the Lib Dems had so transformed his party that it at least made a Tory deal possible. Long before some appreciated quite what he was up to, Clegg's legs were under the cabinet table.

The key document to understanding this thought had been written that March by Julian Astle. He had been an aide to Ashdown in the Balkans along with Llewellyn, now Cameron's gatekeeper. Astle was employed by the hedge fund mogul Marshall at CentreForum. The title of his paper? A Lib-Con Trick. Clegg has sometimes complained that Astle doesn't always recognise the political constraints, but values Astle's role as intellectual outrider.

Astle wrote: "With politics set to be dominated by the need to tackle the UK's massive structural deficit, the over-riding objective for the Liberal Democrats will be to demonstrate they are part of the solution, not the problem. In a hung parliament, the Lib Dems will wield significant power... [They] will increasingly have to think and act like a governing party. The rules of the game could be about to change dramatically." And this for a party which just a couple of years before could sometimes give the impression of believing politics was about hurling bricks of cash at unreformed public service in the hope some of it might stick.

Astle, by the way, anticipated this Tory-Liberal Democrat understanding would fall short of full coalition, but was otherwise correct.

Were there also cultural factors nudging Clegg towards a Tory deal? If politics is tribal then Clegg's tribe was not so very alien to Cameron's. Clegg once complained to me of a colleague who was prejudiced against those (such as himself) who had attended public school, and he joked freely that he was just waiting for the right time to ask the parents for help with school fees.

We probably shouldn't make too much of personal title-tattle quite this trivial. Instead we should focus on the more serious gossip. This concerns Clegg's relations with Brown, which at a stretch could be described as "formal". When the three party leaders met to discuss the expenses scandal, Clegg, more than Cameron, felt insulted by the Prime Minister's bombast. He told the senior man: "there's no point having this conversation, Gordon, if you are just going to lecture us." Even Miriam Clegg, that model of discretion, confided in friends her view that Brown "could never represent change."

Clegg, though, had spurned Cameron's offer of dinner. Huhne was annoyed by this refusal, believing a politician who stands for consensus should break bruschetta with Cameron and Brown.

Clegg, however, wanted to remain detached, which was why in those Politician Idol debates he had referred to the Conservative leader as "David Cameron", not "David".

We should always be alive to the personal, and Brown's slightly crazed displays during the negotiations hindered any deal. As early as the Cowley Street meeting Clegg asked rhetorically whether Brown had the personality to lead a coalition, which tends to be founded on collegiate discussion. But Clegg went on to express more immediate objections to Brown's "rainbow coalition". "I'm not sure the numbers really work for that," he ventured "do they?"

Quickly he answered his question: they didn't. And even if the numbers could be made to do so, as in some imaginatively compiled Enron balance sheet, wouldn't this look like a coalition of losers? The more Clegg dug, the more problems he unearthed. Most seriously, Clegg asked, wouldn't the markets, faced with a rag bag government in the midst of a banking crisis, "go nuts"?

Like the rest of the political class, Clegg was greatly exercised, more away from the camera than before it, by the economy. If 1997 was a time of hope and spend, 2010 was about fear and tax. For all Brown's self-proclaimed mastery of macro-economics, Clegg wasn't convinced that the man who had led us into a massive deficit was the new Moses to lead us to a promised land of sustainable prosperity. The coming parliament could not, alas, be all about social advance. In the first three years it would be about holding the line to ensure the most vulnerable didn't slip further into poverty. There might be room for a couple of new progressive social programmes but they would come at the expense of old, less effective ones. Clegg had spent the campaign arguing against precipitous, major spending cuts, ostensibly because it might push us into recession, but also because gloom doesn't sell. Furtively, though, he had begun to realise it was ignoble to ignore the deficit. The black hole was simply too massive.

But whatever the record of Brown, he could not be ignored. For however disconcerting a Brown charm offensive might be to anyone with the possible exceptions of Mrs Brown and Mr Balls, there were distinct advantages to cooing before a Prime Ministerial courtship. "It's absolutely vital," Huhne declared "to strengthen our bargaining position by making the rainbow coalition a real possibility. If we can do this, we might even persuade Cameron to accept a referendum on voting reform." Clearly Huhne has about him a touch of Madam Shipton, such are his powers of insight. As if on cue Mandelson, that master machinator, rang requesting talks.

Clegg concluded the meeting, to nods of agreement, by saying he would meet Cameron and launch full negotiations with the Conservatives, keeping all options open. There would also be a bit of informal footsy with Labour, exploring possibilities, but this would not constitute "formal" negotiations. This was a nice distinction; the Liberal Democrats had decided to play a dangerous game, but not as dangerous as not playing at all.

Later that night the Tory presses began to roll, and as their words spread across a thunderous night sky their rage was a joy to laugh at. Clegg, they demanded, must graciously capitulate and hand office to the Conservatives as the party that had "won" the election, all on a little over 35 per cent of the vote. Meanwhile, Labourites still with a taste for office were reminding Clegg, very publicly, that he was billed as a progressive politician, not some crypto Tory boy.

But Clegg grasped very quickly that he was in an infinitely stronger position, not only than Paddy Ashdown in 1997, but Jeremy Thorpe in February 1974. Then, the Liberals holding the balance rested as much on the narrowness of the Conservative lead over Labour as any psephological frenzy for Thorpe. The demands of a party which had dominated the campaign and won a quarter of the vote could not be so easily brushed aside. After all, according to the *British Election Study* 45 per cent thought Clegg had fought the best campaign against 26 per cent for Cameron (Gordon Brown was beaten into fourth place behind the 9.5 per cent who went for "don't know"). Only a statistically insignificant 2 per cent thought the Liberal Democrats had fought the worst campaign, with their efforts judged the best by far more than any other party's (35.3 per cent Lib Dem, 21.1 per cent Tory, Labour 8.7 per cent). That counted.

But Clegg had to field calls from two suitors anxious to mark his dance card. He arranged a quick step with Cameron, and the pair agreed—rather in the manner of appointing "seconds" for a duel—for small teams to face each other in detailed negotiations. Meanwhile, it would scarcely have surprised Blair but it took approximately three seconds of Brown's wooing before Clegg found himself, metaphorically speaking, clutched violently to the Prime Ministerial bosom and led careering around the dance floor to a beat entirely of Brown's choosing. The more Brown demanded Clegg's hand in majority government, the more it appeared he didn't understand that coalitions are about consent. At the point Brown announced he was passionately committed to political reform, Clegg just about managed to stifle a chuckle. This was the man who had, for over a decade, been the hulking great concrete block on the road to reform. It was amazing to behold what the prospect of having your dream home repossessed can do to the house proud. Brown the pugilist could apparently morph into Brown the pluralist, if only Clegg would let him stay in Number 10.

As the telephonic interchange—or monologue—continued, the Prime Minister sounded as if he were reading a long list of policy concessions he thought Clegg might like, rather than letting Clegg tell Brown what he actually wanted. When Brown suggested, apparently reading from a pre-prepared text, that he would now read another list, Clegg just managed to cut him off with a "no, please don't". If some suitors are said to be not safe in a taxi, Brown certainly wasn't safe in a tax discussion. As Clegg had feared, Brown was not proving to be a thoughtful lover, and the Prime Minister's dreams of some progressive love-in, a red-orange coming together, were already starting to disappear over the rainbow. Even Mandelson, listening on another line, was later moved to remark in one his majesterial under-statements: "I was a little worried that Gordon might have come across a bit too heavily." It scarcely mattered how thin the ice was—with Brown dancing, it was sure to crack.

As Mandelson was left to ponder a question that had become an old friend these past two decades—how to change Gordon?—the Lib Dem team prepared to meet their Conservative counterparts that evening in Whitehall. There was a sense of unreality about the talks, hosted by Gus O'Donnell. Would the Lib Dems, O'Donnell asked, care to have the governor of the Bank of England summoned to brief them on the economy? No wonder Laws ribbed Huhne when he caught him going through a catalogue of the government's fabulous art collection, available to decorate ministerial offices.

Clegg chose his negotiating team astutely. Much is made of the beefy brains of Tories William Hague and Oliver Letwin, but Huhne and Laws are hardly intellectual bantamweights, and both are capable of delivering left and right hooks to flatten an opponent with a knockout argument. If the media didn't consider either a match for the Tory pair, well, that merely spoke of the media's knowledge of the Lib Dems.

One MP briefed on the negotiations says: "David [Laws] and Chris [Huhne] deserve real credit. They faced top Tory guns, especially William Hague, and rang rings round him. We couldn't believe the concessions David and Chris won."

Alexander also proved an adroit choice as team leader, emollient yet adept at prodding the talks towards a more favourable conclusion. And the presence of no nonsense Andrew Stunell reassured the faithful that this would be no Orange Book/Tory stitch up organised by those rich public schoolboys, Huhne and Laws.

Early Cabinet Office talks were good tempered and found a degree of agreement. The Lib Dems conceded the need for £6 billion of savings, while the Tories agreed to tax cuts for the low paid and £2.5 billion to fund that Clegg/Laws signature policy, a pupil premium.

Laws says: "We were picking the best policies from each party. Each side agreed to drop its least favoured policies while embracing the better alternatives presented by the other. No doubt some in both parties would have been horrified to hear cherished polices being so happily cast onto the coalition bonfire." However, perhaps the Lib Dems were a little too enthusiastic fire-starters, as they would discover.

A Lib Dem, now in cabinet, reports that Letwin was particularly accommodating: "He seemed very familiar with the Lib Dem manifesto and accepted large chunks of it. Indeed, he seemed to agree with rather more of it than his own." According to this source Letwin, on the pretext of appeasing the Lib Dems, pushed the coalition agreement towards a far greener programme than Hague favoured. No wonder Hague was heard to stammer at one point: "I think this side has already conceded quite a lot."

But on the key Lib Dem demand for electoral reform there was little traction. Perhaps Huhne had been too optimistic.

So Clegg played the red card. He dispatched his negotiating team to secret, preliminary, talks in Portcullis House (better to avoid cameras) while the Lib Dem leader met Brown. The second time he took the precaution of taking Alexander as chaperone. At the first meeting Brown promised to step down, but by the second had insisted he needed to hang around to win a referendum on the Alternative Vote, a system of electoral reform. "But we will never win a referendum with you in charge!" the normally diplomatic Alexander rumbled. Even Brown looked chastened. Ashdown, a veteran of many a campaign to reunite the centre left, tells me Brown shouted at Clegg and describes the meeting as "bad". As dates go, it was hardly love at first sight.

When Labour, inexplicably, leaked a story that Brown might, terribly selflessly, be persuaded to stay on in order to see the nation through the economic crisis, Keith Simpson, Conservative MP, gained the measure of it: "It's like Neville Chamberlain saying in 1940 'I intend resigning but not until after the autumn party conference because I'm the best man to deal with this rather large offensive coming through the Low Countries.'"

Ashdown was furious. Like a father who has passed custody of his beloved train set to a younger generation, he was keeping a protective eye on events, hosting a raucous dinner for MPs and ringing Laws throughout the night demanding updates. To his final call of the evening, sometime after 4 am, Laws was rather of the opinion that the only update was that he needed sleep. Initially Ashdown thought the arithmetic ruled out a deal with Labour, but his old desire for realignment of the centre left gnawed. Even though he has grown more economically liberal, to him the Tories have always been the enemy, Labour the competition. He still accepted Blair's analysis that the 20th century had been the Conservative century because of the split in the progressive forces of British politics between Labour and Liberal, and that to make the 21st century a progressive one Labour would have to make accommodations with the Liberal tradition. Unfortunately Blair had been more eloquent in articulating the problem than in fashioning a solution. Like many Lib Dem activists who wear their radicalism on their fair trade sleeve, Ashdown struggled to imagine working with Conservatives. His attitude to them had been summed up by one of Clegg's better quips of the campaign: there is nothing progressive about the Conservatives, "the clue is in the name."

So even though Ashdown's leadership had broken on the wheel of trusting Blair to deliver electoral reform, he retained a romantic attachment to this tattered project. The retired Captain decided it was time for one last daring raid. And like all veterans of the SBS, he launched his sortie in the dead of night. "I got Cherie out of bed at 2.30 am," he tells me. "She got hold of Tony who was in the Middle East." Even in his half-sleep Blair couldn't resist a chuckle when Ashdown said Brown was being "impossible". A key Liberal Democrat condition was that Brown, as architect of an economy blitzed by the banking and spending crisis, would have to go. And Blair, with his monumentally interesting relationship with Brown, agreed readily, even if he did think that whatever the result of these talks, Labour was exhausted and needed time in opposition. "He said 'you are right, he will have to go. I'll make sure he does,'" Ashdown reports. Less happily for Ashdown, Blair was privately convinced Labour needed time in opposition and with the economy deteriorating felt this was the ideal time to let the other parties take the stage—and quite possibly the blame.

But Clegg was playing his hand in mercurial fashion. By keeping the Labour option just about alive, pressure was mounting on Cameron. Rumours circulated that Brown was about to bow to the inevitable, which brought the possibility of a Lib-Lab double act centre stage. Clegg rang Cameron and told him that after consulting his party the price of a deal would be full coalition and a referendum on electoral reform. By now this was Clegg's preferred outcome. Cameron acknowledged Clegg's points and promised to respond soon, acknowledging that a confidence and supply pact would look like failure.

Such deals are inherently unsatisfactory, as earlier Liberal leaders have recognised. In 1965, when Labour was shuffling along with a tiny majority and coalition talk crackled through the Westminster air, Grimond said: "I should be very much opposed to going back to the 1929 system, in which the Labour government and the Liberal Party made practically daily ad hoc decisions on the business of government. I should be very much inclined to say: 'we are in this difficult situation. Here are things both parties want to get through. We will support you on all issues, however minor, until that is done."

But this required an even greater risk. Clegg barely knew Cameron, and texted a mutual friend: "Can I trust this guy?" The answer came back: "yes".

If Lib Dems wondered if Clegg had overplayed his hand, news arrived—so joyously received it was like the lifting of the Siege of Mafeking. It had leaked from the Conservative camp that the leadership had been canvassing MPs on whether to accept a referendum on AV. A Tory MP had told a journalist in strictest confidence who promptly told Nick Harvey, Lib Dem MP. Clearly the Tory leadership wanted to make the concession but were testing their party. As the Westminster jungle drums beat ever louder, Conservatives began to fear (wrongly) the Lib Dems were tilting towards Labour. Osborne advised Cameron he would have to concede a referendum. In the arresting phrase of a Tory MP, "we feel the hand of history on our gonads, squeezing very hard."

No wonder Tories were squealing. A shattered Cameron went home and informed his wife he doubted he would ever be Prime Minister. The first formal talks were arranged for that evening between Lib Dems and Labour. Clegg was privately telling the other parties "we are all losers." But some would be bigger losers than others.

While the Tory leadership remained diplomatic in public,

peripheral figures were growing excitable. Until then Tories had tended to dismiss Liberals as wetter than a winter weekend in Bognor, but suddenly their denunciations of Clegg grew so feverish they were a tribute of sorts. Sir Malcolm Rifkind, revealing a hitherto undetected comedic talent, likened Clegg—the gentle-natured Beckett-aficionado—to Robert Mugabe. Clegg's crime? Daring to consider working with anyone other than the Conservatives, which according to the former Tory Foreign Secretary was evidence of electoral larceny on a lavish scale. If one took Rifkind seriously, which was asking a lot, election monitors from the more mature democracies would presumably soon be uncovering mountains of unopened ballot boxes in the shed at the bottom of Clegg's Sheffield garden, while Ashdown would be accused of using his machete in reprisals on anyone who had dared vote Conservative.

It was highly entertaining, if you were not too offended by this cherished Conservative notion handed down from father to son that they had a divine right to rule. Their party had secured a smidgeon over a third of the vote, considerably more than anyone else but considerably shy of a majority in the Commons, and even more bashful of a majority in the country. They could bluster but they had no right to unfettered power, as their more thoughtful figures now admit. To the credit of the Conservative negotiating team, it grasped this truth long before frights from the Thatcher age growling in the back woods of the House of Lords.

Meanwhile the press had no perspective on coalition-building. It was clamouring for resolution, warning of markets jitters. Actually it was the commentators who were spooked, wondering if the Conservatives they championed would be denied.

The coolest head was Clegg's. The Lib Dem leader realised talks had to be resolved in days—Huhne's assertion that such negotiations often take weeks on the Continent was unlikely to convert the *Sun* to the charms of multi-party democracy—but he was determined to use the time he had to trouser more concessions.

If only Cameron knew how badly the Lib-Lab talks were going, he might have conceded less and returned home to the lovely Sam Cam in perkier mood.

The Labour team arrived late as Brown's last cabinet meeting had dragged on, with ministers paying tributes to the dying man. But a Lib Dem negotiating team, treated as near equals by the Tories, began to look for signs of arrogance from the governing party, and didn't have to peer too hard. Ed Balls looked completely disinterested, and it later emerged Labour's preparation for the meeting had consisted primarily of a quick chat over coffee between Balls and Mandelson. The Lib Dem suspicion was that Balls was playing a longer game, looking for a period in opposition allowing his party to get back in touch with its more masculine, "real Labour" side, under his leadership, naturally. Harriet Harman, never likely to find fresh employment as a goodwill ambassador, was scarcely at her most agreeable. She waved aside Lib Dem demands to scrap ID cards by saying the matter should be dealt with by the Home Secretary and "whoever the Lib Dem home affairs spokesman is." Alexander couldn't resist retorting "that would be Chris", gesturing to Huhne at his side.

If these personal slights should not have damaged as they probably did, there were more substantive differences, within Labour's negotiating team as well as with the Lib Dems. While Mandelson expressed an almost indecent enthusiasm for cuts—and later blamed Lib Dem spending commitments for the collapse of talks—Balls said he couldn't accept any more economies than Labour had already announced. Laws was incredulous. Despite Labour's insistence that they were negotiating as a party rather than the government, they gave every appearance of regarding this process as a useful wheeze to bolt on a few peripheral Lib Dem policies. It would essentially remain the same old programme delivered by what the much lamented Bill Deedes would have called the same old shower. When Laws demanded that those bomb-proof public sector pensions be reviewed, Harman (copied by Ed Miliband and Balls) screwed her faces in such a gesture of disgust it would have impressed Maggie Smith playing one of her disapproving dowagers.

While Mandelson appeared to sympathise with the Lib Dems on pensions, he started to appear as if he were of another party to his three colleagues, perhaps reflecting the different company he keeps. At one point this superior representative of the peoples' party announced, possibly as a joke to rile his earnest colleagues: "Haven't the rich suffered enough?" One must hope Kier Hardy's grave has decent turning facilities.

But it was Balls who really derailed the negotiations when he declared Labour might not be able to deliver AV, about the one long-standing Labour commitment Balls didn't seem wedded to. Laws remarks: "It was a deadly intervention and I felt a calculated wrecking device." Having pushed for Brown to go, Lib Dems now realised that post-Brown Labour had progressed from being unpalatable to ungovernable.

Clegg was shocked when the Lib Dem team reported how badly the showdown had gone. He had faced a triumvirate of former Lib Dem leaders (Ashdown, Kennedy, Campbell) urging him to give Labour another chance. Telephone lines had crackled through the night, mostly leading from Ashdown. A generation brought up longing for the arrival of that Blair-Ashdown baby, Christened far too prematurely the "Progressive Consensus", still prayed for safe delivery. But a younger generation began to wonder if after 13 years this wasn't a phantom pregnancy.

A second Labour meeting next day was less spiky but scarcely more substantive, with Miliband ruling out a major cuts programme. Again public sector pensions proved divisive, with Harman, still in the argot of class politics, questioning the need to panic "our people". Miliband declared flatly: "we cannot go further than our existing agreements with the unions."

Given all this it is extraordinary that Andrew Adonis, one of Labour's negotiating team and a former SDP figure, should blame the collapse on Clegg's supposed determination to deal with the Tories. While he and Mandelson were probably sincere in trying to secure agreement, their colleagues preferred the absolutism of opposition.

When details of the meeting were reported to Clegg he decided very quickly the former leaders of his party had been indulged enough. There had to be a coalition of the willing, and that meant the Conservatives. He ordered his negotiators back to Whitehall to meet Hague's high command to finalise a deal.

As well as AV, his team wrung from the Conservatives two major concessions: tax cuts for the low paid and substantially more money for disadvantaged pupils. However, Lib Dem negotiators didn't put up much of a fight to protect their pledges not to raise tuition fees. In the otherwise informative Laws book on the negotiations, *22 Days in May*, it merits the briefest mention. Another negotiator has insisted this aspect was handled by Alexander, and after discussion with Clegg, the Lib Dems decided not to force the issue. Now one of those negotiators insists a deal with the Tories would have been possible protecting the Lib Dem promise on tuition fees, which doesn't explain why he didn't push this argument at the time. It was a collective failure in the most febrile atmosphere which would later come back to inflict major damage on the party's credibility.

As details of the coalition document were being hammered out it was imperative to keep Brown in office to maximize leverage—the moment Brown's car left for the Palace to hand his seals of office back to the Queen, Clegg would be under pressure to announce a deal, or else face cries of "Will No One Govern Britain?" So as the Lib Dem team worked feverishly with Tory counterparts, Clegg found himself in the uncomfortable position of ringing Brown and asking him to hold off his resignation. How Brown must later have choked back tears of irony. Eventually Brown declared "enough" and stepped outside with his wife and two children to say goodbye. However, Clegg had kept him in place long enough for all but the smallest details to be agreed. As TV footage caught the prime ministerial car leaving, Osborne slapped Laws on the back in a gesture of triumph. For Liberal Democrats it was bitter sweet, realising they would be entering government with their historic enemy.

The document that finally emerged announcing agreement amazed everyone in its breadth, and lent some weight to those who thought feelers had gone out prior to the election. One Tory peer has said to me: "You saw the document agreeing in considerable detail to various policies. Could that have been thrashed out in a couple of days? Or the idea of the 55 per cent majority required to bring down the government? Laws and Hague are clever, but could they have come up with that in minutes? Of course not." All those directly involved insist it was decided then and there, though Liberal Democrats had enjoyed a certain leisure to think up such ideas— after all, no Liberal had been burdened by the chains of office since World War Two.

Norman Baker, MP for Lewes and the first MP to speak in favour of a Tory/Lib Dem deal, tells me: "It went how I expected. It was the only viable option. I'm sure there were informal discussions before the election. Certainly many chats in corridors."

The new generation of Tory had proved less obnoxious to Liberal Democrats than their predecessors, just as a new generation of Liberal Democrats proved far more professional to the Tories. Laws had hit it off with Osborne ever since the then shadow Chancellor had attempted to persuade him to defect, firmly as Laws had rebuffed the overture. And Huhne was a friend of Letwin's. "They had talked a lot together about the environment before the election," I'm told. "Although Chris found Oliver's views on Europe quite mad, on the green agenda there was already huge agreement and they simply downloaded a lot of the ideas they had talked about into the coalition agreement. It's why there is such a lot of surprising detail on the environment."

Whatever, the Lib Dem negotiating team had done well. University College London's School of Public Policy calculated that 75 per cent of the Lib Dem manifesto found its way into the agreement against 60 per cent of the Tory document. Sure, policies are of wildly varied levels of importance and the Conservatives won the biggest decision, the £6 billion of cuts, but for a party with 57 MPs this was an achievement which should not be overlooked, however great the Liberal Democrats later problems.

Labour's complaints were surprisingly muted. If few of the outgoing cabinet could be described as burnt out volcanoes— volcanoes, after all, are towering, magnificent edifices—they did at least resemble a box of rather damp fireworks that, after a colourful early display, had fizzled into disappointment. Mandelson, who often finds much to commend in anybody important, considered Clegg no exception and wished him well. He had opined earlier that if Labour suffered heavy losses it would be pointless propping up Brown. And in this he was not being merely vindictive—though that incidental pleasure was surely not lost on him—for he saw the changing mood. New Labour had become old lags. Given the horrors of working for Brown, as Alistair Darling chronicled in the memoirs, many must have been quietly relieved it was all over. Balls and Miliband, meanwhile, seemed less interested in a "progressive government" than in progressing careers.

Heroically, the *New Statesman* ventured that a Lib-Lab deal "was possible on every issue apart from on the pace and severity of deficit reduction", which even if true is rather like saying Amundsen and Scott could have got along fine if only they had bothered to agree the little matter of who would reach the South Pole first.

Labour's not terribly disguised attitude was to regard the Lib Dems as a vaguely remembered old jumper, to be used in only the most inclement weather. Or perhaps Labour saw them as the token woman ("Sally Traffic") let out to announce various snarl ups approaching the M1 on Radio 2. Either way, if Labour failed to keep promises on electoral reform, well, the poor old Lib Dems would understand—and if they didn't, well, who cared?

Privately several sensible Labour figures acknowledged they hadn't offered enough, though some leftist commentators predicted with *faux* concern that Clegg would become a "human shield".

The wilder howls came from that wing of the Conservative Party that considered the prospect of sharing power an affront to its dignity. Particularly with Liberal Democrats, who to Tory MPs remained the enemy back in the constituency.

As for the Lib Dems, selling this most democratic of parties the deal would be the greatest test of Clegg's career. He convened a meeting in Smith Square of his party's MPs, peers and leading officials. And by most accounts he played a blinder, winning over diehards and ditherers. Flanked by Alexander who fielded questions, he took his seat on a platform facing about 120 politicians, many sceptical. "He set the parameters," says Browne, now from his desk at the Foreign Office. "It was almost like counselling." Campbell could scarcely bring himself to talk to Laws, once such a key ally, when this architect of the agreement sat beside him.

Clegg acknowledged, both for those who were around in the eighties when Margaret Thatcher was prime minister and for those who hailed from areas long sacrificed by the Conservatives, that the dislike for the right was visceral. But tellingly he explained there was a generational shift and he didn't carry that baggage. "He led them gently, never seeming to force them, until a coalition with the Conservatives seemed the only option," says Browne.

Many of the newer MPs agreed, with some shouting "let's get on with it". But the grand old men remained doubtful. David Steel, another leader whose career had been dedicated to realignment, was furious, though insufficiently so to attend. Kennedy is very rarely furious, but had also raised a quizzical eyebrow. Campbell may dress to the right but thinks to the left and could never have dealt with Cameron, though he graciously kept his counsel believing it for the new generation to make its choices.

Alexander was patient and emollient, fielding often irrelevant questions. "They weren't quite 'how can I go back to my constituents and tell them I'm now supporting a party that is opposed to speed humps in our town?', but many weren't much more elevated," says one source.

Kennedy, the source continues, "made a poor speech, basically saying the Conservatives were not very nice." But our mole reserves his greatest ire for Ashdown: "He made a self-indulgent speech, finally saying he would accept [the coalition] with a heavy heart. He had even been on the Today Programme earlier saying he had doubts about a coalition. Imagine if Michael Howard had done that to Cameron. It was totally disloyal."

This was harsh. Ashdown had been talking up a Lib-Lab deal in the media, on instruction from Clegg, but to pressure Tories into conceding electoral reform. This was, no doubt, laced with genuine fear about what a deal with the Tories would do for realignment and the Lib Dems own long-term standing. He entered the meeting wondering if he might speak against the Lib-Con agreement but reading it, was won over.

Now Ashdown tells me: "Nick realised by the Sunday morning we had to go with the Tories. It took me longer. I was very unhappy. Then I did think 'fuck it, it will have to be.' And 'fuck it', I think, was about where the party was."

Cable shared some doubts of the Grand Old Men, but significantly declared it was the only possible agreement. Though his dry fiscal policies had moved his party to the right, emotionally he recoiled at working with Conservatives. He refused the Chief Secretary's job, declaring privately: "I'm not going to be Osborne's hatchet man." Even Laws, often seen as the party's most vocal right winger, was, according to one friend, pre-programmed to expect a deal with Labour.

If alliance with the Tories went against the spiritual constitution of many Lib Dems, it was the more brazen for being entirely the venture of Clegg and his small circle. As one of the party's most important backers says privately: "Others talked about it but I think Nick was the only one at the top who had a real willingness to go with the Tories. I'm not sure if even David [Laws] would have preferred Labour."

As for the vote of the parliamentary party, the only figure who decided he couldn't, in Ashdown's robust phrase, "fuck it", and make policy babies with Cameron was David Rendell, Old Etonian victor of the Newbury by-election who probably more than any Liberal Democrat politician looks and sounds like a patrician Tory. His singular vote against was quickly explained away. Harvey, now Liberal Democrat defence minister, has been heard to joke that if he ever fell asleep in a meeting and was jolted awake in time to vote, he would glance round to see how Rendell had voted. He knew he wouldn't have gone too far wrong if he voted the opposite. Kennedy abstained.

Before Clegg it would have been inconceivable the party would vote, with virtual unanimity, for a Con coalition. If triumph it be, it was his.

His reward was to find himself Deputy Prime Minister, a position

Campbell, Kennedy, Ashdown and Steel would not even have dared dream about after a couple of glasses of crisp white long into a summer afternoon. Further, his team had apparently pulled off a remarkable negotiating coup in extracting more from the Conservatives than Cameron could ever have envisaged conceding. In particular, the suggestion of Cameron giving way on electoral reform would have sounded somewhere between fanciful and laughable.

Yet just as budgets that look good at first glance look grizzly a little later, the coalition agreement contained several landmines that would later blow up in Clegg's face.

That was a problem for another day. Clegg had turned a small, crisis-ridden organisation into one half of the British government. Whatever the later criticisms, whatever the mistakes, this was quite a coup.

But there is nothing naive about Clegg. Because for all the optimism, Britain's new politics was suspiciously like an old European politics, and Clegg was rooted in that. Which was just as well, for the success of this groundbreaking coalition would depend in large part on how vigorously Clegg grew as a politician.

15

THE BLOSSOM OF MAY

As Clegg and Cameron stood in the rose garden of Number 10 sun burst from the clouds, blossom blew in the breeze and enthusiasm seized even this cynical audience, an attack squad of journalistic assassins. Yet while Clegg gazed across the lawn at his new and extremely civil partner as the pair announced the birth of Britain's first post-war coalition government, one thought must have swum through Clegg's befuddled, sleep-starved brain: "could this really be happening to me?"

"Nick Who?", the virtually unknown house-husband from Sheffield of just five years ago, was effectively joint Prime Minister. It is easy to be cynical now. Just as footage of Tony Blair's stroll up Downing Street against a splurge of Union flags was later repeated as a symbol of hubris rather than of hope, so all that Clegg-Cameron blossom and bonhomie is dredged up to show how relations have grown chillier, now the garden apples have fallen from the tree. As those photos are re-shown the couple seem, in retrospect, a little too close, a little too similar, a little too at home in their lovely new house. "There is genuine collegiality," Ashdown told me at the time. "It can't last."

But back then even that most suspicious of audiences felt excited by these two clean-cut young men in petrol blue suits, revving to go. Hard as they tried, questioners couldn't quite hide their optimism, giving rise to a slightly joshing tone, more in the style of an engagement interview for younger royals than a solemn political marriage. No wonder that entertaining old goat David Davis crowned this the "*Brokeback Mountain* moment".

For the rapport seemed—a new sensation, this, for hacks who had survived the Labour years—genuine. It is inconceivable Clegg and Brown could have generated a warmth that gave rise to such apparent trust. So when a reporter reminded Cameron that he had once referred to Clegg as his "favourite joke", Clegg felt sufficiently emboldened to pipe up: "did you really say that?" before shrugging "I'll be off, then", and sauntered from the podium. Only briefly, though. Even then Clegg was convinced he was in this with Cameron for a five year stretch.

And Labour was worried, so "right" did Clegg and Cameron look. Douglas Alexander, who months later was still describing himself on his website as a Secretary of State, admits even he was staggered by the iconography, and feared Labour could be out for some time. Baker relays a telling private remark of a former Labour minister: "While your coalition between Cameron and Clegg seems marked by generosity of spirit and goodwill, our coalition between Blair and Brown wasn't."

Clegg would later play down the love-match, suggesting it had been vital to strike a note of unity to steady the public, parliament and markets. But back then spinners would talk of Clegg helping Cameron assemble an Ikea cabinet for one of his children, a sacrifice almost as painful as tuition fees.

As the pair turned from their inquisitors and marched inside to form their government, they knew they would need more than goodwill. Their task was to form the first peacetime coalition since the twenties, and all against a backdrop of economic crisis. With Cameron "flat on his back" and Clegg devastated he had not won more seats, getting into Downing Street suddenly seemed the easy part.

Nevertheless, Liberal Democrats were united in believing they had stumbled across a leader—or perhaps their leader had stumbled across a party—that was going all the way. Ashdown told me: "the great thing about Nick is he has the ability to grow. And if you see him dealing with civil servants and the full panoply of government, it is hugely impressive." One former party leader even ventures: "He has the potential to be a better Prime Minister than Cameron."

Whatever their respective abilities, the strategy upon which Clegg and Cameron agreed was bold. The priority would be to turn round the economy, primarily by massive public spending cuts which they hoped would generate private sector wealth creation. Then, after two to three years of pain, the economy would recover and government would embark on more positive policies. For Clegg it was vital these measures would resonate with Liberal Democrat voters to justify coalition.

Three other key principles were a direct response to the failures of Blair.

Firstly, Clegg and Cameron were determined not to fritter away their considerable early political capital. If Blair did little in his first term, theirs would, if anything, be a government criticised for doing too much. Both felt that unless they struck early they almost certainly wouldn't strike at all.

Secondly, Clegg and to a lesser extent Cameron were determined not to follow the Alastair Campbell example of seeing all political decisions through a tabloid prism. Success would not be measured by gaining an endorsement from Lady Gaga, but from posterity.

Thirdly, and most boldly, they were determined coalition wouldn't fall into the trap of simply splitting the difference. Ashdown said: "I think what's really impressive is that the agreement is genuinely reformist."

Such were the high intentions. As ever, the actualité proved more challenging.

Clegg quickly learned that if opposition leaders can offer promises, Downing Street delivers disappointments. And soon there would be no shortage of the disappointed. If Sir Ming had expected a cabinet role he was, I am told, offered Australia, or at least the role of Governor-General. Lady Elspeth would surely have been in her element in Government House but alas after three days of pondering Sir Ming told Clegg—in considerably more diplomatic language— that he wouldn't give a "4X" for the job.

Simon Hughes had to be told no red box awaited. Cable made clear he wasn't going to be Osborne's "hatchet man". He, incidentally, failed to climb into his car to take him to his new work place, the Department of Business, because the notion that such trappings should be for him simply hadn't occurred. Cable set off on foot and its driver followed meekly behind.

Laws, at least, was comfortable in his role as Chief Secretary to the Treasury. He was convinced that from there he could protect the vulnerable—be they the poor or Lib Dem policy—and he immediately ring fenced money for the pupil premium and tax cuts for the low paid. Also, he hoped, he would earn the party a reputation for mature, economic competence.

However, not all Lib Dems were sanguine. "We agreed to the cuts, fair enough, but why take all the political flak by associating yourselves with it quite so closely?" one senior figure tells me. "We were left running virtually no departments, and those we did were left with two very difficult decisions: tuition fees at the Department of Business, and nuclear power at Climate Change." Even Ashdown tells me: "Not everyone was in the right position in government."

But while in single party administrations spokespeople tend to slot into the corresponding job of government, dividing spoils in a coalition is hugely more challenging. Given energy levels, the Lib Dems hadn't done badly for a party apparently in permanent exile. I'm advised that when Clegg told Ken Clarke of his concerns about "hang 'em and flog 'em" elements of the Tory manifesto, the new Justice Secretary apparently breezed "Oh, don't worry—we'll ignore all that."

Clegg looked supremely assured, and humbled his predecessor at a meeting of the parliamentary party. Campbell, I'm told, had dared question a decision. One of the party's top MPs recalls: "Away from the cameras Nick has always been a very forceful leader, and more impatient than you might think. Ming spoke out against something in the agreement—I think tuition fees—and I remember wincing as Ming had his legs sliced from under him. You might have expected Nick to show respect to a former leader but he has never lacked confidence. And that willingness to take people on makes them think twice about opposing him."

Personally, friends say Clegg was remarkably unfazed by the adjustment from "modest pebble dash" to Chevening, Prince Charles's magnificent former country retreat in Kent that he was sharing as a weekend bolthole with Hague. He took to inviting staff there on Friday afternoons to brainstorm away from the claustrophobia of his office at Number 70 Whitehall, and even advised Hague on the delights of swimming in the Chevening lake. And in those early days he found Conservatives relatively congenial. As Baker MP tells me: "If you are looking to agree with someone it's amazing how you can find common ground." Baker certainly tested his theory, possibly to destruction. Not only did he address Kensington and Chelsea Conservatives, he accepted an invitation from the Monday Club, where even Eric Pickles is probably regarded as some fey metropolitan pinko. Baker is no quisling, but he does believe in dialogue. As he says, "fighting Tories is what I do." Nothing in his demeanour smacks of Alan B'Stard, the fictional Conservative MP of horror, yet addressing a lunch at his constituency racecourse, Plumpton, he was approached afterwards by a superior sort who asked if he would mind terribly addressing the Conservative Association of Lewes. His interlocutor was quite shocked when Baker had to break the news that he was the Lib Dem MP for the town.

From the Conservative perspective, one Cameroonian minister who is both friend of Cameron's and knows Clegg, was so enthused he told me: "I can see this ending with a merged party. Nick, David Laws, Jeremy Browne and one or two others are basically Tories but didn't join for cultural reasons. A merger would work for David because, oddly, Liberal Democrats would make us more normal. And it would work for the Lib Dems because it would deliver them power. I think this is just the start of a major realignment." Even then it seemed an over-statement, underestimating certainly on the Liberal Democrat side their antipathy for Conservatives, but it did show the zest with which both sides took to their partners.

An underestimated bond was humour, a quality not in bountiful supply under Brown. At a reception in Downing Street to celebrate the formation of the coalition, Browne bowled up to a Tory huddle including Michael Gove and said: "don't worry, I'll instil a bit of backbone to the Foreign Office." Similarly Harvey, marooned in the Ministry of Defence with a bunch of old-style right-wing

Tories led by Liam Fox, had been heard to teasingly refer to himself as "Cameron's man at the MoD."

Lib Dems warmed to the way Cameron didn't appear to take himself too seriously. A minister discloses that in a meeting of the National Security Council Cameron asked "C", head of MI6, whether it had a particular piece of intelligence. "C" apparently replied "It doesn't work like that, Prime Minister."

To which Cameron replied: "I'm sorry, I've obviously watched too many episodes of *Spooks*."

In those early days there was willingness on both sides to be supportive. Cameron was pleasantly surprised when he rang one Lib Dem to offer a ministerial job and was told "I'll consider it part of my job to make you look good, Prime Minister."

The honeymoon was largely as harmonious as anything out of a Jilly Cooper, if not quite a Mills and Boon. Hague, in particular, went out of his way to be gracious in private, while at a reception for ambassadors he pointed out that with a coalition majority of 70 he could actually visit some of their countries. Otherwise he would have to stay home and vote on every dreary sub-clause.

Gove took the new love-in further, quietly suggesting a Tory-Lib dining club to Browne, Laws and other Orange Bookers. Huhne, meanwhile, set up a think tank with Gove to explore how Lib-Con ideas could mesh into policy, called Coalition 2.0. It would attempt to generate ideas for the latter half of the parliament, when most measures included in the coalition agreement would have been enacted.

Though as a breed Lib Dems don't wallow in grandeur, one or two were swooning. A minister could scarcely contain himself when he told me about the helicopters and outriders that met him on a recent trip. If there is any defence it is that for Liberal Democrats politics had been about Orange Books and green waste, not black limousines and red carpets.

For others it was more the sense of achievement that after so many years of campaigning they suddenly had power and purpose. Laws felt close to tears when he sat in the Treasury under a portrait of that great Liberal Chancellor (and later Prime Minister) Lloyd

George. Browne delighted, playfully, in his office once being held by the Secretary for India. "It has two vast doors," he explained. "If two maharajas arrived at the same time, one wouldn't be left to enter behind the other." He paused: "Walking through the Foreign Office I wonder if someone will tap me on my shoulder and say 'can you now hand in your day pass, please?'"

Harvey, a Defence minister, recalls waiting for the call from Number 10 with a beaming Ed Davey, who asked whether Harvey believed 18 years ago when he entered parliament the day would finally arrive when he might be called upon. "Yes," Harvey replied "and I thought it would come about 13 years ago."

Some aspects of coalition life provided even more of a culture shock than power. "I must admit I was a bit surprised," says Harvey "when a fellow Defence minister asked me if he could borrow my top hat." The Tory, apparently, was quite taken aback when Harvey explained he didn't possess one.

Harvey was placed at Defence as something of a human sacrifice with various Tory creatures of the wild. "It is fair to say they are quite a trenchant lot," says Harvey diplomatically.

When his new colleagues asked Harvey where he educated his children and Harvey replied "the local state school", they looked mystified. This only intensified when he explained that quite apart from any political preference "it's all I can afford." Finally, Harvey's attractive young American aide, Monica Allen, was "mildly startled" to walk into a meeting of Conservative Defence ministers to find them ogling a picture of Page 3. Offenders have been humanely put down for less in the Lib Dems.

But on the substance, Lib Dems were initially pleased. A committee on immigration chaired by Clegg in June 2010 saw thinking Tories line up to "savage" Theresa May, Home Secretary, for proposing a cap—even though this was the policy on which Conservatives had fought the election and had incidentally ridiculed the softer line of Lib Dems.

A minister tells me: "First David Willetts said 'so what will happen if the brilliant Peruvian IT expert wants to move from Germany to England to take up a job and we have to turn round and say 'no sorry, we have reached our limit?' Gove then made the classical liberal argument for free movement of labour. And a couple more Tories piled in, saying their party's anti-immigration stance made them uncomfortable." A Lib Dem caught Clegg's eye but stiffed a smile.

If there was any internal dissatisfaction it was that Clegg's man-management skills had briefly deserted him. Colleagues were unimpressed that some staff had been abandoned for days in his old office. They were sacked, eventually. "Surely he could have deputed someone to do it?" asks a minister. Clegg, if he had time, might have retorted that he was just a little tied up.

And what many colleagues didn't grasp was that for all the pomp of the Downing Street rose garden there was no infrastructure to support a Deputy Prime Minister. "The previous incumbent was not perhaps quite so central to government," a senior Lib Dem adviser with top level corporate experience smiled over a chilled glass of Sancere on the terrace of the National Liberal Club. He was referring to John Prescott. "At the beginning, Whitehall just wasn't sufficiently aware of the new role Nick had as deputy PM." Like the media, it had no experience in living memory, or plan, how to deal with a coalition government—a problem that continues to this day. For every paper that was to cross Cameron's desk had to cross Clegg's. Actually, more. For not only was Clegg running more or less in his spare time an ad hoc department—Reform—he also had to monitor every other department. As all bar a few were headed by Conservatives, Cameron could be more confident letting them be. But Clegg needed to see they weren't up to anything that might offend Lib Dem sensibilities.

Clegg managed, but it was a punishing job. Even now Laws says: "Nick and Cameron text each other every five minutes. It goes a hell of a lot better than I ever imagined. The difference between working with Cameron and Brown is so different your jaw drops. I remember when Nick came down to Somerset and someone asked why a particular decision had been announced by government that day. Nick responded with absolute certainty that it hadn't, because he would know about it. If it was Brown he would have found himself hearing decisions in this way every five minutes. It's a genuine partnership. If there is an inner cabinet it's as much Nick and Danny with David and George as it is people such as William Hague." In Whitehall parlance this is "the quad". In addition Cameron and Clegg call each other on private phones on Sunday evenings.

But the dynamics of office life were fraught. "Even now Nick doesn't have a Permanent Secretary," says the corporate source. "His civil servant was a nice guy, but relatively junior. He now has someone else, but still below the rank of Permanent Secretary. You know how any departmental clashes are going to go in the Whitehall food chain. Nick's office has been beefed up but take a look and see how small his staff still is."

The source leans forward and stares at me: "Somebody said to me: 'who does the shouting in that office? Who will eyeball the Permanent Secretary of another department?' Other than Nick and his political advisers, there is no civil servant with the authority." This was endorsed by Catherine Hadden in a report for the Institute for Government, which concluded that the office of Deputy Prime Minister needed strengthening, and Whitehall be forced to recognise it wasn't some adjunct of the Prime Minister's office.

When the coalition was formed there was, I'm told, "a certain hair-shirted desire to spend less than Labour" so far fewer political advisers were appointed—hence the delay in telling Lib Dem workers their fates. But just as cars grow more bloated through the evolution of a model, so do governments, and this decision has been partly reversed with eight new civil servants joining the Number 10 policy unit. There is also growing demand for Lib Dem ministers outside the cabinet to be given special advisers. The management source adds: "If you look at something like the political problems the government has had over Health reform, that could have been avoided if there was a Lib Dem on hand to go through detail."

The civil service is, by temperament fearful of change, but its resistance to giving proper assistance to a party heavily backed by a population that pays its wages is becoming a scandal—and one that

Lib Dems have shown considerable grace in not protesting about far more loudly.

If this was the tired apparatus of state, it only spurred Clegg on to introduce the government's reform agenda, an extraordinary privilege for anyone with a feel for Liberal history. He embarked on what he has called the biggest constitutional shake up since the 1832 Great Reform Act. A key decision was when to hold the AV referendum. Clegg got his way for an early poll, linked to the Scottish and Welsh elections thought likely to boost the "yes" vote, feeling it would be before mid-term blues set in. All that can be said is that it seemed a sensible decision at the time. As Clegg, that quiet puffer, has observed: "A date for the referendum is a bit like giving up smoking: it's never the right time."

Meanwhile, what was that noise emanating from Cameron's (much smaller) office across Horse Guards? Surely it wasn't the Prime Minister singing "I Never Promised You A Rose Garden"?

16

ROUGH WINDS

If Clegg needed reminding that spring blossom never lasts much beyond May it was Laws falling from the political tree. It remains one of the most sombre, brutal moments for the Liberal Democrats in government, and there have been a few. Clegg's vital ally, the intellectual power behind the party's revolution, had been forced to resign after just 16 days. This gave Laws the unenviable record of enjoying the shortest ministerial career in British history, though it was still 16 days longer than any Liberal had managed since Sir Archibald Sinclair in World War 11.

Laws was contacted by the *Telegraph* saying it knew he had claimed £40,000 expenses for rent over five years, and that, contrary to Commons rules, he was in a relationship with the recipient of his rent cheque. This was doubly disastrous for Laws, professionally because it would make it hard to remain in government, and personally because it would expose his homosexuality. For the relationship was with Jamie Lundie, a lobbyist who Laws had met when both toiled as officials for the party, Lundie as press officer and Laws as economics adviser.

The *Telegraph* insisted it did not intend "outing" Laws, and that its interest was financial not sexual. But Laws knew that within minutes of the story hitting newsstands photographers and film crews would be outside the south London flat seeking photos of "the lover", as they duly were. Thus compromised, he had little choice but to issue a statement that evening announcing he was gay. So while he battled to save his career, he also had to endure fraught conversations with his family, telling them about his sexual orientation and why this most personal of matters was suddenly everybody's business. And of course it threw up problems for the previously cheerfully-anonymous Lundie.

To most friends the revelation about Laws' sexuality was no great shock. By now this was a curiously Westminster secret. That is, one known by all. "All", of course, didn't include the public. Lib Dem whip Andrew Stunell had, I gather, approached Laws and tried to unearth any road-side booby-traps about his private life, but was rebuffed. Much to their frustration the red tops no longer feel able to treat homosexuality as a flogging offence, but they will find excuses to throw a politician who is not a "family man" into the dungeon for something else, then ridicule them for their sexuality in passing—as Simon Hughes discovered when he was outed on the flimsiest pretext.

Many friends feared some titillating tabloid expose. With the profile of Laws rising daily and even Conservative commentators mentioning him as the star of the coalition, he had become a target. What no one saw coming was a suggestion, however harsh, of financial impropriety.

Laws realised his position was untenable. He was the politician charged with making the cuts, who would be reminded by every vested interest that if he was so protective of the public purse why had he fleeced it of £40,000?

Clegg, in Paris, rushed home to urge Laws to tough it out. But Laws was determined to make a graceful exit. Clegg was furious, but sad: furious because it was such a trivial scandal to fell such a serious talent, and because it was so damaging to the Lib Dem wing of the coalition. But also sad: he had always had huge regard for Laws, the man who encouraged him to stand for leader that sunny Somerset day.

Laws felt he had no choice but to refer himself to the standards commissioner, yet of all the *Telegraph* expense scandal stories, this stirred least public hostility. It was a sign of a changing Britain that nobody could understand a life of moats and duck houses but they could the desire of a gay man to protect his privacy. Even radio phone-ins were muted.

Laws was not in a civil partnership, so was Lundie technically a "partner"? While Clegg would attend weekend lunches with his wife and children, Laws would travel alone, so certainly he and Lundie weren't a "couple" as heterosexuals would understand the term. Laws didn't, for instance, claim travel from the Commons authorities for Lundie between London and the constituency, which is allowed for "partners". Thinking about it, the more you are struck by the inadequacy of the rule: in this diverse age, how to define "partner"?

That, though, was viewed by Laws as too legalistic an argument. More relevant was that as a backbench MP with a constituency far from London, Laws was entitled to claim from the state rent for his London accommodation. Indeed, he could quite legally have claimed much more if he had rented a large flat on his own rather than an extra bedroom in the flat of a friend. Or he could have nominated the London flat as his primary residence and asked the state to pick up the larger cheque for his Somerset house. Then, incidentally, Lundie would not have needed to have paid 40 per cent of the rent as tax. So the commissioner's only real interest was whether Laws was sleeping with his landlord, which seems at best prurient.

Moreover, when Laws entered into this arrangement in 2004 the practice was allowed, only falling foul of little noticed changes in 2006. Finally, the commissioner lets significant numbers of (mainly Conservative) MPs take out large mortgages against properties they own outright, specifically so the taxman pays off a fresh mortgage, thus giving themselves a massive tax free windfall at public expense. That, surely, was the scandal. But, as Tina Turner didn't sing, what's fairness got to do with it? Wisely, rather than "do a Mellor", clinging on to a tarnished office with his finger tips, Laws resigned swiftly.

Clegg was devastated. He recognised Laws provided intellectual ballast to his political re-pointing. Clegg knew Laws was gay but for a pair who worked closely, Clegg had told me he had never discussed the other's private life. Laws had told me that since Clegg was elected leader talking about anything that wasn't strictly "shop" had been tricky. Even on long train journeys every two minutes of Clegg's time would be allocated to pre-booked calls. Perhaps both now wish they had carved out that time.

The crisis also exposed the old problem of the party's amateurish handling of the press. Lobby hands say Clegg's press officer did not return calls, perhaps in the vague hope the hideous mess would go away. Shockingly, it was left to Andy Coulson, then Conservative spinner, to reduce the damage as best he could. He, of course, would hardly advance the argument that Laws was considerably more frugal than most Tory MPs.

The only Liberal Democrat apparently willing to take a bullet for the man who had done so much to earn them their new importance was Browne. He remained a huge admirer of the Chief Secretary. Alas his studio defence, though eloquent and heart-felt, proved insufficient.

After Laws resigned, the authorities not only investigated this case but all expense claims by Laws, stretching back years. And it took them a year to do so. Nothing further was found. Well, if money was the main interest, Laws would surely have stayed in the City. "He just doesn't talk about his private life," a colleague told me. "It's only in the south of France that he can be more himself." This, though, was speculation as no colleague had stayed there.

"Everyone just assumes it all happened a year ago and is all over," Laws told me shortly before the verdict. "But it is still hanging over me and I can't do anything until I know what it is."

It delivered mixed news. Laws was found guilty on six charges, all stemming from the fault of paying rent to someone with whom he was in a "relationship". But on the central charge that weighed against the Laws character he was found innocent. He had not done anything to profit. That being the case he was, many felt, hardly deserving of censure, but in the body that makes our laws rules are all. He was suspended from the House.

As so often the most interesting aspect was the story behind it. After the *Telegraph* exposure of Clegg's bank details there were those in senior Liberal Democrat circles who wondered if we were witnessing a concerted campaign to discredit the party. Now those voices wondered if the campaign was to destroying the Liberal Democratic wing of the coalition. "This is months after the main revelations about MPs expenses," says one peer. "It will be interesting to see whether this forensic scrutiny of Lib Dem cabinet ministers will be followed by similarly thorough look into the behaviour of Conservative colleagues."

Few held their breath. The *Telegraph* launched a sting on Liberal Democrat ministers, sending undercover reporters to pose as constituents at their surgeries. Most damagingly, Cable was recorded criticising Conservatives and "declaring war" on Rupert Murdoch as the regulator overseeing the tycoon's planned takeover of BSkyB. This aspect of the story did not appear in the newspaper. The *Telegraph* said it had intended to print it the following day, though was beaten to it by the BBC. Cynics were heard to wonder if the *Telegraph*'s unaccustomed reticence might have owed something to its delight that Cable had "declared war" on their rival.

Cable complained and the media regulator censored the newspaper for its "fishing expedition". The *Telegraph* insisted its intention was to expose the hypocrisy of Lib Dems professing support for the coalition in public while rubbishing it in private. Which was a noble argument, and would have been strengthened if it had exposed Tories for harbouring similarly interesting views. Readers might, for instance, have enjoyed hearing what Liam Fox or Eric Pickles, to lob a couple of names at random, thought of their Liberal Democrat friends.

And so it went on. Huhne was exposed for having an extra marital affair, a revelation which wrecked his marriage and tore his family apart. If that wasn't punishment enough, allegations appeared that Huhne had asked his now ex-wife to take penalty points for him on her license in 2003.

Labour MP Simon Danczuk helpfully referred the matter to the police who promised to take the matter "very seriously". We had the spectacle of a cabinet minister being interviewed by the CID, though with Huhne's ex-wife also potentially facing charges of perverting the course of justice if she testified against him, it was felt unlikely there would be evidence to charge Huhne.

You can wonder what the next scandal involving the Lib Dems will be, but you won't have to wait long. Meanwhile, it is tempting to ask is it just men in sandals who have scandals. Have Tories suddenly become whiter than white? If so, they must have undergone quite a collective personality transformation.

While all these controversies are entertaining, The *Telegraph's* political strategy is unclear. Destroy the Liberal Democrat wing and you bring down the coalition. The Conservatives will have no majority and become a minority government with chaos and economic uncertainty. Perhaps it should be careful what it wishes for.

Baker, like many Lib Dem ministers, was stung by the fake constituent routine, sees a conspiracy with newspapers that are "not democratic. They simply don't accept the result of the election. They think Cameron is a bit of a pinko hiding behind the Lib Dems. So they want to get out the Lib Dems and either force Cameron to be more right wing or replace him with David Davis.

"You can see a scenario whereby the Lib Dems are picked off one by one. If you scrutinise any human being enough, there'll be something..."

Of his own entrapment by "agent provocateurs" he says: "I was given a real sob-sob story clearly trying to elicit such comments. I actually said Cameron was doing quite a good job but funnily enough that wasn't quoted." Far from helping break the coalition, in his department it strengthened it. "The ministers were very sympathetic and said they could have been caught in the same way. It actually made me realise I could do business with these people."

There was, I understand, an urgent internal party inquiry to discover if any further skeletons were about to be dragged inelegantly from Liberal Democrat closets. Meanwhile, one rising star reported his own case to police after a rumour was put about in his constituency that he had been cautioned for cottaging. The police were happy to confirm that he wasn't involved. The MP concerned is contentedly married with young children. But so the smears were sure to continue.

Through all this Clegg was remarkably resilient. "Remember Blair and how he was blown off course by trivia," he kept repeating. So he accepted the unpopularity and braced himself to ignore headlines, and kept his eyes cast flintily on the horizon.

17

THE GRANOLA BAR PACT

Through all this buffeting at high altitude Clegg has at least had a strong marriage to act as an important wind-break. This was underlined in 2009 when Miriam gave birth to a third son, Miguel.

It remains a partnership of equals. A journalist asked Miriam at a private party recently how she would feel about a second term, to which she apparently responded that there would be no second term—"that was the deal". The journalist (reliable) was left uncertain if the remark was a joke. Given the domestic nature of these considerations, if Miriam was in earnest this would not so much be a Granita pact—the name given to the restaurant where Tony Blair apparently promised he would stand aside in the second term for Gordon Brown—as the Granola Bar pact. Clegg has insisted there is no deal, though admits: "I'm racking up a lot of debt with Miriam".

She remains a devout Catholic, in contrast to Nick's virtual atheism, but Nick agreed their children would be raised in her faith and be given Spanish names. At the Clegg family home in Putney, SW London, their three boys speak Spanish, a trade-off for the children taking their father's surname and, more importantly, being raised here. Nick is also obliged to spend most of his summer holiday in that Spanish village ("dry", according to Miriam, "dusty" according to Nick) when the Cleggs stay with Miriam's mother, a glorious occasion in the calendar he grumbles about rarely, and never in wifely earshot.

With Miriam working the couple attempt to "split" parental responsibility, so if Nick walks the boys to the local primary, she does bedtime stories (often made up on the spot). Miriam has complained she now sees less of her husband, though insists he does his best. They are helped by a Spanish housekeeper cum nanny. At social gatherings Nick will be as likely as Miriam to resolve boyish squabbles.

Miriam, acquaintances agree, demands a lot from her husband considering his workload, one acknowledging "Nick puts a lot of effort into being with the boys as much as possible."

An old friend says: "It's probably very tough on Nick saying he is going to be a modern dad, and she has held him to that. That's fine, even when you are leader of the Liberal Democrats, but as Deputy Prime Minister it's hard. And Putney is a way from Downing Street, but they feel they have to stay there for the school."

Indeed, even in his exhaustion the morning after his momentous general election, as leader he was obliged to drop the children so she could catch up with work she had missed during the campaign.

A friend claims: "She is certainly very beautiful and from the moment they went out they made a dashing couple. But she is not always the most soothing or sympathetic wife. Nick's domestic and work life is pretty tough. I think it's one of the reasons he has remained such good friends with Corisande. She has always been fiercely loyal and protective. She has never spoken to a journalist about Nick, and their friendship is something that remains quite separate from Miriam."

However, my outsider's impression is that the fiery directness of Miriam remains one of the great attractions. Sherlock offers a positive take on the Clegg dynamic: "To go into their house is to get a sense of a very warm, powerful and modern marriage. And the boys are central to family life, wanting to go out and play football." Indeed, Sherlock recalls a lunch at Chequers with the Cleggs, the Campbells and the Steels which ended with Nick being dragged outside to kick a football. You can normally sense when a couple are staying together for the children. With the Cleggs, they positively purr in each other's presence.

As Miriam is too polite to say in public, she works just as hard as Nick, and has been the primary breadwinner for most of their marriage. She has acquired several roles but her principal job is senior partner in charge of international trade law running a large team at DLA Piper, working from a commanding office overlooking St Paul's in the City of London. Privately, she points out that despite a split in roles, much of the running of a house still falls on the woman.

She describes herself as "supportive without being submissive. I am sufficiently confident to understand I can have a proper career, and I also understand I happen to be married to Nick and people will want legitimately to have a look into who he is—and provided they respect our children, I'm happy for anybody to have a look."

It is a benign attitude, in contrast to various political wives I've met: Norma Major clearly loathed her quasi-official role, and lay lower than an evening sun on a winter's beach. Sarah Brown, so engaging in her earlier role as a PR, could sometimes come across as prickly after such a political marriage.

Miriam, at least, had an ideal apprenticeship, watching her mother. "Being daughter of a politician, I knew what to expect," she has said, shrugging with weary indifference when the press were writing off her husband even after the then newly elected Lib Dem leader pushed Labour into third place in local elections. She stretched to the limit her interpretation of "supportive but not submissive" when she said during the election, perhaps through gritted teeth: "If Nick were Prime Minister and I had to give up my job to support the country, I would have no problem doing so."

But when asked on TV during the election why she didn't spend more time playing the dutiful wife, perhaps carrying flowers a few paces behind "her man" on the campaign trail—á la Samantha Cameron—Miriam gave it both barrels: "Well, listen, I don't have the luxury of a job I can abandon for five weeks, and I imagine that is the situation for most people." "Sam Cam", as the tabloids dubbed her, enjoys the title "creative director" for Smythson, the fabulously expensive stationers. We got the point: Miriam's job is more demanding.

Miriam is deeply serious. You don't write a book called *Regulatory Aspects of the WTO Telecoms Agreements* to give yourself something to do between putting the washing out and slinking off to a cocktail party. It also gives you an idea of the conversation round the Clegg dinner table. She is, with Michael Portillo, vice president of Canning House, which promotes British links to Iberia and Latin America. Oh, and she's an expert in EU law.

So she is never going to be the traditional political appendage. While long seeing herself as broadly "liberal" she only joined the Liberal Democrats a couple of years ago and cannot vote in British elections.

Journalists know instinctively when they are being frozen out and there was a degree of *froideur* at the start of the election campaign. But as Miriam joined in and relaxed, they warmed to her, particularly when she teased that she would send incriminating photos to their editors of them lurking by "I agree with Nick" posters. They discovered her steely demeanour can be overstated. And like her husband, she can be playful. When asked if her children understood what their father did, she replied: "Partly. My five-year-old thinks he's the captain of the Liberal Democrats. My eight-year-old is quite perceptive and understands some of it—he advises on plans to capture Osama bin Laden."

She has been a major asset. Canvassing in the election I found far more voters (male, bloke-ish) keen to talk about Miriam Clegg than the intricacies of the Single Transferable Vote. Throughout the campaign she won praise for glamour. Despite her reluctance to simper, endless pieces about the leaders' wives praised her poise. You know the articles, ones that scream "let's make the election interesting for all those who can't understand politics, like women." Ironic, really, when the subject was Miriam. For what it is worth, even American *Vogue*, one of many admirers, noted approvingly she was "papped" leaving Rigby & Peller, the royal lingerie shop, and wittered: "lucky Clegg!" It is hardly surprising that after he was elected leader Clegg was pushed by advisers to nudge Miriam into the political frame, but he refused, pleading for a degree of separation.

In return Miriam is always loyal in public, however "frank" (a friend's word) in private. That was evident during "Cleggover-gate". To an interviewer she breezed about the incident: "It was a jokey response to a cheeky question that was taken out of context and, in my view, blown out of proportion—probably with political intention." She added: "I married Nick because he was the best man I'd ever met. And nothing's happened to alter my view."

Despite arguments brought on by the clash of strong wills and tired heads it remains, say friends, an unbreakable relationship. And though she comes with a formidable reputation, she also carries a warm smile, a generosity to friends and a memory for details about acquaintances.

Where, understandably, she does grow defensive is over the three Clegglets. Mama and papa both hail from largish clans (Nick one of four, Miriam one of three) and they were keen to create a similarly boisterous brood. "A picture has never emerged of the boys and they would defend them to the death," says Sherlock. "And to defend them you must be around."

Clegg has been less prepared than most modern politicians to sacrifice his children on the altar of state education, saying he was a "father before a politician" and that he would not use his children as a "political football". Instead he acknowledged that in London, especially, many parents felt, secondary schools were not good enough, reflected in the 25 per cent who go private. Indeed, he has even joked to friends about whether he should ask the grandparents for money towards school fees. He has been criticized for not demonstrating the fervour of the convert for the state system, unlike Old Etonian Cameron and his discovery of municipal provision. Miriam was baffled that even Lib Dems should attack her husband: "Some colleagues were actually thinking: 'What a weird thing to say.' I was thinking: 'Surely that is normal?'" The weirdness to Miriam was the political obsessiveness that put loyalty to failing branches of the state above new branches of their own families.

Anybody who watched Tony Blair walk out of Downing Street, *faux* casually cradling a mug that flaunted his fatherhood status, can be cynical of any mention of family and politicians. But an endearing characteristic of the Cleggs is the cheerful admittance that they struggle with parenthood like the rest of us.

This was shown when Clegg blurted out his views about Gena Ford, the baby-rearing "guru". Looking worse for wear, he revealed he had been up with his newborn. When it was suggested he might try Ms Ford's book he dismissed it as "absolute nonsense" and likened it to "sticking children in broom cupboards."

He revealed that one night when the Cleggs were still following this "bible", Antonio woke crying. A drowsy Miriam had turned and murmured: "what does the book say?" Nick replied, probably in less polite terms, that they should ignore it and do what they felt best as parents. He picked up Antonio, who stopped crying. As a father who similarly cast his Ford to the four winds, I warm to Clegg on this. After all, isn't it a bit suspect, the ability to leave your child crying for hour after hour?

However, newspapers solicited condemnatory quotes from Ms Ford, even suggesting millions would turn against Clegg—proof that it is often the lightest observations that provoke the heaviest criticism.

Certainly Miriam is discovering the spotlight shines ever brighter. Pauline Prescott, Britain's previous "second lady", rarely did anything more threatening than sport a particularly livid-looking hat, and in any case engendered universal sympathy for being married to John. Miriam's career, in contrast, has given the press excuse to do what it does best: sniff and dig.

Shortly after the election she was given a non-executive director-ship by Acciona, a Spanish energy company. Newspaper men suggested she only gained the post to help win contracts. Well, Liberals were the masters now. However, the move had been sanctioned by the Cabinet Office and it was promised she would remain removed from any such activity.

More controversially, DLA Piper was accused in early 2011 of lobbying for the Libyan government. This provoked questions from Labour and even Lib Dem MPs, though Miriam has nothing to do with the company's lobbying arm. The row also seemed slightly confected for although Col Gaddafi had suddenly become the west's new Saddam Hussein, Blair had taken tea in his tent just a couple of years before. But as Cherie Blair discovered, it's hard for wives to maintain high-flying legal careers while husbands skulk in low politics. And unlike Cherie, Miriam has not sought to cash in on her public position. Indeed, far from moving towards the media flame, her wings have flapped to carry her towards the shade.

Yet as Nick has flown ever higher, the media sun has glowed stronger. In the summer of 2011, an interview with *Grazia* magazine provoked comment when she admitted her husband "kills himself" to be a father and politician, returning from early morning meetings in Whitehall for the school run. It was clearly a figure of speech, but the comment proved too much for traditionalists. Why, demanded the *Mail's* Quentin Letts, didn't she put aside her career to help her husband in the national interest?

But waiting at home with a G&T and an ironed newspaper was never going to be Miriam. That was evident earlier the same summer when she addressed the Santa Fe Club for Lib Dem donors, talking with passion and eloquence about feminism, recalling how in 1970s Spain women could not open a bank account or travel abroad without their husband's permission. She took her talk seriously, researching the backgrounds of her audience, enabling her to slip in personal questions as she circulated before dinner. Often donors have to be dragooned into attending these evenings, but Miriam's talk was over-subscribed massively.

She recalled a recent visit to Tanzania, pro bono work for her law firm to raise awareness about women's rights, organised in conjunction with the Annie Lennox charity The Circle. There she had met victims of female genital mutilation, which she said afflicts up to 60 per cent of girls in some areas.

She did not pander to her audience, even a questioner of Asian origin who was told there was indeed a clash between aspects of religion and feminism, and that this shouldn't be ignored purely because it was inconvenient. When I asked if she might consider a political career of her own, Miriam answered with equal aplomb. "Typical journalist!" she laughed. "The answer is 'not yet'." One could imagine her in the Spanish senate, like papa. Either way, the career of Chevening's music-loving chatelaine is a long way from its last waltz.

18

AN ECONOMY OF GOODWILL

The economy is what both promises to bind and break the coalition. Both parties know they could be punished if they don't address the deficit and then deliver modest, sustainable growth. But the precise measures required to bring about recovery were always going to cause the partners severe strain.

Osborne demanded of Liberal Democrats that they backed a programme of £6 billion cuts. Laws, who led the economic negotiations, needed little persuading, while the mercurial Cable was not a negotiator, but accepted the argument.

The interesting figure is Huhne. I can disclose that senior ministers have told me of fierce cabinet rows over the initial decision to introduce cuts of this magnitude. Huhne, an economist of mildly Keynesian instincts, argued that the reductions in spending were so severe they could drive the economy into double dip recession. But more than this, he felt cuts this big were both inhumane and undeliverable. I am told that privately he went so far as to warn Clegg he was "mad" to submit to Osborne's axe. Intriguingly, the arguments crossed party lines with, I am told, Huhne and Cable being supported by that "wet" who refuses to dry out, former Chancellor Kenneth Clarke. He apparently warned: "Margaret Thatcher baulked at cuts half the size".

A senior of senior sources described the cuts that began on April 6th 2011 as "just an *amuse bouche* for the bond market. The real cuts—I'm just not sure we are going to withstand that. And we are going to have to face that before the election."

However, rivals have suggested that this was about providing an exit strategy for Huhne if the recovery is slouchier than hoped. Publicly Huhne has only said the government shouldn't "lash to the mast" precise figures to cut, as government spending can be altered to reflect the health of the economy. However, he has never spoken out publicly against the level of cuts already agreed by cabinet.

One who has sat round that cabinet table said: "I don't recall any arguments in the run up to the decision [about cuts]. I think some of the noises were raised by Chris after the GDP figures were published. He shouldn't try to exploit differences that weren't expressed at the time. If the economy goes well, we won't hear of this again. If there were concerns being expressed, they were expressed incredibly quietly."

The source added, none too charitably: "Chris is a very ambitious person. He is planting various landmines in the hope one goes off and that this leads to further advancement."

Clegg and Alexander, now Chief Secretary in place of Laws, found themselves somewhere in the middle. They took no pleasure in major cuts, but as well as coming to see them as necessary economically they also saw them as essential politically. The Conservatives were the senior partner and they were determined to cut rather than spend out of recession. Labour's strategy of spending had hardly been an unalloyed triumph. Austerity would have to be the future.

In a rare blunder Clegg was quoted saying the middle class would hardly feel the cuts, reinforcing an impression he and the equally well-padded Cameron didn't always empathise with Brown's "hard working families". It wasn't what he meant but that was the message newspapers conveyed.

Bar some massive calamity such as war, the economy was likely to define the government. It would also determine the success of Clegg's leadership.

If Huhne really thought the cuts should be more modest he accepted that if they went to plan the coalition would be well placed. The first three years would be deliberately and necessarily bloody. That would allow two years of largesse—or at least medium-esse—prior to the election, particularly to the less advantaged. It would also earn the government political space to introduce "higher" policies that exercise Lib Dems more than technical questions of economy.

It would also buy the Lib Dems some definition against the Conservatives as Osborne looked to "share the proceeds of growth" with tax cuts. Several influential Conservatives suggested, fairly quietly, that war on public spending was not merely welcome because it balances books but because it slims the state. Lib Dems, unlike Labour, have no ideological commitment to a large state. But nor do they have a fetish for a small one. They are far more interested in what works for people who might use public services, aware also that well-funded services depend on a thriving economy. A Liberal Democrat wants a state that is localised, responsive to the needs of communities and individuals, and helps the needy. Orange Book Liberals share with Conservatives a desire for more providers and market mechanisms to drive up standards, and where affordable, tax cuts; but what they won't accept is tax breaks for the already well off if it leaves the under-privileged to go to the wall—particularly with social mobility scandalously slow.

So senior Liberal Democrats intended to argue heavily for surplus resources to be steered towards the vulnerable, whether through tax cuts for those on modest incomes or increased spending.

But first the economy had to recover, and with inflation up and growth flat-lining, Lib Dems were sweating like Cyril Smith in a sauna. They knew that to a worrying degree their future rested in the gamble of one they would hitherto have dismissed as a trust-fund toff, Osborne. "There is," winced one with gallows humour, echoing their Thatcherite partners "no alternative now."

But intriguingly, the key word there is "now". The Liberal Democrats have plans to hit the Conservatives with a major renego-tiation of the coalition agreement, or according to some sources, they might even threaten Cameron with withdrawing from the coalition and moving to a confidence and supply arrangement, whereby the Lib Dems would resign ministerial seats and support the Conservatives from the backbenches on limited measures. It would bring paralysis. The hope is the stakes won't get so high, that the Conservatives will concede enough to keep the Nick and Dave show in business.

All this depends on the economy recovering. As Cable warned

starkly in the summer of 2011, our economic model is "broken": "Britain is no longer one of the world's price setters. It is painful. It is a challenge to us in government to explain that, and it is a pity the political class is not preparing the public to understand how massive the problem is.

"They are in a state of denial that there is a big structural problem with the UK economy. So we stick to this short term, tit for tat; why has the growth in this quarter been slower, the scale of the cuts should be slower... Ultimately, it comes back to this unwilling-ness to accept Britain was operating a model that failed." He flagged up that the economy contracted by 6 or 7 per cent and was 10 per cent below trend. The structural problems in conjunction with the banking crisis were the real issue, he said, rendering debate about cuts almost frivolous. Not only did he feel Miliband was wrong to criticise the scale of cuts, to Cable it showed he simply didn't get it— that Britain faced a major economic crisis.

Increasingly talk of a recovery towards the end of the parliament was looking optimistic, with talk of recession lasting a decade. Then there will be no windfall to fight over and the coalition will have to present itself as a safe haven in a very powerful political storm.

Another area which will be crucial if Liberal Democrats are to demonstrate they have made a tangible difference will be on the green economy. In the summer of 2011 Clegg was finally able to announce real achievements, in particular the establishment of the world's first Green Investment Bank. With an initial £3 billion of public funds it was intended to raise a further £15 billion of private money for low carbon investments such as offshore wind farms and energy efficiency.

Huhne also launched his Energy Bill to encourage businesses and households to reduce carbon emissions. Householders and business could see up to £10,000 invested in insulation at no up-front cost, paying back the investment through reduced bills.

Huhne announced he had reached agreement with Conservatives—and as trickily, Cable—to seek dramatic reductions in greenhouse gases. Which was a relief: days before he had warned friends this was "far from a done deal". Privately he was furious

Cable had used the "write-round", a log of ministerial comments that goes across Whitehall, to express scepticism. "He is meant to be a colleague," a senior source complained. "If he had doubts, why didn't he express them privately rather than somewhere that attracts leaks?"

"He's an economist trained in the seventies before the environment was a serious issue. Even if you don't care about the environment per se, many of the fastest growing companies in China are those developing green technology. Wake up and smell the coffee." The row took place with already strained relations owing to Cable's continued friendship with Vicky Pryce, with whom Huhne was now at war. Cable was understood to take a dim view of Huhne for leaving his wife and the pair's relations have not recovered.

"We must make sure we deliver on the green agenda," I was told. While Huhne won backing from Tories such as Letwin and Tim Yeo, he is said to still bear the scars from less forward thinking Conservatives who consider anyone who cares about the environment a Swampy figure. One Tory minister in Huhne's department baffles Liberal Democrats by constantly saying the government must "look after" energy companies.

In announcing his "carbon budget" on the floor of the House, Huhne committed Britain to becoming the world's first country to accept "legally binding" targets on greenhouse gas emissions beyond 2020. Not only was this historically significant, it prompted major companies to announce they would invest in green technology, a crucial demonstration of Lib Dem arguments that green policy need not be anti-growth.

Huhne was forced to concede that energy-greedy companies would receive relief from rising energy prices. The budget would also be reviewed in 2014 to see if targets were burdening British companies unduly.

Huhne told MPs the budget would "set Britain on the path to green growth", but had the savvy to pitch his message to Tory MPs, pointing out it would "establish our competitive advantage in the most rapidly growing sector of the world economy."

That done, Huhne faced the difficult decision whether to allow a new generation of nuclear reactors. Privately Huhne was understood to have warned this was as challenging in its way as tuition fees. "It's extraordinary," a senior Lib Dem source complained "that the two policies on which we will be accused of betrayal—tuition fees and nuclear power—have both fallen to Lib Dem Secretaries of State."

Huhne decided early to back nuclear power in defiance of party policy as a necessary evil to tackle climate change. However, as over tuition fees, there was dithering over how the party should vote. One suggestion was that ministers would vote for and MPs against, apparently failing to realise that even an unpopular decision makes for better politics than a confused one. At the time of writing there were anxious calculations as to whether MPs could be brought round before party policy could be changed at a future conference.

A report on safety of nuclear power following the Japanese disaster was likely to show no reason to stop Britain, unlike Germany, going ahead. "The Japanese problem was their sea walls were lower than historic flood levels."

Huhne could at least claim support from experts with impeccable green credentials. James Lovelock and George Monbiot were among converts to nuclear power for its ability to slash emissions. Lovelock in particular made a powerful emotional appeal, and certainly went a long way to convincing me when I sat in his charmingly eccentric Devon mill. He ventured that the planet had to embrace the atom or shake hands with Armageddon. "It is much too late for insulating your house and all that," he said. "Fifty years ago it would have helped. What we need now is sustainable retreat."

However, the economics of nuclear power were nearly as fraught as the politics. Because nuclear power stations require huge start-up investment there was scepticism over whether private companies would build them without subsidy. Huhne's solution, I understand, was to guarantee prices for providers—in contrast to gas, whose price fluctuates wildly. Greens were sure to call this subsidy by another name, but given that there has been insufficient investment in renewables to meet energy needs, no one offered a better idea.

Whether increasingly fractious backbenchers, stoked by the anti-nuclear lobby, would realise this was a time to back their government was less certain.

Vitally important though these green decisions were, Clegg knew he would stand or fall by the green shoots from the old economy—and much of that was still looking a rather withered brown. Call it, if you will, Gordon's parting gift.

19

"KNACKERED" AT WORK,
NAPPIES AT HOME

"I have plenty of friends," Clegg reflected, in the manner of one who feels friendless. Well, there is nothing like finding excrement posted through your letter box or effigies strung around Parliament Square to highlight you need allies. It was not, he admitted with feeling, "a time for triumphalism and bunting".

Speaking to Clegg's colleagues in the wake of the coalition's first year there was palpable anger at what the Liberal Democrat leader had been put through, with some suggesting the public hadn't the faintest idea what was being thrown at him. For not only did students protesting against tuition fees post their displeasure—less "disgusted of Tunbridge Wells", perhaps, than disgusting of Tooting Bec—a steel worker spat at him in Sheffield.

And I can also reveal that his children were drawn into the tumult—which was, understandably, his lowest ebb.

"I think having shit put through your letter box was pretty bad," Harvey told me "but it was the child-minder who was spat at when she collected kids that was particularly upsetting. It was a real shock to him. He did go through a bad patch towards the end of last year. All this was happening when he hadn't had a day off in two years."

Politically there was certainly a spot of light turbulence. If the Liberal Democrats had benefited from being the "none of the above", anti-politics party for those who refused to accept politics was a choice of either/ors, then this core constituency was demonstrating its fury that under Clegg there would no longer be honey for tea—well, not if you also expected porridge for breakfast.

As one Lib Dem cabinet minister told me: "I always thought it likely Lib Dem support would take a real hit, maybe to as low as 5 per cent. What I hadn't expected was this would all happen so soon."

And personally it was bumpy, too. Public vicissitudes don't occur against a domestic vacuum. Unlike Cameron who had moved into Downing Street, Clegg was neither granted—nor requested—a London residence. He remained with his family in South West London's Putney, some six traffic-clogged miles from Downing Street, so his two older boys could continue at primary school.

Miriam, far from reducing work since her husband became Deputy Prime Minister and she became a mother for the third time, took on more. On Sunday mornings Clegg was often dragged to church—hardly the preferred haven of relaxation for an exhausted atheist—to ease his boys passage to the elite Catholic state school, the London Oratory. And there was a baby in the house, with the sleep deprivation that entails. The one novel he is thought to have (re) read over this period was Lampedusa's *The Leopard*. It is beautifully written but decidedly melancholy, describing the decline and decay of a once noble figure.

However, Laws says now we should not exaggerate his angst then: "I don't think he felt depressed, he is really, really enjoying the job. I've never detected anything but relish. But there have been times when he has been very tired, starting out in the coalition after the election.

"And this is a very awkward party to lead without the resources of the Conservatives. Nick for instance has to see a lot of donors. And as well as looking after his constituency, he has to make sure every department is being run to his satisfaction. Plus he also runs his own department, of Political Reform. I suspect he is more stretched than Cameron. I think Cameron manages his time very carefully and doesn't clutter his diary. But because Nick has less people around him, more things fall on him. He lost into the Treasury Danny who had been effectively his right hand man as Scottish Secretary. With Danny suddenly leading the Treasury review, co-ordinating everything across government fell to Nick."

Laws adds: "From June to October he was knackered. The first year was the most challenging. The space in his diary is better from here on in, and I think he will find the second much easier."

Clegg did suffer a difficult period with uncorroborated rumours of raised voices in his office. Hacks also noticed that at a lobby reception Cameron worked the crowd and was his usual smooth, charming self. Clegg, by contrast, struck a lonelier figure in a corner, protected by a press guard, apparently reluctant to engage. It is not a sage strategy and again shows the Lib Dem failure to work or even understand the media, however reluctant Clegg felt to clap on the back people trashing his friends.

Harvey now says it is easy to criticise Clegg for calling the AV referendum at a wrong time "but we were all asked for advice and I was one who also thought we had more chance of winning if it was held early with the local elections. We all make mistakes, yet it was all heaped on Nick."

The most sombre decision Clegg faced in his first year was sanctioning military action in Libya. For a party that broke under the strain of the exercise in human mulching that was the First World War, no Lib Dem could send military personnel into battle with any flippancy. The party had made great hay opposing war in Iraq, though Clegg had been determined to keep the party to its commitment to help the international effort to defeat the Taliban in Afghanistan. Clegg agreed with Cameron to support the international effort for a people's uprising against a dictator.

But the desire of politicians to be rid of an egregious ruler is not always mirrored by military means or even strategy. "It was very much a Downing Street/Foreign Office caper," a well placed minister tells me. "David Cameron's attitude to the MoD was 'go along and do it, chaps.' It was a real eye opener. Everyone at the MoD, including Liam Fox and the generals, were opposed. They realised a no-fly zone was a complete no-no. They knew from bitter experience, force from the air wouldn't be enough. Yet there would never be international agreement to finish the job on the ground. So there was always a big risk of stasis.

"A negotiated settlement would have resulted in Gaddafi staying, unacceptable politically. But it is very difficult to take out a dictator, particularly with both arms and one leg tied behind your back."

However, with the rebels proving more effective than the MoD calculated and Gaddafi overthrown, the Cameron-Clegg decision appears vindicated.

Intriguingly, the source notes Fox's gradual distancing from Cameron, on Libya and more recently in calling for Britain to scrap its commitment to give 0.7 per cent of GDP in overseas aid. "He sees himself as the prince across the water," said the Lib Dem. "He thinks Cameron never faced a proper challenge for the leadership because he [Fox] was edged out in the first round by Davis, whom he considers flaky. Liam is not going to blow his shot too early and it's a good way off, but I do think he wants to challenge Cameron for the leadership." Here, then, is comfort for Clegg: madness is certainly not confined to his party.

Inevitably the mechanics of working in coalition are far harder than the ideals of talking about coalition. In a typical department the Lib Dems are represented by a junior minister and are not allowed government-funded special advisers. This hampers Lib Dem performance and thus public perception: "It makes it very hard for our ministers to find out what's happening across government," says Allen, aide to Harvey. "For instance, in a spending department what the view is from the Treasury about the availability of funds."

Betraying modesty rare in a politician, one minister admits: "The Tories run the department much as they would if I wasn't there. If I am any influence at all I think I am fairly benign, but I'm not sure I have much influence at all."

He pauses: "It's a bit like that American saying 'every time I climb another rung on the ladder, power seems a little further away'. It's quite surprising just how little power ministers have." How different this sounds to the joys of May. More positively he says: "A lot of ministers are doing well, and although there is short-term cost we are actually pushing back those credibility barriers which held us back for so long."

At least two junior ministers I've spoken to complain of "a bit of control freakery" in their Tory bosses. "They want to run their departments on their own," says one. And if politicians are still receiving coalition training, the civil service are at an even more elementary level. Allen says: "When Lib Dem and Conservative ministers set out different positions on Trident, the civil service went into complete panic. They didn't understand that from our perspective it was good people saw there were two very different views on this inside government."

The Tory emotional dislike of Europe has also proved problematic, with Ken Clarke a lone exception. Lib Dem ministers were mystified when Theresa May, Home Secretary, said she intended to opt out of an EU charter on human trafficking while Clarke at Justice said he would opt into an EU charter on child trafficking. "The arguments were virtually identical, so it was a nonsense," I am told. "Cracking down on trafficking, like anti-pollution legislation, needs to be at a European level." Similarly, Conservatives who complained about France or Italy not tackling illegal immigration blanched at the very measures that might have helped. Depressingly the May argument won, so while the free movement of skilled labour was unacceptable to many Tories, the un-free movement of unskilled slaves was apparently fine.

In November a meeting of the parliamentary party was addressed by European Liberals on their lessons of coalitions. In front of Clegg, the leader of the Dutch Liberals warned that the rose garden moment and Clegg slapping Osborne on the back had been a mistake. "He said the two leaders looked too similar and that to survive coalitions it was important to be distinctive," I am told. But this was difficult for Clegg, operating in a culture unused to coalition where any disagreement or even distance is framed as a "split."

Still, if it was looking bad for Clegg it was about to look much worse.

20

DOOM AT THE TOP

THE AV CAMPAIGN AND LOCAL ELECTIONS

"Technically," Cameron allowed "he is probably a better player than me. I was just a bit more wily." Such was the Prime Minister's verdict after he beat his deputy 8-6 in a tennis match at Chequers. Clegg had lobbed back questions on the same *Dispatches* documentary, with the cheeky little reply that the result was a "state secret", a novel line for a campaigner for "freedom of information". Off-camera Clegg marvelled at how competitive Cameron was on court. Did the result vindicate, after all, the verdict of that tennis captain who judged Clegg a fine stylist lacking the killer touch?

After truly atrocious results in the May 2011 Alternative Vote referendum and local elections, even some Lib Dems were wondering if Cameron's greater wiliness was the problem. For not only had Lib Dem candidates up and down the land attracted scarcely more votes than a typical Maltese entrant to the Eurovision Song Contest, they had possibly lost the chance of electoral reform for a generation. And they couldn't help but peer over the fence to next door where the Conservatives at Number 10 seemed remarkably chirpy. Indeed, so at one with the world did Family Cameron look they were finding it exceptionally difficult not to smirk. Only the impeccably brought up father of the house managed a statesman-like wave of cheery sympathy for the folks in the hovel next door.

The Tory vote had remained virtually unchanged from the general election, even if it had been Osborne driving through major cuts. Indeed, far from suffering their predicted losses, the Conservatives gained four councils. Virtually the entire change in vote—in England if not Scotland—was a massive shift from Liberal Democrat to Labour.

In the fall out Clegg's position was hardly strengthened by a succession of defeated councillors paraded on television like pilots shot down over enemy lines, denouncing all they one stood for. In faltering voices they seemed to argue that because they had lost their jobs, so should Clegg. Whether this was part of some grand strategy of recovery or simply blood-letting to make them feel better, they didn't explain.

Perhaps they were too shell-shocked. Across Orange Britain it was like the Blitz revisited, with Lib Dem victims left badly mutilated in England's great industrial cities: Manchester, Leeds, Bolton, Stoke, Telford, Newcastle—even in Clegg's "home city of Sheffield", Miliband's raids bombed Liberal Democrats out of their council homes.

In years to come this will probably be looked back upon as the time the party grew up and realised it could now be the victim as well as beneficiary of bad mid-terms; whoever said power buys you friends couldn't have been a Lib Dem.

But uppitiness among the grass roots cannot be dismissed easily. The Lib Dem ethos is localism, and the party's resurgence has been built on diligent work in local government. From London these disloyal calls seemed to betray a monstrous lack of perspective, but particularly in the north—where the loss of government spending and the toxicity of Toryism is felt most keenly—it is hard to exaggerate the bitterness. Many voters told Liberal Democrats "you are worse than the Tories", which hurt. This confirmed the experiences of the human sacrifice that was the Lib Dem candidate in the Barnsley by-election who was told "I wouldn't spit on you if you were on fire." He emerged sixth, though thankfully un-singed.

Yet the punishment of voters was a compliment of sorts. They wanted to show the Lib Dems they expected more of them. The Conservatives, in a sense, had got their betrayal in first. "Conservatives slash public spending" is hardly a shocking headline: "Conservatives in massive splurge of human generosity" would make even the least political choke on their morning Crunchy Nuts.

If it were just a set of poor numbers from the local elections the Lib Dems could probably have breathed slowly and, in the argot of spin doctors pretending to pass on great wisdom, "moved on". But the greatest victim in this blitzkrieg was turning out to be the party's tallest spire and hitherto greatest monument, Clegg. For the party not only lost the referendum but went down so heavily—two to one—it prompted the question "how could the Lib Dems have ever imagined they could win?" Yet this was meant to be the electoral kick-back the Lib Dems were granted for the painful kicking they would take for the cuts, the great concession Clegg had wrung from the then desperate Cameron. Was the figure about to topple in Clegg's coup Nick himself?

The Conservatives had managed to do precisely what, as Laws ruefully recalls, Letwin had threatened in those negotiations: grant the Lib Dems their referendum, then thrash them in it. "No to the Yes Men," *The Times* chortled.

But what had happened to the so-called "gentleman's agreement" between Cameron and Clegg to keep the campaign as something of a phoney war, perhaps with a spot of light, occasional bombing but avoiding key installations and civilian casualties?

For here was Clegg himself being carried off on a stretcher, with some Lib Dems even calling for his honorary discharge. "The most popular leader since Churchill": how painful for Clegg to remember the popularity that had echoed in his ear, and how loud the cries of protest had grown in a year. Cartoonists, the most accurate readers of the political weather, were now as merciless about Clegg as they had been about Kennedy and Campbell. For somebody so evidently capable—at least to those who knew him—the "Calamity Clegg" label was proving hard to shift. Particularly when it was reinforced in election literature of the "no" campaign, funded, devised and executed almost entirely by Conservatives. But the really low Tory blow was to detail, under the inevitable "Calamity Clegg" headline, how Cameron's right hand man had supposedly changed his mind on a long list of policies—overlooking that it was Cameron in conjunction with the electoral arithmetic that had forced him to do so. The Lib Dems were not pumping out literature attacking the Tories for abandoning their promise on inheritance tax, say, yet it seemed that for the Old Etonians running the Conservative Party, gentlemen's agreements weren't worth the White's Club notepaper they were written on.

It was hard to exaggerate its harm. "There is a real loss of trust," said one of the party's most senior frontline figures. Tories who accused Lib Dems of triumphalism after they massacred much of Andrew Lansley's health bill in June 2011 should have stopped to ponder when and why the warm spirit of co-operation ended.

Another source close to Clegg suggested the Tories started the campaign reasonably decently, but then "Osborne panicked" and sent in the attack dogs: "Someone persuaded George Osborne that it would be fatal for Cameron to lose." Swiftly dismissed in all Lib Dem circles were claims by Tim Montgomerie, Conservative commentator, that the anti-Clegg leaflets of the "no" campaign were devised by those nasty Labour people. "I just don't buy that," said a senior Lib Dem source.

In Cabinet Huhne slapped down on the cabinet table a couple of offending leaflets and demanded Cameron sack any Conservative activists implicated. Osborne replied, a little pompously, that cabinet wasn't the forum to engage in "sub Jeremy Paxman interrogations". In fairness Osborne did try to mend decidedly smouldering bridges with Huhne and was "very sympathetic" in a chat behind the speaker's chair over the media fall-out from the Lib Dem's divorce debacle. But that hardly atoned for the political manure he had chucked at his coalition "partners". "At the top level of politics," said the senior source "it is not about the personal. It's political." And the politics of the campaign stank.

A Lib Dem cabinet minister fumed to me: "Disraeli said the Tory Party is organised hypocrisy, but the level of hypocrisy was gasp-making."

As the public delivered its deafening "no", Clegg must have felt like screaming "what was I supposed to do?" Except he couldn't scream, for that would have de-stabilised the coalition. He had no majority and was necessarily the junior partner. He had, by most independent evaluations, negotiated a good deal. Even allowing for the usual posturing of a referendum campaign it was breathtaking that Clegg should have been savaged for U-Turns by the Tories. The level of disinformation was astounding, particularly posters of soldiers in the front line with the message that money should be spent on them rather than new voting machines for AV. In fact AV ballots could be counted manually in only slightly more time than first past the post voting papers, but this was lost in a blizzard of absurdity. Chief culprit was the Conservative Sayeeda Warsi. However, Huhne's furious response to compare her to Joseph Goebbels probably did little to elevate debate or entice un-decideds into the "yes" camp. In marked contrast to the bonhomie of a year earlier, I understand Huhne withdrew from the Lib-Con dining club Gove established to foster relations between the two parties.

Cable, fresh from a row with Cameron over immigration, felt moved to comment: "Some of us never had many illusions about the Conservatives, but they have emerged as ruthless, calculating and thoroughly tribal. But that doesn't mean we can't work with them. I think they have always been that way, but you have to be businesslike. That is being grown-up in politics."

But while Cable and Huhne were accused of rocking the coalition, their Conservative tormentors remained smugly silent.

And if Lib Dems were attacking the Conservatives in public, they were positively savaging each other in private. One of the party's very most senior figures told me in the wake of the rout: "If John Sharkey is ever let near another campaign I won't be involved." A blistering reference, this, to the former joint managing director of Saatchi & Saatchi UK who ran the "Yes" campaign, and is arguably Clegg's most trusted adviser. Clegg also ennobled him. "The 'Yes' campaign was unbelievably incompetent," the source rumbles. "Truly disastrous. Actually, we didn't have a 'Yes' Campaign."

So furious was this senior of seniors that he could barely contain himself about Sharkey: "He has now run two campaigns. He also ran our general election campaign and I didn't think that was very good. [The "Yes" campaign] had plenty of money. I spent 10 years of my life raising money for Electoral Reform Services and Sharkey frittered it all away."

However, Harvey defended Sharkey: "He's no Chris Rennard [former party chief credited with masterminding great by-election triumphs], he's an advertising man. But to lay all blame on him is totally unfair." That said, Harvey didn't find the campaign theme of making MPs work harder resonated: "It was too long after the expenses scandal. Our canvassers were startled in Yeovil to find an old lady who said she would be voting Lib Dem but had decided not to vote 'yes' in the referendum because those wicked people wanted their MPs to work harder 'and my MP David Laws couldn't work any harder...'" Baker was blunter: "The campaign was completely useless."

The Sharkey critic rattled off the tiny enclaves where the "Yes" campaign won (Hackney, Oxford, Cambridge, Edinburgh Central...the list soon peters out): "It's all places where they read the *Observer* and *Independent*." So not too many. "And we wouldn't even have won those if a few of us hadn't taken the initiative late on." The source had a point: having spoken at length to Eddie Izzard I can confirm he has a surprisingly serious interest in politics, for a comedian, but to have him fronting the campaign was too cool for school—a classic case of a political class not realising that the taste of the broader public is not always synonymous with its own.

Clegg largely kept his counsel. A statement issued under his name to party members could scarcely have contained more clunking clichés if it had been penned by Tony Parsons, full of calls for activists to dust themselves down and pick themselves up. It didn't quite tell them to keep a stiff upper lip, but that was the message.

According to some allies Clegg had largely written off the AV campaign some months before. Though committed to electoral reform, it had never been the obsession to him it had to his party. After all, he had proved he could win under the rotten old system, and he thought it more important that Liberal Democrats established a reputation for competence in government.

For all the criticism, the "Yes" campaign would probably have lost anyway due to Miliband's lukewarm support and refusal to share platforms with Clegg. "It was such bad politics," says Baker. "All Miliband did was drive us towards the Tories. If Labour wanted to cause Nick awkwardness in the coalition they should have been nice to us. Miliband can't win without us and is showing every sign of being the new Michael Foot. He just demonstrated he is not fit for the job." According to Baker, Labour antagonism springs from their lofty assumption that Lib Dems would only go into government with them, despite years of false Labour promises over electoral reform: "It is the mindless Polly Toynbee argument. She said the deal was terrible before the ink was dry."

While Clegg braced himself for more stray bullets—including friendly fire—whistling round the dark alley of Downing Street, he was determined to remain embedded with Cameron for five years. A little wearily he recognised his fortunes were linked, inextricably, to his rival's. As Sir Ming has said, it was the judgement of Cameron and Osborne that cuts rather than spending was the way to lift Britain from recession, and that upon their good judgement Clegg had "bet the farm".It was left to Ashdown to plead for calm, quoting to colleagues Wellington at Waterloo: "Hard pounding, gentlemen, let's see who pounds the longest."

It is always tempting when a party is under attack to find a policy scapegoat. The Health reforms came under sharp focus, and Clegg heaped pressure on Andrew Lansley, Health Secretary, to water-down his bill. Clegg demanded the health bill be changed in thirteen specific areas. Cameron conceded totally on eleven, and partially on the other two. This was after Clegg arrived in Cameron's office and told him: "I don't want to see three words in a headline: 'NHS', 'Tory' and 'privatise'—its toxic".

A change, critics said, from the earlier Clegg position which was to welcome a greater plurality of providers. It was, after all, two decades since the health service had starting buying in treatment from outside. In *The Times* Ian Birrell reminded Clegg he had bravely challenged his party, thronging with public sector workers, by attacking a system which treats patients as "passive recipients of a second-rate state monopoly". As Alan Milburn, a Labour Health Secretary, had said, all evidence shows increasing the range of providers raises standards.

But Lansley's proposals were a mess. "He was allowing private contractors to cherry pick potentially profitable parts, leaving the NHS with the difficult parts," commented a Lib Dem minister. "If he was going down that route he needed to make sure private contractors took bite-size bits, as with the railways, so they took profitable and unprofitable sections together."

The minister conceded there were "Liberal things you can do with the health service, but I'm not sure you'll find them in Lansley's bill. I appreciate Mrs Lansley is a GP but I don't see the GP as a proxy for the consumer. I think the patient should be given far more choice, not the GP."

But the precise argument about the relationship between private and public was not the primary factor. A minister, normally associated with the party's right, told me: "Nick had no choice but to cut up a bit rough." So not only did Clegg decide the measure had to be dramatically changed, he also saw it as an opportunity to distance his party from the Tories. As one outside adviser told me: "This is not a time to leave the philosophers in charge."

And Lansley presented an attractive target. Clegg rubbished the Health Secretary's requirement that cost be the over-riding factor in determining whether a private or public contractor should carry out a procedure. He even engaged in a bit of light arm-wrestling with Cameron, using a meeting of the parliamentary party to attack a Tory adviser who had earlier consulted companies on how to take advantage of these very "reforms". The public, warned Clegg, would find this "confusing". Cameron was said to be "relaxed" about Clegg's attack, Lansley perhaps a little less so.

At least there was still time to offer a different prescription for Health, but not for the policy that had proved most damaging of all.

If "toxic" is the politician's favoured word of warning then tuition fees were a giant oil slick lapping Lib Dems shores. It was a rare policy that cost two votes for the price of one, for not only were students outraged, so were parents. Clegg had looked shaken after a stint on Mumsnet, when his apparent duplicity on tuition fees dominated questions. This was his equivalent of Tony Blair's Womens Institute disaster of 2000, when the cake-bakers of Britain deflated a Prime Minister. Clegg signed off: "Ps: I'm not a Tory!"

Afterwards one organiser said he looked so depressed puffing a melancholy fag "I just wanted to hug him".

But that was mild compared to excrement and effigies. And Clegg more than Cameron was the recipient of this hate because he was the one who had changed positions, or in that favourite student charge down the years, "sold out". It was a harsh charge, as Baker tells me: "The great message we haven't got across is this is a coalition. There is still an expectation you deliver your manifesto. But we are 269 seats short of a majority. If you know how we could deliver our manifesto, please tell me."

Still, protecting higher education had not been a passing fancy but a grand Liberal passion. Clegg had even signed his pledge in Cambridge promising not to raise fees. Had he forgotten Mill's dictum about the sanctity of education ("better Socrates dissatisfied than a fool satisfied"), or even Matthew Arnold's attack on Philistinism in *Culture and Anarchy*?

But with Labour and Tories both supporting tuition fees the Lib Dems were, in the evocative word of the Deputy Prime Minister, "stuffed". The Lib Dems had wrung significant concessions during negotiations—particularly that there would be no up-front fees and there would be increased help for poorer students—but everyone understood the headline figure: "£9,000". Worse, in the panicky speed in which the coalition was agreed, nobody on the Lib Dem side had thought out the nightmare of Cable, as the responsible minister, having to push through the legislation. How Tories must have cried—with laughter. For Lib Dems had, cleverly they thought, negotiated the right not to vote for tuition fees in deference to their election commitment. But it was a nonsense that Cable might vote against the very measure he was commending to the House, and his suggestion under fire that he might abstain was howled out of court. Subsequently Tories have reminded journalists they had offered Clegg the choice of abstaining, but this would probably only have made him look doubly slippery.

"It was a cock up of fairly immense proportions," a Lib Dem minister admits. "Tuition fees should never have been conceded but after it was it was like a slow motion car crash. It took six months for the shit to hit the fan, during which they should have realised opts outs were worthless. It still would have conceded to the Conservatives a majority for a measure they hadn't earned. Our conference had saddled us with a completely unaffordable policy, but we could have compromised on, say, £5,000 a year rather than £9,000, and announced details during the general euphoria directly after the coalition was formed."

That Lib Dems voted all three ways—for, against and "dunno"— was nothing if not even handed, but did little to dispel an impression that they were unprofessional as well as untrustworthy.

Opinion was divided over where Liberal Democrats had gone wrong, but not that they had gone wrong. The party's left said the negotiators should have rejected increased charges. In retrospect they were surely right, though this would have been a hard concession to extract. The senior of senior sources intimately acquainted with the coalition negotiations insists: "I think we could still have got a deal without compromising on tuition fees. Electorally it was vitally important to us as one of the groups most likely to back us is graduates." However, if this was the view of such figures they might have voiced it a little more loudly when it mattered.

But there is another take on tuition fees, less often expressed for fear of venomous tirades from the National Union of Students. A former adviser, from the party's right, argues that actually Clegg's mistake was not ditching his promise before the election: "It's the trust issue. During the election he was shown in a party political broadcast trudging down a street rained on by bits of paper, repre-senting broken promises of the other parties. The message was 'no more broken promises from the Liberal Democrats: we aren't going to lie to you.'"

But here's the controversial bit: "Nick had done very good work transforming us from a stodgy, centre left social democratic party to a genuinely centrist liberal party, but he didn't quite get there. *The Orange Book* was an-unfinished revolution. He went on to do a lot more but there was probably still another 20 per cent of the revolution he had to complete by the general election. Sadly he was either too scared or too weak to take the party on. That is the real story, and that is why he has suffered since."

It is a rigorous verdict but not a charitable one. Clegg had force-fed his party a large dollop of Orange medicine. No leader can be in a state of perpetual antagonism with their party and survive, which is why even such an arch-moderniser as Blair made so many concessions to Brownites. If Clegg had have got his betrayal on tuition fees in first, this would have cost him dear in university towns, many Lib Dem target seats.

Indeed, a source on the left who describes himself as a "former friend of Nick's" and sits on the committee which agrees party policy says Clegg did fight tooth and nail to drop the policy, but lost the vote. And, the source still contends, rightly.

"Nick had ditched a vast number of our spending commitments such as free care for the elderly. He argued very strongly that a progressive case could be made for higher tuition fees. But I don't think he grasped what a touchstone issue this was for our party. We don't have many core constituencies but this is one. The Clegg leadership likes to contrast their 'realism' with the lack of realism among activists. But in this case it was the leadership not under-standing the politics."

This source blames Alexander. "I understand from one of our negotiating team that he was left to deal with tuition fees. Presumably after discussing it with Nick he decided it was something we could concede. It appears the leadership didn't get how toxic it would be."

As the reverberations were felt across Liberal England, the party's senior figures looked rattled. Cable made it clear he would insist on banking reform while Lord Tyler in the Lords questioned whether Lib Dems would support boundary changes that would help the Tories at Labour's expense—and they would reconsider on grounds of money. After all, Tories had opposed AV on the nebulous claim that it would cost more to administer: "Two can play that game," said the shrewd-eyed Tyler.

Meanwhile, to quote again the very senior source: "There is no point getting mad, we have to get even. It's against the collective ethos of government but we are going to have to make it clear where we differ with the Tories. We will have to break some rules."

Implicitly the source also criticised Clegg for not making a more abject apology for breaking trust over tuition fees: "When a brand in the corporate sector has suffered a lot of damage—Perrier, BP, Ratner—all the literature shows that what you do is fess up to the problem and apologise to victims. You don't put in lots of excuses because that undermines the apology. Instead you give assurances it won't happen again, and finally you have to make amends. That doesn't mean you have to undo everything but it does mean doing something like giving additional help to school kids. I don't know if that is happening."

But Browne expressed the alternative view eloquently: "There is a limit to how much you can campaign against the government of which you are part."

This is an argument whose reverberations threatened to rumble and rattle on through the life of the coalition. Our senior of senior sources again: "You can make a case for saying 'don't do anything to rock the boat'. My instinct would be that it's better to be a bit more pro-active politically."

Worryingly for Clegg, he was starting to resemble a football manager who is told that if he doesn't land some trophies he could face the sack. Huhne was the most obvious challenger, though problems arising from his motoring arrangements dampened his ambition.

Those around Clegg remained wary of Huhne, while acknowledging his contribution to Team Clegg after losing the leadership. "He became part of the inner core, though now Chris is running a department they see less of each other", says a well-placed source. "They have probably grown more reserved again." The source pauses, then says: "there's always a sense with Chris that he has one eye on the main chance."

Everywhere lurked danger. As for the tiger, suddenly Clegg was expected not merely to ride it, but shoot it and turn the skin into a decorative ornament. It wasn't going to be easy.

21

FROM CIVIL PARTNERSHIP TO
MARRIAGE GUIDANCE

The posturing of a political post-mortem often has a higher testosterone count than the pugilism of the campaign.

And Clegg knew he had to fight the Lib Dem corner and slug Cameron a few left hooks. But unlike some colleagues he realised that the party was likely to be judged ultimately for its performance in government, not its showing in some media-contrived boxing ring.

"Nick understands instinctively how to calibrate it," said an adviser. "The danger is some colleagues might go over the top."

Clegg made a short hop to the National Liberal Club to deliver a speech, appropriately enough, on "muscular Liberalism", vowing to fight for Liberal values. Gerald Scarfe responded with a cartoon depicting the model of a massive muscle man—and Clegg's tiny, terrified head peeping out from the top.

Yet Clegg is a thoughtful operator and his speech was intended to send a new message. If the aim had been to "own the coalition" and work with Conservatives, now it also seemed about wrestling the Tories to win trophies.

But he realised that real victories would be achieved through mediation, not a megaphone. And we soon started seeing the results.

Even the press felt obliged to represent Cameron's U-Turn on Health as a Clegg triumph, to the chagrin of Tories. However, a commentator who talked to Clegg just before the compromise was announced told me: "I think he did brilliantly over Health but he seemed rather other worldly about taking the credit. He desperately needs someone who will ruthlessly drive home to the media his achievements."

In another hard-fought compromise, £3 billion pounds of

preparatory work for a replacement Trident system was agreed. But the final decision on whether to splurge the really serious money and build the thing was kicked into the long (possibly radioactive) grass until 2016, after the next election. Then both parties could argue their cases during the campaign, with Lib Dems not only putting distance between themselves and the Tories but possibly outflanking Labour by being the only party to oppose these hugely expensive phallic forget-me-nots of the Cold War. Says a minister: "It will certainly make it harder for Labour to paint us as right-wing cryptos."

Clegg's hand is likely to be strengthened by an official MoD cost benefit analysis exploring alternative uses of the money. Harvey launched a successful air-raid, warning that if the Tories pursued Trident it would be at the expense of other military programmes which Tory MPs profess to cherish.

"It is now quite clear," Harvey told me "the money we are pushing towards a new nuclear deterrent is taking its toll on the rest of the Defence budget." It will be interesting to hear the Conservative explanation for "our boys" going without vital equipment now Fox and friends cannot blame it on the apparently exorbitant cost of AV voting machines.

And there were plenty more skirmishes playing behind those bomb proof curtains in Whitehall, many minor but all showing the different mindset of the two parties. For instance one suggestion was that Baker, hardly the most fervent monarchist, was keen to scrap the expensive Queen's Flight. Responsibility for this was transferred from the Ministry of Defence to Transport where Baker labours. However, it would scarcely have annoyed Tories more if Baker had proposed a tax on roast beef. The Flight can trace its roots to 1928—15 years before the American president gained a dedicated aircraft—and after the acrimony that greeted the scrapping of the Royal Yacht, it would by a symbolic gesture to flag up contrasting Con-Lib priorities.

A more substantial battle in which Clegg found himself embroiled was House of Lords reform, a bill Clegg piloted through the Commons personally. It was an historic ambition of the party to shoo the blue bloods from parliament and create a genuinely democratic elected assembly. It was exactly a century earlier that Asquith had fought his titanic battle with the Upper House, after Tory peers fought in the last ditch to defend the landed interest by voting down Lloyd George's "People's Budget" of 1909. The King (reluctantly) sided with the Liberals and threatened to flood the Lords with (turn away now gentlemen of delicate sensibilities) commoners. The blue bloods blinked, and from then on their political club would no longer enjoy the privilege of blocking "money bills". The aristocratic hegemony was broken, but the watchword of the British ruling class had long been "reform, that you may preserve". Once again it had conceded just enough to keep the aristocratic peers in place—Tory, almost to a man.

It only took another nine decades—a mere blink of an aristocratic eye—for Blair to turf hereditaries from what was always a little optimistically called the parliamentary home of democracy. But not all: a little under 100 remained, clinging like ivy to a crumbling balustrade. Oh, and they took to electing themselves—a comically British solution. Other peers were appointed. So as Deputy Prime Minister, Clegg proposed to complete the reform, giving us a wholly elected Upper House. In 2011 it hardly sounded revolutionary. But it proved too much for certain Conservatives who talk in sonorous, statesmanlike tones about the wisdom and expertise of this higher chamber, so a compromise was agreed of 80 per cent of members being elected—still representing a change of historic proportions.

Tory traditionalists didn't welcome the compromise, even though Lords reform had been in their manifesto. Edward Leigh, apparently with a straight face, asked Clegg at the latter's Question Time to adopt the Conservative approach of "gradualism, and drop the proposal". Presumably reform that had taken a century to complete was all just a little too hurried. Perhaps, he felt, Conservatives needed another century or so to digest the change.

Meanwhile Labour betrayed the ambivalence that has always marked its attitude to "the other place". It shared Liberal Democrat revulsion for a group of law makers assembled through the vagaries of the old-boy network, but feared a reformed second chamber would have greater legitimacy and thus feel emboldened to block the will of the Commons. But why shouldn't a legitimate second chamber have genuine power, as in virtually every other mature democracy—especially when the MPs of the governing party have often barely gained 40 per cent of the vote?

When Clegg announced his plans he faced a Commons that from both left and right displayed all the decorum of a hen party during a performance of the Chippendales. If Tory whips told their MPs to show support—or at least respect—their instructions were ignored. At a meeting of Tory MPs one called their Lib Dem colleagues "yellow bastards". But in the context of Lords reform it was quite hard to understand—still less accept—the basis of their vitriol.

Here is Dangerfield's atmospheric description of the opposition Asquith met fighting a similar battle a century before:

"The most primitive idols, even those which have been long abandoned to the jungle and the sand-drift, are landmarks in the journey of the human soul: they represent a search for coherence in the confusions and fears of the living. So this venerable House of Lords was not simply a constitutional relic of the great landed fortunes; it was also a fetish, it meant the ideally paternal responsibility of the noble few. And though this meaning was quite irrelevant to the twentieth century, yet those who tried to preserve it were not merely idle men or arrogant men. They saw the passing of certain values which at their best were very high and at their worst were very human; they did not realise that life consists in change, that nothing can stand still, that today's shrines are only fit for tomorrow's cattle. Clinging to the realities of the past, they prepared to defend their dead cause to the finish."

Strike out "twentieth century", replace it with "twenty first century" and work in the name "Edward Leigh"—then you have some idea of the reactionary opposition facing Clegg, after a century of enlightenment.

Little of this resonated with the public, but if Clegg were to succeed it would at least be a little harder for radicals to demand of him "what are you actually DOING in government?"

22

THE FUTURE OF LIBERALISM

"The only purpose for which power can be rightfully exercised over any member of a civilised community, against his will, is to prevent harm to others...Over himself, over his own body and mind, the individual is sovereign."

To the Liberal, John Stuart Mill's principle precedes all others, and came to define both Liberalism and the British way. To grasp the vastness of this Victorian vision, visit London's National Liberal Club: grandiose porticoes remembered in oils, busts of Gladstone, sweeping staircases, all leading to a magnificent view of the imperial capital. And in the centre of that panorama, the remorseless river, demanding free trade in goods and ideas with the world it dominated.

Here was a party of extraordinary confidence. This derived, not from Conservative landed privilege nor even the mercantile money of the Liberal Party's industrial backers, but from a huge sense of moral purpose. Now so much of politics has been trimmed to a technocratic squabble over statistical outcomes it is hard to appreciate how much Liberalism felt like a crusade. When Gladstone summoned all his evangelical fervour to demand Home Rule for Ireland or Mill denounced the subjugation of women, they were preachers more than politicians. Even when a Liberal stood commending a budget, the dispatch box became a pulpit as the House was lectured on the moral imperative of free trade.

Disraeli dismissed his great Liberal opponent as a prig, while Gladstone viewed his battle with Disraeli as Conservative licentiousness verses Liberal righteousness. For all Disraeli's Machiavellian brilliance, Liberals were unshakeable in their classical creed. This could be traced back to the time of Charles II, with the anti-monarchical and anti-church sentiments of the Enlightenment influencing the pro-parliamentary stance of Whigs, the aristocratic forebears of the Liberal Party. Liberals did not assume they would win, but they did presume to be right. And though High Church and high born, Gladstone bucked the historical trend by growing more radical with age. According to one wag, the castle-dweller was "Tory in all but the essentials." Gladstone's evangelical desire for justice, abroad as much as at home, was scarcely lost on Queen Victoria, who renounced her early Whigery and became irredeemably Tory.

Gladstonian Liberalism defined its era, an epoch which itself defined the country, and with British power at its zenith, ultimately helped shape the world. Unquestionably, Britain was the global superpower and expected its values to be received gratefully around the world. Gladstone became Prime Minister four times, and while he was resoundingly popular, he remained resolutely un-populist. With his Midlothian campaigns he would tour the country addressing the common man—considered scandalously revolutionary by London rivals who resented his acclaim—but he would demand of his audience an erudition that a modern politician could never assume.

His train would be stopped at small stations by adoring crowds, and he would be urged into impromptu speeches. In the great cities of the north and Scotland he would address open-air crowds of 20,000 without microphone, often for an hour and a half (a mere sound-bite to Gladstone; introducing a budget he spoke for four hours). Far from growing restless, working men who might have spent a night and day walking to the venue would hang from lampposts, just to see the Grand Old Man. The crush became so great some fainted, and whenever Gladstone spoke of extending the franchise, the applause was so thunderous it could feel more like a modern-day pop concert than a stilted Victorian meeting of our imagination. No wonder crowds broke into song.

Whatever Gladstone's subject, morality was his theme and seriousness his tone. He was repulsed by what he saw as the cheap patriotism of Disraeli, and it is a mark of his skill that he could leave an audience believing that, far from revelling in imperial adventure, it shared his high-minded concern for the native. He would denounce the slaughter of 10,000 Zulus "for no other offence than their attempt to defend against your artillery with their naked bodies, their hearths and home, their wives and families." In a line that will surely resonate down the centuries he warned over an earlier Afghan adventure that "the sanctity of life in the hill villages of Afghanistan, among the winter snows, is as inviolable in the eyes of Almighty God as can be your own."

Domestically, Liberalism stuck up for what Americans call "the little guy", against the deadening weight of brutal power, rigid class dominance and dull prejudice. It is no coincidence that many Liberals were Nonconformists in their faith; for conformity reduces humans to cattle, and Liberals have always been wary of received opinion.

The Liberal Party was formed in 1859 in the Willis Tea Rooms, an alliance of Whig aristocrats who believed that great statesman could re-direct the tide of human history for the better; "Peelites", including Gladstone, who split from the Conservatives to defend free trade; and Radicals, who sought social reform. The Whigs had already granted the middle class the vote in 1832, and by the early 1860s Liberals were pushing to extend the franchise to working men. Their conversion to democracy and opposition to arbitrary power placed them firmly on the progressive side of political argument.

Sir William Harcourt remarked in 1872: "A despotic Government tries to make everybody do what it wishes; a Liberal Government tries, as far as the safety of society will permit, to allow everybody to do as he wishes. It has been the tradition of the Liberal Party consistently to maintain the doctrine of individual liberty. It is because they have done so that England is the place where people can do more what they please than in any country in the world." This Liberal ethos is also why Britain has for several centuries been a haven for those escaping tyranny and poverty, and also been a Mecca for free thought and experimentation. Britain's society and economy have been the beneficiaries.

With education and freedom, Liberals held, the individual could do remarkable things, an idea Conservatives variously denied and feared. Burke's sombre view, at least as commonly interpreted by

Conservatives, was that individuals fitted into society best when everyone knew their place; to dream was to despair. The Liberal, in contrast, insisted that human improvement was no utopian fancy but an ethical imperative. Take away the possibility of progress and you took away man's purpose. When Barrack Obama wrote of "the audacity of hope" he was actually being audaciously Victorian.

Improvement, then, was central to the human adventure. Crucially for these Liberals it would be achieved through free trade and self-reliance. Public bodies were to be run rigorously— Gladstone insisted civil service and military appointments should be made on merit alone—but society would be driven by individual endeavour.

Liberals did, though, have a sense of society. Our towns are adorned with statues of concerned Liberals who bestowed on their communities libraries and public baths. Jeremy Bentham, an early Liberal, had inculcated the party in his philosophy of Utilitarianism, which argued that public policy should be made to bring about the "greatest happiness of the greatest number." To even think of happiness represented a paradigm shift in a society mired in duty and suffering. As the 19th century progressed and society grew more complex, new voices argued that government had an obligation to improve the material well-being of its people. Traditional Liberals were shocked as they realised just what a radical idea the happiness principle was their party had unleashed upon the world.

In class-bound, industrialised Britain it was growing painfully apparent that the greatest number was not free in any meaningful sense to achieve the greatest happiness. As Queen Victoria died in 1901, Rowntree and Booth produced painstakingly researched, empirical reports into the conditions of the working class that cast a retrospective moral shadow over the bombast and pomp of the Victorian age. In detailing mortality rates to standards of sanitation they shocked Liberal opinion.

Radicals, pushed by Lloyd George, plundered these findings to argue poverty was frequently caused, not by fecklessness, but by powerful forces outside the individual's control: humble birth, illness and old age. A complacent, jingoistic society suddenly questioned the supposed glory of the British Empire when its sons were suffering degradation at home—a degradation "respectable" society witnessed only fleetingly from the window of a Hansom-cab, festering as it did down the shadowy alleyways of Britain's sprawling industrial cities.

And Liberals started to link the Conservative government's neglect at home to its brutality abroad. The same year Sir Henry Campbell-Bannerman, now Liberal leader, denounced the government's "methods of barbarism" in its prosecution of the Boer war.

This gave rise to the New Liberalism of 1906, which saw the party sweep back to office with its greatest—and last—majority. Its programme was free trade, land reform and peace, but in office grew more radical. This ministry of glittering talents, Asquith, Lloyd George and Churchill among them, argued that the individual could only be truly sovereign if freed from poverty, ignorance and squalor. The state was no longer the enemy but the enabler of liberty, because for individuals to enjoy genuine freewill there had to be a greater equity of means and equality of opportunity. It is a point that exercises Liberals today, after the last Labour government actually presided over a decline in social mobility. New Liberalism also foreshadowed by half a century the famous essay by Isaiah Berlin, *Two Concepts of Liberty*. The first concept was "freedom from" liberties, for example, from persecution; the other was "freedom to" liberties, for instance to lead a prosperous life. When government started to think, as it did under Asquith, that it had a duty to promote not only the first kind of liberty but also the second, it set itself a monstrous challenge. It is one that governments of all persuasions have wrestled with ever since.

As the need for a fair start gained greater purchase on the ministerial mind, a tension arose within Liberalism. Classical Liberals such as Mill, author of *On Liberty* and himself a Liberal MP, had advanced the cause of Utilitarianism, but he also feared "the tyranny of the majority". For might not the happiness of the greatest number be achieved at the expense of individual freedom, such as through higher taxes? It was balancing these two great competing demands—the wants of the individual versus the needs of the masses, upholding "freedom from" liberties while advancing "freedom to" liberties—which marked Asquith's mercurial premiership.

This stress fracture would undermine the very foundations of Liberalism for a century. How much easier to be a socialist who does not believe personal effort needs reward, nor that freedom to create wealth is essential to a successful economy. Alternatively, how much easier to be a Conservative who does not worry overly about the grinding injustice of so many being born poor, and all that human possibility snuffed out, merely by lack of luck.

Still, for nearly a decade the government flourished, skilfully synthesising the powerful forces of freedom and fairness. Those forces, incidentally, are evident in the coalition. The challenge for Cameron and Clegg is whether they can meld them as successfully as did Asquith and Lloyd George.

The New Liberals, who came to prominence when Asquith succeeded Campbell-Bannerman to the premiership in 1908, founded the Welfare State by introducing pensions, unemployment pay and a contributory form of national insurance. There were free school meals, scholarships to enable hugely more working-class children to attend secondary school, and probation which saved young people from prison. Medical check-ups were introduced, and made free for children. Labour-exchanges were established, while public works such as forestation provided work. And there was much more.

Where these reforms drew on the public purse, Lloyd George determined to pay for them with his 1909 "People's Budget". With customary fire, he spat: "This is a war Budget. It is for raising money to wage implacable warfare against poverty and squalidness. I cannot help hoping and believing that before this generation has passed away, we shall have advanced a great step towards that good time, when poverty, and the wretchedness and human degradation which always follows in its camp, will be as remote to the people of this country as the wolves which once infested its forests." The House of Lords and Conservatives agreed that this was indeed war, and broke the understanding of the constitution by voting down the Budget. It was to prove one of the bitterest and longest running disputes in twentieth century Britain. Inheritance tax and curbs on the Lords signalled the end of aristocratic dominance, and the rise of meritocracy. Meanwhile, in giving the poor pensions, unemployment pay and health insurance, Liberals ushered in modern Britain, though unlike socialists expected contributions during good times from recipients.

Throughout, the government remained mindful of old Liberal concerns. After the outbreak of war in 1914, who but a Liberal Prime Minister would have visited captured German prisoners, and grown so exercised about their treatment? To the Conservative, Asquith's forays were at best a distraction, to the Liberal, a command from conscience.

But a conscience is an expensive commodity in wartime. Liberalism is the gentlest of the mighty political philosophies, and it broke in the Great War under the strain of running the fiercest exercise in state slaughter the world had witnessed. Asquith, dubbed "Squiffy" after he was once said to have swayed at the dispatched box, had already been weakened by a Conservative-led armed-mutiny in Ireland. He found wartime measures such as conscription more than merely painful; they lost Liberals their religion. As Asquith tried to comprehend the enormity of human suffering—his son Raymond fell at the Somme in 1916—he channelled his anguish into love letters up to thrice daily to the young Venetia Stanley. At the very point defeat seemed a real danger and Lloyd George was conniving with Tories to hound him from office ("don't fail me now" he wrote), Stanley left him for his most trusted ministerial protégé.

So in 1916 Lloyd George replaced a broken Asquith in Number 10. Lloyd George was a Liberal to the left of Asquith but was sustained as Prime Minister by Conservative votes as the Liberals split as fatally as a mighty oak felled by Gladstone's axe. He proved a more ruthless and consequently more brilliant war leader than Asquith, and led the Allies to victory in 1918, but at the expense of Britain's super-power status and Liberalism itself. In victory Lloyd George was lauded and the Tories backed him in the post-war election, pitting Liberal against Liberal.

By the mid-twenties Asquith and Lloyd George united the Liberals, but too late. There was one last hurrah as the great pair toured the country by train—Asquith retiring to a hotel at night with his family, remarking *sotto voce* that Lloyd George was probably enjoying the hospitality of a nearby castle.

For a party whose electoral heart had apparently stopped beating, the Liberal brain continued to tick as vigorously as in its Victorian youth. The *Yellow Book* and *We Can Conquer Unemployment!* of 1929 were thought-changing Liberal responses to the great depression, foreshadowing by several years FDR and his New Deal in looking to stimulate the economy by paying the unemployed to engage in public works. Indeed, through the inter-war years the Liberal Party produced Britain's two most influential economic thinkers of the century, Keynes and Beveridge, while Liberal Summer Schools bloomed with the darling—and daring—buds of fresh thought.

But the Liberals would never be the natural party of government again. By the thirties the party was no longer a roadworthy vehicle for ministerial ambition. From the Liberal Unionists to the National Liberals, too many Liberals seemed open to Conservative blandishments, subsumed in the right wing party—hence the Liberal fear that Clegg is leading a dangerous dance. David Butler has invoked the rhyme *The Lady of Riga* to warn of the risks of riding the Tory tiger: "There was a young lady of Riga, Who went for a ride on a tiger; They returned from the ride. With the lady inside. And a smile on the face of the tiger."

If major ideas, combined with the memory of what had been, kept Liberalism alive, Liberaism continued to vanish—with Liberals from Chamberlain via Lloyd George to "Simon the Impeccable" gobbled by that Tory tiger.

Dangerfield argued In *The Strange Death of Liberal England* that Liberalism was fatally wounded before it went walking with any tiger, or even before it wandered madly onto a Flanders field. This, he said, was due to the philosophy's inherent tension: the Labour movement demanded more "New" Liberalism while Conservatives had stoked up civil war in Ireland to kill off even old Liberalism.

The age of Liberalism was closing. In the aftermath of what was touchingly still called The Great War, WB Yeats wrote in that fine modernist Poem *The Second Coming*: "Things fall apart; the centre cannot hold/ Mere anarchy is loosed upon the world".

Still, at home the mood was less one of anarchy than lethargy. For the next half century the country trudged grumpily between paternalistic Conservatism and centralised socialism. The individual was no longer sovereign, but a cog in a terrifyingly banal, class-crazed machine.

Should the Liberal Party have remained in any doubt about its declining popularity, the electorate delivered a fairly broad hint in 1945. Even its leader, Sir Archibald Sinclair, was defeated. By 1951 a party that had ruled the largest empire the world had seen could muster only six MPs, having performed more splits than an *artiste* at one of Mr Stringfellow's late night dancing emporia, becoming a soft target for music hall comedians: 97 per cent had voted either Conservative or Labour, their preferences almost entirely predetermined by class loyalties. And as Conservatives tended to poll slightly better than Labour, this meant Britain was mainly ruled by what Liberals saw as the forces of reaction, not progress.

If Liberals found the psephology sour, the zeitgeist was really foul. With rationing continuing until 1954, the post-war world was less sun-dappled uplands than bread and dripping. Liberals tend to do better when folk are having fun, and there wasn't much fun to be had. Conservatives retained Labour's state-superstructure, undermining individualism. But they did periodically privatise what Labour had just nationalised. Economic policy—you could not, with entirely straight face, call it strategy—pogo-ed drunkenly, often in response to growling industrial unrest. Class resentment became a defining national feature. Liberals looked forlornly to the Continent, where meritocratic societies were building healthy market economies which in turn afforded generous welfare states. And this was based often on social insurance as advocated by Beveridge, not Labour's universal welfare. Labour assumed demand for healthcare would be finite, and that standards in public services would rise even without a plurality of provision. It was a colossal miscalculation, only now challenged by the coalition.

At the point the parliamentary Liberal Party could meet in a public telephone box, along sauntered the swashbuckling Jo Grimond. The party went from securing 2.5 per cent of the vote in 1951 to fleetingly topping opinion polls in just over a decade. Why, Grimond demanded, were Labour and Conservatives conspiring to make the state ever grander, further removing it from the people it governed? He tapped into the sixties realisation that convention, snobbery, staleness, bigotry and authority could be challenged. He commanded his troops to "march towards the sound of gunfire". The individual, he insisted, mattered. And all this feverish activity resulted in many claimed sightings of the Liberal ghost. Most tantalisingly there was "Orpington man" after Eric Lubbock's great by-election triumph of 1962, which claimed to see the emerging skilled manual worker as a Liberal voter. Most such sightings proved, upon closer inspection, to be but shadows in the long night.

Still, slowly Grimond breathed new life into his party. As significantly, he showed both in manner and ideas how the Liberal Party should be led. It was a lesson learned by Clegg. The great movements Grimond's party helped into being have flourished in Clegg's time: social mobility, classlessness, environmentalism, racial equality, feminism, vegetarianism, gay-rights, peace campaigns, internationalism, concern for the Third World, organic farming, animal rights, localism, consumerism, the craft movement and of course civil rights. It would be crass to claim Liberal ownership of all or even any of these causes but they did find a warm welcome on Liberal pews not always afforded them in the chillier churches of Socialism and Conservatism. The idealistic, non-materialistic crusades such as the anti-Apartheid movement, that initially only interested Liberals, gradually became the crusades for which people took up politics. This was no phantom; this was a living, campaigning, thinking political party.

I had joined the party aged 14, inspired by one of the most retrospectively ridiculed speeches ever delivered by a top politician. After the Labour right broke to form the SDP and an Alliance with the Liberals, David Steel proclaimed himself the first Liberal leader since Lloyd George to be able to say at the end of the annual Assembly "go back to your constituencies—and prepare for government".

In my defence there were reasons, some cogent, why an impressionable, serious-minded boy might have jumped up and joined in the almost orgiastic applause—in my case in front of the family television, still black and white. According to one poll in 1982 the Alliance was tipping 50 per cent, heady even for a party used to popularity; for Liberals, then, it was so disorientating it was as if the celestial furniture had been re-arranged.

Britain was glowering. The least likely people were talking politics, even we children. Later, the political consensus was that a significant quantity of Thatcher's medicine had been necessary. But back then the political thuggery of the "Chingford Skinhead" repulsed as much as the madness of "King Arthur". Liberals saw where two class-driven political parties had brought us—to blazing streets, dole queues into the distance, entire nations of the "United" Kingdom laid to waste—and wondered how this could possibly represent a sane future. Even Italy's spluttering Fiat 500 was zooming past us, the sick man of Europe, the rusty Austin Allegro. My youthful exasperation, I later learned, had been shared by Clegg.

As a nation we were tearing at each other's cheeks over class, quite the most useless invention man has made, denying the possibilities of each individual. Growing up in north London my contemporaries—sons and daughters of senior civil servants, human rights lawyers, those sorts—founded a magazine called *Class War*, and spent highly agreeable weekends on "bash the rich" marches. Their proletarian duty done, they would retire to Hampstead for a good supper (there were embarrassments, alas, when for some inexplicable reason the "Bash the Rich" route led them past a schloss of their own).

My political activity was less revolutionary, and so less heroic. While classmates talked—I'm not sure how far they progressed from the planning stage—about throwing Molotov cocktails, I was delivering my own political message, popping thousands of

Spotlight leaflets through doors in which the Alliance launched local campaigns for recycling bins and pooper scooper facilities. It was a curious youth, yet perhaps not entirely misspent. Within two years West Hampstead went from being a Lib free zone to a forest of orange posters that spread from this tiny enclave to cover Camden. Remarkably few contemporaries manned the really important teenage barricade, to embark on the love war; this was a time, so unusual in Britain, which was entirely political.

Like my extremist contemporaries and more moderate citizens, I also viewed the governing party as spivvy, cruel and divisive. Did it not care, we wondered, about the misery it made for the real underclass? The economic violence unleashed by the right and left was ratcheted daily, a domestic arms race. How much more boring—and sensible—seemed the Alliance's proposals for profit sharing and broader share ownership. Thatcher was surely right to seek a "property owning democracy", but shouldn't capitalism's fruits be sufficiently low-hanging to be plucked by what she might have called "the little people"? Only then, I felt, might we heal the class wounds seemingly draining the country's life-blood.

But as the eighties snarled on, the Thatcher fortress proved impregnable. Meanwhile Neil Kinnock, having dropped Labour's pledge to nationalise Britain's 200 leading companies, tackled the "obscenity" of Militant. It was painfully obvious the Alliance had missed its chance; the seas had parted, and now they had closed. So after failing to "break the mould of British politics" once more at the 1987 general election, the "Alliance" embarked on a favourite past-time, upturning the life-raft to unseat a fellow survivor. Was David Owen pushed or did he jump? It didn't matter because the party scarcely deserved to be asked a question. By now I was "president" of the Liberal Society at Durham University, but the party at Westminster was virtually un-leadable.

The Liberal Party and all but a festering rump of the SDP merged. But it had the aroma of a marriage where childhood sweethearts are re-united half a lifetime too late, neither retaining much attraction for the other but both being too kindly to say. There was a sense that Liberalism had, in Ashdown's criticism, been living too long on the intellectual piggy bank of Grimond.

On my first day working for Ashdown, just elected leader of the new party, our poll rating had slumped to 4 per cent, while that magnificently sturdy Highland Liberal Sir Russell Johnston MP would cheerfully tell his new leader to "fuck off", sometimes between medicinal sips of oak-aged malt.

Absurdly, the newly married couple took the name "Social and Liberal Democrats". Sketch writers dubbed us "SaLaDs", confirming us in the public mind on rare occasions it paused to ponder us as a bunch of enfeebled Tofu munchers. In reality at Ashdown's HQ we interns would have devoured anything from a wilting salad to a bloody T-bone steak. The former captain of the Special Boat Squadron had declared lunch was for wimps, so all we did was work and starve. Another of Ashdown's notes from "P" to "J" read: "call me tomorrow on my car phone at 6:47 am." It wasn't purely the earliness that distressed; it was the preciseness in a party hitherto more comfortable with vagaries.

Even Ashdown struggled to improve the party's standing. Fortunately, perhaps, a tabloid then revealed the ex-MI6 agent's action-man persona was not confined to his working life, reporting a relationship with his secretary. Headline writers laughed at a man ("Paddy Pants Down") who—in public—seemed reluctant to laugh. But in private Liberal Democrats were soon the ones chortling. Suddenly their support was also displaying unexpected potency.

Ashdown didn't so much lead the party back to the battlefield as bark it there. He deployed leadership skills learned in one of the world's great fighting forces on a band of Liberal irregulars that sometimes had more than a whiff of Dad's Army.

During university holidays I worked for Ronnie Fearn, whose qualifications for becoming an MP were being deputy manager of his local bank and a dame in Southport Amateur Dramatic Society's annual panto. He was hugely generous, fun and driven by an unwavering zeal to do good by the people of Southport. He had been standing for election in the town since the early sixties, then the safest Conservative seat in the country. When this redoubtable Victorian seaside town finally fell to his tireless charm in 1987—

probably in a bout of nervous exhaustion—it could scarcely have contained a puppy, baby or hyacinth he hadn't loudly admired. But he wasn't necessarily the most predictable choice as "shadow Health spokesman". The Lib Dem press office would complain Ronnie was more interested in "Southport in Bloom" than in the blooming health of the country. But unless he cultivated Southport, the apparatchiks would have no Health spokesman upon whom to dump their compost.

Despite its apparent irrelevance and occasional viciousness the party was an intoxicating place to work. Later, toiling for newspapers, I would frequently hear it said of executives that they were "drunk in charge of a newspaper". And though almost too sober, I sometimes found myself, aged 18, a delinquent in charge of a political party. So short-staffed was it that I was able to issue press releases and launch campaigns at will. Some even provoked a slight ripple on the deadly-still Westminster pond, such as a major petition against charges for eye and teeth check-ups. On one occasion I announced a campaign against drug abuse in the army, nominally in the name of Ronnie, which had every newsdesk in the country demanding details of the press conference. This came as some surprise to Ronnie, enjoying a well-earned summer sojourn in his Welsh caravan.

These vicissitudes did occasionally have me wondering if I had stumbled on to a particularly eccentric village fete committee, but I felt I was doing my miniscule bit to restore Liberalism to its rightful place at the heart of British life. It was a philosophy with a political programme as distinct and as deliverable as Conservatism or socialism, and one that even after eight decades of attracting mildew in the history section of municipal libraries had done at least as much as any other to shape the country.

The Liberal accepted the socialist's contention that society was unjust, and that it was government's fundamental duty to make it equitable; and it accepted the Conservative's rejoinder that you don't free the poor from poverty by making them benefit slaves. But it rejected the contention of both that this was the sum-total of political choice. Government could take from the comfortable to give to the uncomfortable, but the trick was to incentivise them to help themselves. More than this, the Liberal saw human existence as higher than a purely mechanical process of labour spinning unthinkingly in the capitalist wheel: for what of education, thought, human rights, the environment, culture, enlightenment, generosity, personal growth, good conversation, better argument, love, sex, humour and above all freedom? Money, the Liberal contended, was important, but only up to the point that it enabled us to get on with the really vital stuff of life. Perhaps it is pure prejudice but I don't think its coincidence that Liberals are often simply more fun.

Liberalism's support was no longer wide but it remained deep, demanding—and receiving—a fanatical loyalty from remaining adherents. A party that had long drawn strength from its very unpopularity felt strangely invigorated by its precarious position. And while opponents made the mistake of believing jokes they told about the hopelessness of Liberals, our squadron of woolly jumpers were the deadliest campaigners in the business. Liberals would carpet bomb areas with niceness, cased in *Focus* leaflets, with an indefatigability that would have impressed "Bomber" Harris. And it worked. Here were politicians who actually seemed interested in people and their neighbourhoods.

Just as Grimond led Liberals in the late fifties and early sixties to "the sound of gunfire", now Capt Ashdown commanded them in the dark arts of guerrilla warfare, ignoring Westminster's unforgiving terrain. And he found a willing brigade or two. I caught an echo of the party's enduring determination canvassing at the Kensington by-election of 1988 with Jo's elderly wife, Laura. We realised we'd missed one flat at the top of a particularly unresponsive block (sans lifts). To my shrug she bristled that if I wouldn't run back up seven flights, she would. After a lecture I saw she was right and we became firm friends.

She had been born a Bonham-Carter, part of the Asquith clan, and there was among some Liberals—me included—a nostalgia for a time when Liberalism was the natural guide to government. The National Liberal Club, that wonderful Victorian wedding cake, survived, like Miss Havisham's, long, long after every crumb should surely have been swept into a dustbin of political biography. And there in its vast tile hung caverns—rendering it, according to one unkind visitor, the most convenient public lavatory between Charing Cross and Westminster—packed meetings of the Liberal History Group would continue to savour the achievements of Mr Gladstone and Mr Asquith. Only Liberal International, anxiously discussing fraudulent elections in some far off land they had little hope of influencing, could attract a greater number of wise, concerned heads.

But in the airless basement more urgent discussions were taking place among younger workers and volunteers, arguing over new policy on every conceivable subject, even Health. And slowly the party found its voice, notably over Kosovo, where a discernibly Liberal critique—moral, crusading, high minded and perhaps a little pompous—could be heard once more. And the public began to cock at least half an ear.

Ashdown, though, was deceived by Tony Blair after Labour's victory in 1997. In agreeing to turn the Liberal Democrats into a sort of UN peacekeeping force—neither of the government, nor entirely of the opposition—activists felt he had been beguiled by that notorious charmer. For a born-fighter Ashdown had kept his dagger sheathed, and in return for few spoils: a half promise on electoral reform and a few seats on desultory committees (how Liberals are seduced by committees, much as Conservative grandees traditionally are by non-executive directorships and nightclub hostesses). Lance Price, Blair spin doctor, tells me even he left a meeting uncertain if Blair had been sincere in promising Ashdown PR: "And I suspect Blair wasn't sure either".

In his desperation to see investment in our brutally run down public services, Ashdown had overlooked that the progressive forces of British politics split almost a century before with reason. Labour was incurably tribal. And its prescription for improving the lot of the poor had long been about pumping billions into centralised state institutions, not helping individuals to help themselves. So Brown did as Labour knew best—spent, always with a new strategy, but rarely with much sagacity. And in doing so he undermined, perhaps for a generation, the progressive case for public investment.

To Ashdown's credit he later realised his mistake, and warned that the party was like a faulty car—without a strong driver, it would veer left. His speech resigning the leadership in 1999 called for the liberation of "the great institutions that deliver our public services—education, health, justice, welfare—from the clammy embrace of corporatism." This was surely right, but incendiary—fitting, really, from one who had spent his working life lobbing grenades at the unsuspecting.

The Liberal Democrats, he warned, should look for their brain food in an entirely different trough. They should, he said, seek nourishment in raw Liberalism, not soapy social democracy. After he had flirted so long with Lib-Labery, this represented a departure. Ashdown was standing down because he felt stood up by Blair, both by the Prime Minister's failure to form a coalition and his pliant acceptance of Brown's statist solutions. And now Ashdown was all but hurling Blair's engagement ring across the conference floor.

Without his speech there might have been no Orange Book movement, nor coalition government. At last Liberal Democrats were questioning the Blair domestic record. What, they demanded, was progressive about Labour's strategy of funnelling billions into unreformed public services which only entrenched poverty, offering no escape to a better life? Labour was merely increasing benefits sufficiently to lift a little the least poor of those fairly arbitrarily defined as living "in poverty", out of that bracket. Was Labour fundamentally raising life chances or aspirations? And what of all those stuck further down the heap, for whom poverty was increasing? Anger at this failure was the inspiration for *The Orange Book*. The state was no longer working in a purely benign way to alleviate poverty, as envisaged by New Liberals a century ago. The Welfare State, as now defined, was feeding on the poor to grow itself. It was an instrument of enslavement as deadening as the satanic mills from which welfare had supposedly saved them. It was keeping the poor alive, but to what life? Orange Book Liberals argued that all society—but especially its poorest—needed to be liberated; not left to their own devises as Thatcherites had proposed, but helped to build better lives.

But before this idea's time, the party endured terrible tribulations, even by the standards of its turbulent history. Much as I warmed to Kennedy, valuing his political skill almost as much as his conversation, under his leadership the party grew intellectually the worse for wear. He was the only senior British politician brave enough to say it was wrong to fight in Iraq, but closer to home he seemed to regard fresh thought as something akin to a hazardous material. When I ventured, with Greg Dyke, to give a talk to the shadow cabinet at an away weekend in a Buckinghamshire hotel to suggest how the party could improve its profile, only Laws seemed to appreciate my message: that this was the time for Liberalism. Big government hadn't worked, particularly for the poorest, and individuals were craving more independence—so why weren't we exploring how the disadvantaged could enjoy the benefits of Liberalism? In short, why weren't modern Liberal Democrats more liberal? Through David I came to meet a small but highly impressive group in the party who, to my relief, shared these thoughts.

Meanwhile, they would explain their ideas. *The Orange Book* woke up the party, and media. It was attacked from within as "right wing", even "toxic", but what was "left wing" or organic about pumping millions with just enough benefit to keep the poor in drowsy, state-sponsored perpetual poverty? The driving idea of *The Orange Book* was actually about raising people from the bottom. Its trick, influenced by consumerism, was to see how supposedly right-ish means like choice could bring about socially desirable ends. After all, policies such as vouchers for school places had originated in America on the left of the Democratic Party to gain black children places in hitherto "white" schools. Clegg's pupil's premium was in that tradition. The money attached to a poorer child would be worth more, encouraging better schools to offer them a place.

As the party was gaining face time with the media's size 10 boot in the wake of Kennedy's resignation, it underwent a crucial period of renewal. Still the press restricted their enquiries to whether Kennedy had kicked the booze or if his replacement Campbell wore posh socks. Hacks couldn't see it, but there was a more significant story developing which even they couldn't ignore forever. The Liberal Democrats were going to become a party of government once more, and that government's guiding idea would be Liberalism.

If there is a laurel politicians seek, more than honorary degrees or titles, it is an "ism". Because this denotes they have not merely a programme but a philosophy. Thatcher earned one after her name, but she is one of the few post-war Prime Ministers who have. Butler and Gaitskell shared one ("Butskellism") to symbolise the mushy, corporatist consensus of post-war Britain. But you would have to look hard to find anything worthy of a philosophy in "Majorism", with all due reverence to the traffic cones hotline.

It would, then, be over-arching to claim an "ism" for Clegg, for this is bestowed after the event. But his coterie of Orange Book Liberals has spelt out very trenchantly an ideology. Contrast this with Cameron, who is either purposefully vague or simply doesn't believe that policies should fit into a paradigm of consistent beliefs. We see this when the Conservative leader talks about law and order, veering violently between authoritarianism and liberalism. Nor do we know if Miliband shares Brown's fondness for big business and an even bigger state or whether he has a new progressive idea.

Clegg, in contrast, is easier to define. He is progressive because he identifies the most pressing domestic concern as raising the life chances of those almost entirely cut off from mainstream society, giving them more "freedom to" liberties, such as to experience a genuinely first class education. But he is no socialist because he wants collective action through the state to deliver individual progress. The successful should be allowed to flourish and be rewarded, while the unsuccessful are helped to help themselves. He embraces the techniques—even the language—of the right, including "choice". But the least advantaged must be given extra help, so that choice becomes meaningful for all.

Asquith would recognise the approach. Freedom would be strengthened, by making it a reality for the many. Meanwhile, "freedom from" liberties would be fiercely guarded, protecting the citizen from big state interference and small town prejudice.

Liberalism, Clegg found, was like an old overcoat—or perhaps in honour of those Victorians and Edwardians, Gladstone and Asquith, a greatcoat—lost for years in the back of a dark, National Liberal Club cloakroom. It should not have surprised that it still fitted snugly round the frame of modern society.

23

THE MAINSTREAM

WHERE DID ALL THE FLUFFY BUNNIES GO?

In a joke the Irish are fond of telling against themselves, a driver finds himself hopelessly lost in some rural backwater and stops a local to ask the way. Said yokel scratches his head and ponders. "If I were you," he finally responds "I wouldn't start from here."

But "here" is where Clegg found himself. The question was which way to turn, left, right or straight ahead.

Or so you might assume. But Richard Grayson, former Lib Dem director of policy, placed himself firmly with our Irish friend in suggesting Clegg simply go backwards; if the Tories had a No Turning Back Group Grayson was founding a Turn Back and Scarper as Fast as You Can Group.

"Nick Clegg has taken the party to the right throughout his leadership, especially on public spending," he complained. "But the party now needs to realise that the shift to the right has made centre-left voters who have backed us steadily over the past 15 years desert us and vote 'no' on AV."

How the Liberal Democrats could have implemented a programme of government based on the Father Christmas school of politics he presided over ("a bauble for you, another for you..."), he does not enlighten. Moreover, if Clegg had refused the Tory offer and skulked in opposition, or perhaps tried to cobble together some improbable deal with Labour, the Lib Dems would almost certainly have faced an early election like in October 1974 when they were punished for causing "instability". And incidentally, as party managers have told me, another quick election could have driven the party close to bankruptcy.

But whether or not Grayson offered any answers he did at least proffer the key question: if there was a constituency for a genuinely centrist, free market party of government, where were its voters? For just because Grayson's solution could be dismissed as a depressing attempt to keep the Liberal Democrats as some pressure group of perpetual and immature opposition, the party still needed to work out who and where it's new voters might be. Grayson was not alone in fearing that if Clegg were to plough remorselessly forward through the wilderness, he would end up stuck in the bog of unpopularity.

An answer was suggested by Browne. Many, he argued, refused to vote Lib Dem because they believed the party could not win, was not a party of government and was not serious; but significant numbers *did* vote Lib Dem precisely *because* the party could not win, was not a party of government and was not serious. These, in a sense, were the "none of the above" voters who wanted to demonstrate ideological purity, or nudge Labour into a more righteous position. The challenge, argued Browne, was to swap voters who didn't want a serious Lib Dem party for those who did. And, he posited, it was already working in small ways: when, for instance, was the last time you had heard the dismissive phrase "beard and sandals"? Patently, that cliché no longer held. For every idealist the party was losing, might it not have gained a realist who recognised that the party went into a difficult coalition to lift the country from recession? By the Lib Dems proving able and conscientious administrators, new voters would emerge.

"But emerge from where?" I could hear Grayson howl. There was no very easy answer. In the referendum and local elections Clegg had proved more adept at losing the first type of voter than attracting the second. The centre ground is notoriously crowded and even one of Browne's ministerial friends, a fellow right winger, said bluntly: "Unless we can get some of the fluffy bunny voters back, we are done for. I'm not sure there are enough centre ground voters. The Lib Dem base has been public sector workers, students and intellectuals. We have contrived to fuck them all off."

This was echoed in less gynaecological terms by Dr Andrew Russell, senior lecturer at Manchester University and co-author of *Neither Left nor Right?*

He said the centre-party voter Browne described only existed in the minister's febrile imagination, though conceded the Lib Dems could create such voters. The problem, he said, was this meant reversing the path (and some progress) the party made in attracting voters of the centre-left.

Lib Dem supporters, he said, were often "fairly affluent", like their Tory counterparts, but while a typical Conservative might be a manager in the private sector, a Lib Dem would be manager in the public sector: "They work in hospitals, schools, the BBC. Politically they are more like Labour, particularly on welfare issues. A significant number are what we call 'student plus' who include first jobbers, often in socially caring occupations." Not only was the coalition almost certainly cutting the budget at their place of work or study, the essence of Orange Book Liberalism was to shake up these vast public monoliths, to make producers more responsive to consumers. Liberal Democrats were becoming anti-statist—but their voters *were* the state.

No wonder Clegg felt under pressure over Health reform. Or that the left spat that snuggling up to Conservatives would lose the "Kennedy coalition". This included voters in Labour outposts attracted by Kennedy's attack on the Iraq war and his defence of public services.

Kennedy went courting converts many miles from the sunny glades of suburb and shire, where throughout the party's post-war recovery it had snapped at Conservative heels. This is why figures such as Huhne were warning privately that the party might alienate its newer leftish supporters. "We are not talking Aberavon or Tonypandy as seats we need to defend," says one senior source. "Our voters are not the horny-handed sons of toil. They tend to be professionals with degrees. A typical example of seats we were winning from Labour was Lynne Featherstone's Hornsey and Wood Green [North London]. But they were urban, and this was the historic base of the party. It was never just a rural party. Indeed, even in our rural seats we gain most support from towns within them. It's always been like that. It's why Tories would always look down on Asquith for being a 'villa dweller.'"

These seats will be harder to hold now Clegg has engaged in

political congress with Cameron. And they will be susceptible to the blandishments of Miliband, who as a new leader helps voters forget that tuition fees and spending cuts were Labour ideas. As one minister grumbles to no great purpose: "What does fuck one off is Labour making such capital out of cuts when there is such a wafer thin difference between ours and what they were proposing."

However, the party was where it was rather than where Grayson, Browne or indeed Clegg would have it be. The next election looked to be about holding on to as many seats as possible rather than embarking on the optimistic crusade of the last campaign to capture new territory.

And that could be tough. Liberal Democrats did a fine job in the early stages of coalition making Conservatives feel more comfortable voting Tory, yet polls suggested a horrific six out of ten Lib Dems were considering deserting. Especially worryingly, Russell said the party was walloped particularly hard in the 2011 local elections in those areas where they had previously flourished. "Where there was no Lib Dem presence, the Tory vote suffered more."

Paul Whiteley, co-director of the British Election Study and professor of Government at the University of Essex, pointed out that on the three previous occasions when Liberals went into government with Conservatives (1895, 1918 and 1931) it was followed by a period of two party rule and Tory recovery. However, if there was a chink in Whiteley's comparison it was that then, unlike now under Clegg, the Libs were hopelessly split.

The Lib Dems, put simply, were on a road without maps and everyone was merely hazarding a way ahead. Actually, through the summer of 2011, the party's wrist slitters were already starting to look a little foolish. The Lib Dem poll rating was rising modestly, and the Tory one was plummeting. With Clegg forcing concessions on Health and toughening the government's response to Rupert Murdoch, the Lib Dem contribution was growing more apparent. Nobody was suggesting Clegg was leading his party down Victory Avenue, but nor did he appear to be leading them over a cliff.

And even if "events" had not started to go a little more Clegg's way, there were fundamental factors that should have given the party a little optimism. If Dangerfield identified four powerful forces driving a dagger through the Liberal heart, I'd like to suggest four factors pushing the other way. And for all the gloomy talk about Liberalism's health, I'd suggest that the local and AV elections revealed it to be suffering nothing more terminal than a mild dose of influenza. These four factors actually speak loudly about the renewed life of England, not about the death of Liberalism.

Here are the four major changes: the breakdown in class identity, increased educational attainment, the flowering of liberal values and the enthusiasm of young people.

First, class. Just as the emergence a century ago of an organised, politicised, industrialised working class helped Labour eclipse the Liberals, so the rise of mobile, classless individuals points to the centre party's revival. The breakdown of class identity since the fifties has coincided exactly with a massive fall in support for the two class-based, socially authoritarian parties—and a rise for Liberals. Union membership, large industrial workplaces and Labour's heartlands are all in steep long-term decline. Instead, the successful progressive politician must appeal to the aspirational. Clegg showed at the last election he can do that.

After questioning voters during the last election Whiteley found that the campaign itself rather than class loyalty is slowly becoming the primary factor in determining votes. Base support is eroding across the spectrum, and here the Lib Dems have least of the three parties to lose. With the Clegg pitch based on rational argument rather than class loyalty, this should continue to boost support.

Second, education. People become massively more likely to vote Liberal Democrat if they attend university. The party's membership contains a far greater proportion of graduates than those of the other two. Many seats Lib Dems have won or nearly won have been varsity towns. Education, and the belief in human improvement, has always been a core Liberal ideal. The tuition fees debacle aside, the huge expansion in university education can only boost the Lib Dems. And what an expansion that has been, with just a shade under 40 per cent of adults under 30 attending university the previous year. Three decades ago just 600,000 people were in full time higher education, now it is 2.5 million. And even allowing for budgetary restraints, demand is only going to increase, with 80 per cent of the children of graduates themselves attending university.

And educated people are more likely to be mobile, exposing themselves to different influences. Online and on the go, they are less influenced than their parents by the nostrums of shop stewards, employers, parents, priests, journalists, rock stars and other spouters of received opinion—including, it should be said, politicians.

The third factor, the growth of liberal values, is the hardest to substantiate, both because of difficulties of definition and because liberal people don't necessarily vote Liberal Democrat. But it can only benefit a party if its ideas are shared by potential voters. And the change in social attitudes has been breathtaking. Because we are living through it we don't appreciate how fundamental—and fast— change is. While traditional right wing concerns such as immigration and crime remain, gut instincts are more liberal than a generation ago. When Conservative MP Patrick Mercer ventured that ethnic minority soldiers should expect to be called "black bastards" and that they were often "idle and useless", the typical response was less outrage than amused pity: poor chap, had modern life so passed him by that he simply had no understanding of the country he presumed to govern? The racist jokes Jim Davidson told on prime time 20 years ago wouldn't even be acceptable now late at night in a working men's club. And this isn't purely because some BBC commandant has banned them. As tastes have grown more sophisticated, comedians have had to craft cleverer jokes that chime with modern values.

When Clegg was a young adult and Davidson was still getting work, judges would draw attention to the length of a rape victim's skirt ("she was asking for it"). Yet when in 2011 Ken Clarke blundered into a conversation about "serious rapes"—with its possibly accidental inference that there were somehow unserious rapes—there was no need for Germaine Greer to call for mandatory castration. Even the Conservative blogosphere spluttered that we had sorted all this out years ago. The *Sun*, which once fulminated against "bra-burning feminists", remarked that Clarke had gone to prison after this offence—but regrettably only for an hour on an official visit. That's progress.

So with apologies to Richard Littlejohn, political correctness hasn't gone mad, it has gone main-stream. And while it is only fair to acknowledge that the social mores of Labour and Conservative politicians have (generally) modernised, the Liberal Democrats, as Clegg emphasises constantly, remain the truest upholders of liberal values.

And finally we come to young people, whose enthusiastic embracing of Clegg was such a striking feature of the general election campaign. The emerging generation is a keen consumer of designer fripperies but also, judging by the massive upturn in support for single-issue causes, of political ideas. The question is whether they can be encouraged to see themselves as party political: whether, for example, a community's fight to save its cottage hospital or open a free school can be seen to be a small part of a much broader struggle to enable local groups and individuals to make more decisions about their lives.

But there is one significant drag on this emerging Lib Dem support: idleness. According to Whiteley, while the Conservative vote was once boosted by so-called "shy Tories" (folk apparently too embarrassed to tell pollsters their voting intentions) Clegg's vote suffered from what Whiteley dubs "lazy Lib Dems".

"We looked at this very carefully and in the 18-26 age bracket, the Lib Dems were in the lead by a long way," Whiteley said. "This group doesn't have strong party loyalties and is prepared to be influenced by the campaign. The problem is they didn't turn up on the day." So while polls showed Clegg ending the campaign nudging 29 per cent, he actually polled 23.5 per cent. And the primary reason for the disparity, said Whiteley, was that less than half of those young Clegg-lets bothered to do their duty.

"Older people feel guilty if they don't vote," Whiteley said. "They also feel government decisions have more bearing on their lives. Younger people have a different view of social responsibility and citizenship. They don't feel stigma in saying 'why should I vote?'" The British Social Attitudes Survey suggested interest in party politics among young people had halved in a decade.

The key question for Clegg—and democracy—is whether this is what academics call the "cohort" effect or the "life cycle" effect. If the latter it's good news for the Lib Dems. Then, "lazy" young Lib Dems will, as maturity and responsibility kick in, rouse themselves from their Fat Boys and saunter those few hundred yards to the polling station (hopefully for the Lib Dems). If, however, it's the cohort effect and citizens are now feeling fundamentally disconnected from their government, then the Lib Dem vote will flat-line.

The worrying news is Whiteley is among several academics who suspect, increasingly, that the change is growing and permanent. "You have to be taught how to vote," he says. "The first time you are normally taken by parents. That no longer appears to be happening. People are learning NOT to vote."

But Russell rejects this view: "For the cohort effect there needs to be a major shock to the system. The Second World War changed the way people vote. Paul's analysis might be right, but I have big doubts. I don't think it's as bleak for Liberal Democrats as he suggests." Undeniably, though, if we are to derive enthusiastic voters from the apathetic young we will have to do so from far lower levels of interest than a generation ago.

My hunch is that expecting young people to vote in the conventional way is a losing battle. But that doesn't mean they are lost to politics. We have seen the same with the media. Companies that rely on the next generation to buy newsprint are dying, but those with a strong online presence are expanding readerships.

Given the importance of the young to Liberal Democrat fortunes in particular and our democracy in general, I offer one small suggestion that will probably require me to don a tin hat in party circles. With electoral reform off the agenda, might not Clegg turn his focus from how votes are counted to how they are cast? For a move to allow remote electronic voting alongside the traditional ballot box could give the Lib Dems as many seats as AV if it tempts the young and undecided to vote. And this is just the start. The electronic age has the potential to bring into being Rousseau's dream of a more direct democracy, with voters being given regular referenda. If Clegg led the campaign for the new democracy it would also demonstrate that he and not Miliband is Britain's leading progressive.

Meanwhile, there are more immediate factors that will determine the next election.

Firstly, as the crescendo against "the cuts" grows, and with voting intentions tied to economic optimism, Whiteley believes Tory popularity will continue to decline. "If there were a snap election the likelihood is the Tories would lose, with Labour winning a majority." This will strengthen Clegg's hand in future wrangles, as Lib Dems remind Tories that elections are won on centre-ground. Already the narrative of this government is changing from strong Tories v weak Lib Dems to a more equal partnership. The electoral advantage Conservatives enjoyed over Lib Dems, Whiteley suggests, will become a "declining asset".

Second, polling evidence indicates that the heaviest drags on Lib Dem support has been the "wasted vote" argument. But as Whiteley and Russell agree, "that is no longer valid" when the party is in power.

In two-thirds of Lib Dem seats the Tories are the nearest challenger, and as Browne says of his Taunton Deane constituency (majority just under 4,000), Tories have relied far too heavily on the "wasted vote" line—even if Browne wins in Somerset, Tories have insisted he will remain a sideshow on the Westminster stage. As Browne observes, this argument might be harder to advance when voters are offered a Lib Dem Foreign Office minister who has made countless decisions in government and learned his way round Whitehall. As the Lib Dems are shown to have been reliable coalition partners capable of drowning kittens—or at least making hard decisions—some Tories might even back them.

Third, while Lib Dem voters are considering defecting, an even larger proportion of supporters of other parties don't rule out voting Lib Dem in the future. Indeed, according to this analysis the Lib Dems have a larger *potential* constituency than any other.

Fourth, Labour under Miliband, so far, hasn't done enough to rebuild Blair's hard won coalition that united a progressive middle class with the old working class. This opens a gap in the middle for the Lib Dems. It also makes a mockery of Grayson's argument that there is still fertile Orange territory to Labour's left. As Russell says: "The body of supporters Labour relies on is insufficient to give it a majority. That makes the Lib Dems viable partners." Looked at another way, Labour needs Lib Dems more than Lib Dems need Labour.

Fifth, the Liberal Democrats have grown much better at playing the electoral system they are stuck with. Alliance support only wavered 2 per cent either way across each region, and for every percent of support the "Two Davids" gained, they were rewarded with a meagre one seat in a parliament of 650. Now each percentage point can give the party nearly three seats.

This was Rennard's brilliant contribution to the Lib Dem revival. His targeted seat strategy pushed volunteers and money into small clusters of seats they could win. This, incidentally, was controversial at the time with one senior figure telling Rennard the strategy was "underhand and dishonest". It is fortunate he was ignored. Russell looked at how Rennard's approach transformed Lib Dem fortunes between 1992 and 1997. The party's vote actually dropped a smidgeon, but its MPs doubled. As Russell says: "Once Lib Dem MPs get embedded, they are hard to dislodge."

A limitation of the Rennard strategy was that it led to intellectual fuzziness, with Lib Dem candidates accused of jumping on local bandwagons that didn't always resonate with national themes. However, one of Clegg's achievements was to take the best of Rennard-ism and of Laws-ism: so candidates are encouraged to campaign on issues that matter in their patch, but which chime with national policy. It is an approach which seems to work.

It shouldn't surprise us by now, but none of these factors were being discussed in the media. Instead, journalists took pleasure in recalling Dangerfield's book. *The Spectator* headline read "The strange death of the Lib Dems", decorated rather fetchingly with the yellow Liberal bird speared by an arrow. The argument was that normal service was to be resumed, the gentleman's agreement we call democracy, whereby two parties consent to take it in turns to occupy Downing Street. The Lib Dems, it held, would be punished by its idealistic supporters for going into unpopular coalition. This would achieve the unthinkable—make Labour popular.

One takes the point. Germany's Free Democrats have enjoyed virtually uninterrupted power since the Second World War on a quarter of the vote of the normally powerless Liberal Democrats. German voters, it seems, would rather nudge their government a little to the right or left rather than back the centre party that will be in government anyway. This might start to happen to the Lib Dems. Moreover, the ambiguity of opposition will be lost and Clegg will be judged on his record.

But while the right and left love cuddling to crush the centre— how predictable the conservative *Spectator* commissioned the socialist Nick Cohen to write the obituary—shouldn't they have realised by now that reports of Liberal deaths are often a little exaggerated? Even given the low Lib Dem poll rating, the massive collapse in support for two-party rule is the real historical trend the enemies of Liberal Democracy should worry about. Do they believe a process of realignment that has gone on for half a century is reversed by one set of local mid-terms? Moreover, with Labour reverting to faithful friends (unions, tax and spend, placards) will Miliband look quite so attractive under scrutiny?

There are strong grounds for believing Liberalism is back in the game. Like modern Britain it is classless, internationalist and open-minded. It has every chance of going from being the dominant political philosophy of the 19th century to the guiding idea of the 21st. It was hardly surprising Liberalism sat out most of the 20th century because that was about treating people less as individuals than as insects. The emerging century promises to be about the inspiration and invention of the individual, not the march of the masses. People have discovered a sense of self, and Liberalism is the philosophy of the self.

Signs in the distance all seem to point the British people towards a destination called Liberalism. With the finest Liberal leader since Lloyd George doing the driving, he could yet take them there.

24

THE CHALLENGE FOR VELCRO MAN

If the polar icecaps of the two old parties continue to melt as rapidly as they have over the past half century, then Liberal Democrats are sure to benefit from this warming of the atmosphere.

But political change, like climate change, is growing ever less predictable and as parliament hit those wintry mid-term blues, the attitude of the public towards both governing parties looked decidedly chilly.

And conventional wisdom holds that only economic resurgence will warm their cockles. "Then we might get some benefit," says our senior source. "I'm concerned about getting through the immediate danger. A full five year coalition is still the most likely scenario, though there is less trust and goodwill. As cuts bite both parties will become less popular—and neither will be keen on an early election.

"Even when the Tories did well in the local elections I don't think they did well enough to win an overall majority."

In one of the key revelations of this book a hitherto loyalist architect of the coalition rewarded with a cabinet post suggests a startling solution that certainly surprised me—and will rock Cameron to the core of his Combats: re-negotiate the coalition with a list of policy demands. And whatever Osborne may intend, a new programme will have to be based on increased public spending as well as tax cuts.

"These are areas we will drop on them," my mole tells me. "It would be wrong to go into detail. Hopefully later in the parliament we will be in a better position to spend more and tax less. Both parties will have to resolve what will be their priority. People will want tax cuts because real incomes have been so squeezed, but also by then the public sector will look pretty threadbare after several years of cuts."

Wouldn't Cameron feel bounced? "There is going to be a second stage coalition agreement. We've agreed this." But hardly to renegotiate the agreement quite so dramatically on Liberal Democrat lines, surely? The mole smiles.

Will, I ask, Liberal Democrats support further progressive tax cuts or more public spending? "Nick recognises we have to be associated with tax cuts. But people will be looking to us as the progressive party in the coalition to help schools and hospitals that are over-stretched. It can't just be tax cuts. It will be a very delicate balance." It promises, then, to be a brutal encounter, more like a divorcing couple fighting over the chattels than the hopes of that May day.

The politics of this economic analysis are confirmed by a ministerial Lib Dem: "The Conservatives might say the Lib Dems are in too week a position to make demands. I disagree. It is important for Cameron to make his administration look Rolls Royce, smoothly burbling along. He doesn't want to be left in a minority administration. And given the move to fixed five year terms, he would find it intensely difficult."

And this is one reason Liberal Democrats are not as pessimistic as commentators would have them be. If Clegg persuades Cameron to accept his demands, he will have yet more to trumpet at the election. And if, as a final resort, he does play the nuclear option of withdrawing from the coalition he can shake a weary head and say "we tried so hard to make Osborne do the right thing, but ultimately we discovered Tories will be Tories."

I simplify. These will be extremely hard hands to play, and other considerations will come into the equation. While many senior Lib Dems wouldn't be averse to pulling out, Clegg is determined to make it work.

And any discussion depends on the economy turning round, which looks ever more doubtful. If we have grown wary of Greeks bearing gilts, so we should be sceptical of British politicians spending the "proceeds of growth". As Laws says: "There is a limit to how much the government can drool about that at the moment. Perhaps we can return to that when we are south of a deficit of £50 billion, rather than the £141 billion of today." Indeed, economic cycles cannot always be made to shadow political cycles and with this downturn potentially so major it is possible the governing parties will have to go to the country in recession. However, need that be as fatal as conventional wisdom assumes? In frightening times will the public trust a free-spending *ingénue* like Miliband who is so obsessed with denouncing "the cuts" he simply doesn't get the scale of the crisis? Sober times might just work electorally for Cameron and Clegg.

But that won't stop ministers arguing in private over what to do with imaginary growth figures. According to one source the priority will be to draw at least some poison from the tuition fees debacle, perhaps by pushing the Conservatives to halve the fees. One weekend late in May 2011 Clegg convened a meeting of the party's Forward Strategy Group, comprising all the major players, to discuss precisely how the Lib Dems were to climb out of the electoral hole in which they found themselves.

I am told: "Chris said 'tuition fees are a major, major, problem. We have to really apologise, promise we won't make the same mistake and then put it right.'" Simon Hughes agreed. However, Cable asked how on earth they *could* put it right. "No one," I am told "had a solution."

Nevertheless many are still hopeful the coalition review presents Clegg an opportunity to rebalance the coalition. "The agreement hasn't given us enough to do for a full parliament," says Harvey. "You can see the need for further agreement, perhaps through Coalition 2.0."

However, even Huhne doubts major concessions could be won. One source close to him says: "The problem with this re-negotiating scenario is your bargaining power is not very good. Cameron has to believe you are mad dog enough to call it out."

The problem for Clegg—and indeed Cameron—is that there are senior Lib Dem figures who are feeling sufficiently "mad dog" to want out. Even Huhne is thought to have at least discussed the possibility of making demands which Lib Dems know the Tories cannot accept, and use that to withdraw. At the very least the agreement for the second stage must be approved by conference, and disquiet grows. But if the agitators succeed it is conceivable it will not even go that far.

"Some are certainly saying we should not continue," I'm told. "John Pardoe [former Liberal MP] did say that hatred of Tories is the beginning of all political wisdom. Breaking up the coalition would be one very good way to flag up our differences."

But it might also flag up that the Liberal Democrats are not serious—undoing the good and only a little of the bad that has come from coalition.

The same source, incidentally, argues that withdrawal of Lib Dem forces would have to take place alongside a change in leader. Only in the Lib Dems would anyone consider toppling a leader who so wowed the country a year before.

And worryingly for Clegg, some of this treacherous talk is thought to be endorsed privately by a few of the party's most senior figures, including Huhne. "A leader change is one of the things that could happen," says a major player within the party. "Tim Farron or someone like that might challenge him." And what of Huhne? "I think it very, very unlikely." But not, you notice, unimaginable. Certainly there are friends of Huhne who say he still harbours ambition, though his career has to some extent skidded off the road since claims about his now famous drive down the M11. Huhne's detractors say he is biding his time, and even his "helpful" interjections (defending Clegg from Tory mud-slinging in the AV referendum) are designed to project him as the doughty defender of Lib Dems against nasty Tories. If Huhne were to argue for Clegg's resignation before either standing himself or throwing himself behind Farron it would be cast as an attempt to draw a line under tuition fees.

But loyalists dismiss talk of a challenge. Baker, a pragmatic figure on the left, said in the summer of 2011: "I told Nick last week I don't regret backing him for the leadership." Harvey put it well: "The party has never loved Nick and never will. And he has never courted or craved that love in the way Charles did. But it respects him. He is a very determined figure. He had a very clear idea about where he wanted the party to be and will stick with it. He is going through hell. No one should go through what he is going through."

Harvey said the party doesn't grasp simply how hard Clegg works: "He is a very powerful figure in government. He chairs lots of committees and sits on the government Security Council. Yet you hear Lib Dem MPs say 'why don't we see more of him?', and in the wider party 'why isn't he out on the rubber chicken circuit?' He is working like a whirling dervish, he has a huge job. He must feel like shit half the time, yet never shows it."

Harvey paused and stared at his book shelf. "I see him at meetings quite a lot and he must have dark moments. The party is reeling. But the party has also been in many dark places before." He also dredged up the Thorpe parallel: "When you have had your party leader in court on a murder charge, this is quite tame." Whatever Clegg is accused of, he cannot be accused of being a dog killer. Not yet, anyway.

"Anyone who challenges Nick would be a complete idiot," another minister suggested. "Vince is not the power he was two years ago and is quite in the doldrums. Chris is on the edge of a catastrophe and even if he survives will be weakened. And for Farron it would be a ridiculous gamble."

For Clegg, the minister reckoned, the question is whether he will retain the "appetite" to carry on through the next parliament "if one of the other parties looks on course for a landslide. Nick is a really gifted man. He is very versatile. If you asked me if Nick would be in parliament in ten years I would say 'no'. I think he will pursue another career, perhaps two more, he is only 44. I can't see him doing an Alan Beith, minding his constituency postbag aged 70." Perhaps the Granola Bar pact mooted earlier is not so outlandish.

Harvey continued: "But I think he will lead us into the next election unless he gets really fed up. The only reason he would go is if he decided to, not because he was pushed. If this bile is heaped on him indefinitely, then even the most indefatigable spirit will buckle." More optimistically he posited: "While I don't think we will have another dose of Clegg-mania, he could morph into a different kind of Lib Dem leader. David Steel was called the boy wonder in 1979 but looked very careworn after dealing with David Owen. Paddy was a very different Paddy later on."

Whiteley, however, insisted Clegg will have to go: "The Liberal Democrats can recover in time for the next election if the economy improves and they reinvent themselves with a new slate of policies and new leader. Then people may look at them again." But with Huhne (semi) becalmed, do the Lib Dems have a leader in the wings even half as good? And what would "reinvention" entail, other than denouncing the party's own work?

Surely Liberal Democrats must stand by Clegg and their record. The most successful Liberal Democrat leader in eight decades needs the party's help to show the coalition has been a success. And as the terms of the debate for the next election are slowly framed, it is likely to open an inviting vista for Clegg. Perhaps some moanier Lib Dems need to, as Browne might put it, "man up". Harvey has told me the party should avoid romanticising the Kennedy era, which was a "shambles". And as Baker said: "Every time I don't like something the Tories do, I remind myself that there are hundreds of them going through the lobbies to vote for our policies because we are in coalition." After the love-in followed by talk of divorce, gradually a more balanced marriage is taking shape, if not quite staying together for the kids, then maybe toughing it out for the pupil premium.

"I've spoken to Tories who are much nicer than I thought," reflected Baker. "And I've also met vile ones. But then they probably think the same about Lib Dems."

What all agreed on—in principle at least—is the advice of the senior of senior sources, when he told me: "The absolutely crucial lesson of the 1930s is the party must stay united." One threat the source foresaw was the Conservatives announcing they would not field candidates against favoured Lib Dems to keep their coalition partners in line. "I think you could see for instance no Conservative candidate standing in Sheffield Halham." Cue: eyebrows twitching, theatrically—a reference to Clegg's seat. And then, warns the source, the Lib Dems would cease to be an independent force: "Certainly until the AV campaign the Tory strategy was absorption by love and cuddles. But then we saw how quickly the Tory strategy changed and it became a very ruthless destruction of the Lib Dem brand."

He reminded Lib Dems that they "didn't go into this for careerist reasons. In the Twenties a substantial number chose the party as a vehicle of power." He doesn't quite say so but in modern times a careerist would have been certifiable to go into politics as a Lib Dem.

"Our parliamentary colleagues ought to be made of sterner stuff. But some are young with families and have grown used to the salary. What do they do if the Tories come to them and say 'it doesn't look very good for you, let us help you'? There are some young members of the parliamentary party who will be tempted."

As if on cue one young-ish Lib minister told me: "Nick should have left himself some wriggle room to form an electoral pact with the Tories."

Another intriguing possibility, this mooted by a different highly placed Lib Dem: that if the coalition lasts, then at the 2015 election both parties enter into a limited but highly secret pact. And the source revealed that this was, astonishingly, precisely what the Liberal Democrats and Labour did privately in the three elections between 1997 and 2005. Clegg has vowed that the Liberal Democrats won't enter into an electoral deal with the Tories but that, after all, was pretty much what Ashdown and Kennedy—and Blair—told voters, too.

The source revealed: "There were lists between the two parties. It was formally agreed but very privately, involving Chris Rennard. In about 20 seats each neither party would make any serious challenge to the other." For the party that did not challenge, victory in those seats was impossible anyway, but its voters making a tactical switch to the other progressive party could just give it victory.

"The *Mirror* published the list, leaked by Labour, so both sides could put on their election leaflets 'the independent *Daily Mirror* recommends....' It ensured we didn't clutter each other up. I suppose we could do the same with the Conservatives if we are still in coalition and leak the list to the *Sun*. But that depends on how the coalition goes. After being in coalition, the party is more likely to feel equidistant between the other two than before."

The possibility was half confirmed by a minister: "Yeah, it might be possible but if I confirmed it for your book it would hardly be secret." Mainly, though, he echoed the earlier warnings that the party must heed the lessons of the National Liberals in the 1930s and not allow itself to become breakfast for the Tory tiger.

The strategy for the next election, I have been told, will be similar to the last: "We will make a big thing of five key policies which we will seek to deliver. And if we hold the balance, we will speak first to whichever party has most seats and say 'it is not our job to decide, it is for voters.'" The source conceded there is a certain ambiguity "in how much weight you give to the phrase 'speak first'."

As for the rest of this parliament, there was agreement on both wings that there will be few attempts to reprise the Clegg-Cameron rose garden serenade. The senior of senior sources said: "Nick doesn't look so comfortable now with Cameron. He probably recognises that was a mistake." This was echoed by our other top source, more on the right: "We have to get the balance better. It needs to be somewhere between the first day of that Morecombe and Wise love-in and the more recent 'You support the BNP' stuff of the AV debate."

Harvey reflected: "People will be cross if lessons are not learned. But our supporters realise we can't rebuild our image overnight. Nobody goes into the Lib Dems to join a social set. It's been a big shock but we are well aware there will be a battle ahead."

The Lib Dems are likely to find the next election harder pounding than the Samoan contingent will the Olympics. How, for instance, does it put clear orange fire between itself and Cameron without burning down its record in the coalition? But it won't find it nearly as hazardous as an election would have been straight after the last.

And if the Lib Dem bird has been shot down, at least Clegg will have grounded a few air-borne animals of his own, especially the flying pig that contended coalitions are "un-British" or "un-workable". However this coalition ends, there will be tangible improvements which Clegg will show are a result of his decision to enter government.

By the autumn of 2011 there were also signs of gentle up-lift.

Clegg followed his success in changing Health reforms by titling the free school programme to help disadvantaged children. Cable was again talking about breaking up the banks, and this time there was no slap-down from Number 10. Even more significantly, Cable was talking of the need for a "plan A plus" for the economy, a clear retort to Osborne who insisted there was no "plan b" to cuts. In doubting that cuts alone would deliver growth he was not merely putting pressure on the Chancellor but reminding him that their responsibility for the economy is shared. Even the emollient Alexander said Tories considering abolishing the 50p top tax rate were living in "cloud cuckoo land". And in insisting on a tougher line on Murdoch, Clegg not only shored up his base but proved that just as the Tories had a clear function—to tackle the deficit—so too did the Lib Dems, namely to keep the coalition fair and honest.

The Clegg of the next election will appear a little battered and bleary-eyed. He will no longer represent "new politics". He will have been run over more times than a speed hump, and been abused more roundly than a typical guest on *Trisha*. But the public might warm once more to a leader who, despite remorseless punishment, has that rare political ability to send himself up and carry on doing what he believes right. He was heard to reflect recently that rather than being "Teflon man" (nothing sticks) he is "Velcro man" (everything sticks). It reflected a charm (Ed) Miliband might struggle to match.

More substantially, Clegg has not merely given Liberalism back its voice; he has put its philosophy into action. If Clegg completes his coup he will have proved that Liberal Democrat governance works for the country and not the classes, unlocking the possibilities of individuals and communities. A few Liberal ghosts will then surely look down with modest satisfaction. But let us finally leave the fallen to the obituarists, and even—recalling the dead animal in Ashdown's office—the taxidermists. Instead, through the success of Clegg, it is time to celebrate the Liberalism of the living.

25

COALITION BRITAIN

THE YELLOW PERIL

"Coalitions are detestable, are dishonest," declared Ramsay MacDonald upon becoming Labour's first Prime Minister in 1924. Why they were more detestable and dishonest than a minority government disliked by a majority in the country and in parliament, as MacDonald had just formed, he did not enlighten the House.

And despite its intellectual vacuity, the MacDonald doctrine already passed for ancient parliamentary wisdom by the time he enunciated it. For Disraeli had famously declared in 1852: "England does not love coalitions." And this old chestnut was even hauled out of retirement to criticise Cameron and Clegg when they entered Number 10 in 2010, despite coalition being precisely what "England" appeared to have just chosen.

The criticism rested on an assumption that had gone unchallenged for a century and a half. This held that coalitions were, like properly edible food, white teeth and decent plumbing, suspiciously "un-British". While almost every country in Western Europe had been governed since the war by a combination of parties working together in the national interest, here the prospect was greeted by reactionaries of left and right as a foreign contagion; if not quite Black Death then certainly something unpleasant, like German measles or Dutch elm disease.

But to Clegg, rooted in the European tradition, it was the British system of alternating single party rule that appeared fetid and unhealthy. He wondered if, rather than delivering endless lectures in democracy to other nations, we could for once take a lesson from across the Channel. After all, the British people seemed ambivalent towards its system of government, complaining about it at home while boasting of it abroad.

The left, Scotland, Wales, the north and large swathes of the traditional working class had railed against the injustice of the "get on your bike" Thatcher years, unleashed upon them despite the majority of the country seeking refuge in other parties; there *was* an alternative, and most people voted for it. Even in Thatcherism's finest hour of 1983 when the Iron Lady gained the largest parliamentary majority since Labour's landslide of 1945, she only secured 42.4 per cent of the vote. Yet this bagged her just a smidgeon under 400 of parliament's 650 seats.

Conservatives and their well-upholstered southern supporters were liable to grouse equally loudly that Brown was knocking the stuffing out of them—and that this was unjust, as Labour had secured a minority of votes and seats in England. Indeed, a Labour constituency in the shires took on the rarity of a museum curio, smuggled back from a foreign land to surprise the public. Throughout the Labour years there was resentment that these aliens from Edinburgh were inflicting on the apparently more entrepreneurial English a centralised socialism. Tories huffed that Tony Blair was elected with a veritable swarm of Labour MPs (418) that were stinging the middle class for more tax. And all on just 43.2 per cent of the vote.

The Thatcher and Blair parliamentary majorities suggested a mandate for radical change, and the former was taken as such by Thatcherites, as was the latter by many in the Labour movement. Yet even during those "landslide elections"—the two most decisive since 1945—over half who bothered to turn out actually voted against the "winner". Moreover, by the electoral system so exaggerating the support of the larger party, the other two were left routed, unable to provide credible opposition. And this is why Britain has, at most given times, scarcely seemed a duopoly, never mind a democracy.

No party has managed to gain half the vote since the war, yet it took 65 years after that seismic battle for Britain to experience the consensus and relative contentment of coalition. In 2010, finally, an administration could claim at least qualified backing from 59 per cent of voters, the first peacetime moment since 1922 when Britain lived under coalition. Before 2010, on one of the very few post-war occasions when a party did approach the 50 per cent mark—Labour with 48.8 per cent in 1951—it contrived to lose to the Conservatives, who secured slightly fewer votes.

When virtually everyone voted for one of two parties, perhaps this didn't matter; if Labour was prepared to accept the injustice of 1951, that was its call. The two leviathans gained 96.8 per cent of the vote between them, so they could make the rules. But by 2010, voter endorsement for the two old bruisers had slumped to 65 per cent. The Liberal Democrats secured 23 per cent, while regionalist parties were increasingly dominant in three of the four countries of the "United" Kingdom. Even the Greens bagged their first seat, and UKIP was tempting Tory ultras. Through it all the electoral system continued to behave like a hectoring waiter, harrying diners to choose between one of two dreary dishes left over from yesterday, even though the menu offered fresh alternatives.

Before we examine the merits of coalition we must dispense with one canard. For, contrary to Westminster mythology, there is nothing "un-British" about a combination of rival parties working together. Indeed, looked at historically, you might argue that it is the single party governments of recent decades that have been the aberration.

As early as 1715 the "c" word began to make its foreign entry into polite discourse, courtesy of a book called *An Essay towards a Coalition of Parties in Great Britain*. In 1782 we effectively had a three party system that the following year produced the Fox-North coalition. For much of the Regency period different alliances shuffled for favour, such as the original "Ministry of All the Talents" (1806-7). When Disraeli thundered that "England does not love coalitions", what he actually meant was that he didn't like Gladstone, and Gladstone was one of several rebel Tories ("Peelites") entering a "mixed" government with Whigs and a Radical. This laid the path for the creation of the Liberal Party. And as well as establishing the economic orthodoxy for the rest of Victoria's reign—low tax, free trade—the government proved that old enmities could be, if not forgotten, temporarily mislaid. After all, Palmerston, the new Home Secretary, was thought to have been referring to the man who was now his boss, Aberdeen, when he complained of "antiquated imbecility". That surely rendered Cameron's earlier assessment of Clegg (his "favourite joke") almost affectionate. Surveys of public attitudes show repeatedly that nothing turns off voters more than politicians hurling insults back and forth that are clearly as synthetic as they are hysterical. For a leader, the realisation that he might have to work across the cabinet table with an opponent serves to tone down the invective wonderfully, and make compromise easier later.

Anyway, the newly formed Liberal Party traded office with the Conservatives, but soon further cross-party alliances were forged. In 1885, Gladstone's Liberals combined with Parnell's 86 Irish nationalists to block the Coercion Act announced by the Conservative Prime Minister, Lord Salisbury. Just as significantly, when Gladstone formed the next government, several of his grander Whigs—Liberal from historic family attachment more than conviction—combined with a group of Radicals led by Joseph Chamberlain in joining the Tories to defeat the Grand Old Man's historic mission to give Ireland Home Rule.

Liberals were appalled to see not only their right but their left wing jump into bed with their Conservative enemy. Still, coalitions can draw out qualities in parties they didn't know they possessed. Thanks to Chamberlain and his Liberal Unionists, the Conservative-led government introduced several long-cherished Radical measures, including reform of local government, the extension of free primary education and worthy reforms concerning allotments and smallholdings. And when a Conservative-Liberal Unionist coalition returned in 1895, the Tories also benefitted, landing them the country's leading Whig, the Duke of Devonshire, and its most powerful Radical, Chamberlain. This increased Tory popularity, and not just by the 70 seats Liberal Unionists brought to the coalition. Indeed, Salisbury could have governed without Liberal Unionists but recognised their value, so offered its leaders plum jobs.

We should concede that this unlikely alliance also showed the dangers of coalitions, for they are combustible, and the contagion can burn down not just one party, but two. This the Conservatives learned when Chamberlain called for Imperial Preference, which not only split Liberal Unionists and Conservatives every which way, it contrived to unite the bickering official Liberal Party, which swept back to power in 1905. The coalition did, however, result eventually in a merger of Liberal Unionists and Conservatives (in 1912), just as the Aberdeen coalition had united Peelites, Whigs and Radicals. And this was a lasting boost for the Conservatives, giving them a metropolitan presence previously lacking. It also highlighted another effect of coalitions, their ability to bring about realignment when parties in government realise that new problems call for new friendships. We are already seeing early signs of that in our current coalition, with moves to disband the Scottish Conservatives.

What these earlier coalitions had in common was a need to tackle what Gladstone called "a great and palpable emergency of state". So it should be scant surprise that much of the period from 1910 to the end of the Second World War saw Britain ruled by some combination of politicians working across the divide—because for most of that period global events buffeted Britain from one squall to another.

In 1910 when Asquith called an election over Lloyd George's "People's Budget", the Liberals returned to power with Labour and Irish support. True, this was more pact than coalition. The Irish remained on opposition benches and appeared indifferent to British domestic arguments, their support contingent on Liberals delivering Home Rule. The 42 Labour MPs elected with Liberal help were uncertain allies, with several voting against Lloyd George's National Insurance Bill. Nevertheless, the administration focused on the needs of the poor, demonstrating a great strength of partnership government—because it drew support across the classes, it could not rule in the selfish interest of one. Instead, it had to govern for the nation, and it can be no coincidence that Asquith's ministry is often sited across the divide as one of the great governments of the 20th century. In March 1914 the Liberals did offer Labour full coalition, a progressive alliance against a Conservative Party stirring civil war across the Irish Sea and blocking reform on the mainland. While Ramsay MacDonald was keen—particularly on the dangled cabinet seat—Labour refused, seeking to supplant the Liberals rather than prop them up. Nevertheless, this is probably the moment Tony Blair had in mind when he expressed regret that Britain's "progressive majority" failed to unite under one banner.

In 1915, with the British offensive bogged down in Lowland mud and blood, Asquith felt compelled to invite Conservatives into government, hoping they would help prosecute the campaign rather than snipe from the opposition benches. Lloyd George took this further the following year by usurping Asquith, becoming Prime Minister as head of a government that suddenly felt more Conservative than Liberal, though it did contain a token Labour member. So successful was the coalition in winning the war that Lloyd George and Bonar Law, the Tory leader, continued their alliance after November 1918's armistice. At the following month's general election, candidates who supported the government were given a "coupon", a letter signed by Lloyd George and Bonar Law, and they swept the country, with disastrous consequences for Asquithian Liberals who rejected the coupon—including Asquith, who lost his seat. Meanwhile Lloyd George was so lauded that Bonar Law suggested he could remain Prime Minister "for life". As this presidential figure pursued a policy between "the revolutionary and the reactionary", many suggested party loyalties were redundant. In the event, the new politics gave way to the old after just four years. It was not the leading lights of the Tory Party that ousted Lloyd George but a rebellion of their disappointed backbenchers—a hazardous phenomenon for coalitions—which led to the formation of the backbench 1922 Committee (which was actually founded in 1923). Far from being immovable, Lloyd George was never to return to office, and for years symbolised all that was considered dangerous about coalitions (deals and intrigue, the sidelining of parliament).

Not only has history been kinder to that government, the end of Lloyd George did not mean the end of cross-party co-operation. Once returned to parliament, Asquith helped Labour into power in 1924 as did his successor Lloyd George in 1929.

Then, virtually throughout the period 1931-1945 we had some variation of national government, formed to lift the great depression. MacDonald, Prime Minister since 1929, found Labour had no response to the crisis. It baulked at spending cuts with unemployment doubling to 2.5 million, yet clung to the classical economic model of free trade, fiercely rejecting Lloyd George's modern Keynesian solution of spending out of recession.

Finding governing impossible, MacDonald resigned in 1931, yet the King persuaded him to form a national government with Liberals and Conservatives taking most key positions. If much of British politics is explained by loyalty to tribes—what Roy Hattersley calls "the Sheffield Wednesday factor"—MacDonald's old Labour friends never forgave him. Still, he soon made agreeable new Tory acquaintances, notably Lady Londonderry. Gradually, Tories grew more dominant and assumed real charge, first under Stanley Baldwin, then Neville Chamberlain, son of "Old Joe", once the radical conscience of the Liberal Party branded by Tories a "Sicilian bandit". Again the Tories benefited, gaining legitimacy from their more progressive partners that a harsh economic programme scarcely warranted.

What was still notionally referred to as the "national government" continued beyond the declaration of war in 1939, but by now was Conservative in all but name. It remained under the chilly leadership of Chamberlain ("the Undertaker") until he was buried by the Norway Debate. A coalition was formed with Liberals and Labour, whose leader Clement Attlee went on to become Deputy Prime Minister. This lasted to the end of the war. Churchill and Attlee wanted to continue their alliance, but with peace came the return of party warfare. Giving a farewell Downing Street dinner for leading figures across the parties, Churchill declared: "the light of history will shine on all your helmets".

And then darkness. Cross-party friendship was snuffed out as swiftly as the Number 10 candles. Far from continuing to mature, post-war politics returned to sulky adolescence. Indeed, the period is marked by two characteristics, perhaps not unrelated: the longest period (1945 to 1977) of one party rule since the Whig supremacy; and the most dramatic decline in the country's relative economic standing ever.

The two major parties reflected rather neatly Britain's class divide, Conservatives ruling for their middle class supporters, then Labour extracting working class revenge. This merely completed a process started when Labour began to supplant the Liberals as the primary progressive force in 1924, or perhaps even as far back as 1867 when the working class were given the vote. For while the Liberals had been a middle class party reaching out to the burgeoning working class, the emerging Labour Party was undeniably the voice of proletarian struggle. A frightened middle class then fled the Liberal Party and united behind the Conservatives as the best bulwark against socialism.

But as political exchange degenerated into class spite—through what defenders of the status quo would have to regard as the glory days of strong, single party rule—there was still much coalition chatter. For a decade after the war, Churchill sought an anti-socialist alliance, a project he had first supported in the Twenties. After going into opposition, he offered the Liberals a clear run in 60 seats. It must have been hugely tempting to a party looking into an electoral abyss, but the centrist rump rejected the offer, realising that survival as an independent party could not be at the caprice of a Conservative. After all, few of Churchill's likely successors shared his nostalgic affection to the Liberal cause (even late in life Churchill referred to "the honoured name of Liberal" and his wife Clemmie remained a Liberal till her dying day). National Liberals, meanwhile, continued to sit in Churchill's shadow cabinet and he ensured they were given free runs, though they insisted on taking their own whip until finally being submerged into the Conservative Party in 1968— the last remnant of the national government formed in 1931.

In October 1951, with a Tory majority of just 17, Churchill again made overtures, offering Liberal leader Clement Davies a seat in cabinet. Churchill's offers were invariably undermined by Hailsham, arguing with some justification that deals would be impossible to deliver on the ground. Yet the Churchillian longing for coalition was not purely sentimental. Contrary to the wisdom of Disraeli, as late as 1967, two years after Churchill's death, a Gallup poll indicated that 52 per cent of the public wanted a coalition.

And this talk was not confined to the right. Labour leader Hugh Gaitskell, opportunistically, suggested a popular front with anti-war Tories as the Suez affair developed in 1956. After Labour's narrow victory of 1964, Harold Wilson adopted "parallel courses" of introducing purely Labour legislation and measures which might find a sympathetic hearing on the Liberal bench.

But post-Churchill, activists in both large parties came to view sharing power as a sign of feebleness, and only to be considered due to crises, not common sense. So as Northern Ireland became an inferno in 1972-3 there was widespread support in Westminster for power-sharing between the province's two warring tribes, protestant and catholic; but despite the mainland being gripped by often violent industrial unrest there was no consideration that power-sharing in London might bring peace to Britain's middle class and working class.

Then in February 1974 the modern two-party system faced its first serious challenge. The election produced a hung parliament. The Liberals under the swashbuckling Thorpe secured 20 per cent of the vote, their finest showing for 45 years. Yet even without a majority, Wilson expected to replace Edward Heath as Prime Minister. Thorpe held talks with Heath, who clung on grimly, but a deal was impossible. With just 14 seats the Liberals could not give the Conservatives a majority. And Liberals had made gains largely at Tory expense. Activists were furious at the prospect of propping up a discredited Heath. More fundamentally, there was acceptance across the spectrum that one party had to be left to govern. Even with a Liberal voting block of 20 per cent, the establishment wasn't ready to admit that Britain was returning to three-party democracy. So Wilson formed a government with just 37.2 per cent of the electoral cake, even though the Tories had polled slightly more.

Yet even during this bleak period for consensus-seekers, there were calls for a government that would soften rather than accentuate national divides. It is rarely remembered now, but in the second election of 1974 Heath's manifesto called for a government of national unity, promising to "consult and confer with leaders of other parties."

Labour won, but in 1977 when Jim Callaghan lost his narrow majority he negotiated a pact with Liberal leader Steel. For years Tories would be unable to mention "the Lib-Lab pact" without sneering, but it reassured markets and led to noticeable economic improvement.

If Thatcher thought she had swept away Lib-Labery with her resounding victory of 1979, within two years the British political landscape was briefly re-drawn. Labour's economically literate wing broke away to form the SDP, forming an Alliance with the Liberals. For the first time in living memory it was the Liberal Party gobbling old opponents, rather than being eaten itself.

But despite briefly topping 50 per cent in polls, the Alliance lacked the strength in depth to defeat a Thatcher transformed by the triumph of war. When Blair was elected Labour leader in 1994 he flirted outrageously with Ashdown, but never consummated their relationship. A couple of desultory committees, fair votes for EU elections and lots of sweet nothings about electoral reform at home was all Ashdown received.

Soon, the history of bi-partisan government in Britain came not merely to be forgotten, but denied. Yet as the political and media elite regarded talk of coalition and realignment as some dreary specialist interest for Liberal obsessives, voters spoke differently.

By 2010, the truculent two-party system had lost a third of its support since its high watermark of 1951. In 2005, a Blair drained by Iraq slunk back into Downing Street with the good wishes of just 35 per cent of those who voted—and, disturbingly, with just 22 per cent of those eligible to vote.

With virtually every passing election for over half a century Britain had become more multi-party, but the Commons remained unshakeably adversarial. Inevitably, debate remained as shrill as it was shallow. The old class-based prejudices of both Labour and Conservative had become hollow rhetorical relics in a multi-ethnic, globalised society, yet this apology for parliamentary discourse was what passed for national conversation.

Most voters, then, had been at any given time in a state of revolt against their government, increasing year by year. Then in 2010 even Westminster's first past the post system finally broke against the sheer force of the multi-party tide. It had been a third of a century since the Lib-Lab pact, just as that pact had been virtually a third of a century since the wartime coalition. For the first occasion since Churchill, an administration could claim support of 59 per cent of the electorate.

There is a caveat. Nobody voted for a Con-Lib coalition, because that choice was not on the ballot. The coalition was decided after the election, and critics would say by politicians rather than voters. But a larger proportion of people than in any post-war contest secured a very substantial chunk of what they voted for. Clegg had said, explicitly, he would try to deal with the largest party after the election. It was for the people rather than him to decide which party that would be. And it was clear as the campaign developed that the largest party would be the Conservatives. If a Con-Lib deal was abhorrent, voters could have united against it.

What Labour refuses to acknowledge is that even many of *its* voters were sick of Brown. Such voters could take comfort that Conservative enthusiasms would be tempered by Liberal Democrats. After all, a Lib-Con government is closer to what they voted for than one that was pure Con.

In France coalitions might be formed before an election, but in most European democracies they are agreed post-election. This is certainly true in Holland, familiar to Clegg, where there are few cries that the government lacks a mandate. Parties that negotiate post-election coalitions are aware they will face the judgement of voters a few years later. If they betray an election pledge, they will be punished.

If there had been a Lib-Con ticket it is arguable that far from being hit, it might have done rather well. The Conservatives would have been boosted by appearing to occupy the centre ground. Their only possible loss might have been a few blazered Euro-sceptics tempted by the Little Englanders of UKIP. Lib Dems might have received fewer votes—roughly a third of its voters are viscerally anti-Conservative—but they might have bagged more of the support they needed to win seats. My hunch is that such an alliance would have been returned on a landslide.

Still, we face a paradox. Whatever the public's early enthusiasm for coalition, in government Lib Dem support fell more spectacularly than the late Oliver Reed in a "speakeasy". So while voters felt alienated from the Conservative-Labour power-swap, they were sceptical of the inevitable alternative. Yet if the electorate continues to vote for a panoply of parties, power will have to be shared.

One reason for the dip in support for the coalition in general and Clegg in particular is that voters report that Clegg is "anonymous" or "invisible". Even at dinner parties of the *bien-pensant* there will be expressions of surprise that "the Conservative government" has not given rise to a new Norman Tebbit, but there will be no acknowledgement that a little of this is thanks to Clegg and the coalition with Liberal Democrats.

Coalitions sideline extremists, and this has drawn much of the anger from marches against the spending cuts. An unleashed Eric Pickles, for instance, appeared to have great potential to be a new Tebbit, but in coalition he comes across as almost emollient.

It is tempting to blame the media for the apparent invisibility of the coalition's orange flank. Just as politicians have had to learn how to "do" coalition, so has the media. In fairness to the Lobby, it has no experience of coalition. Few contemporary hacks were around even during the Lib-Lab pact. So they have described the coalition much as they traditionally have parliament, a battle between two snarling dogs, with one (mainly Cameron) running off with the bone.

As discussed elsewhere in this book, Lib Dems have to take responsibility for their press coverage. But over the course of a coalition, if the press is serious about explaining our governance it will have to grow more sophisticated. Much as adversarial shouting matches make for good copy—or did, until the public stopped paying attention—journalists need to grasp that in coalition real debates are conducted behind closed doors. As for disputes, as shown by the historical analysis above, they are just as likely to break out within as between parties. And while both Lib and Con will continue to lunge for the bone, Cameron and Clegg realise that if they don't remain reasonably well behaved the last they will see of that bone is in the jaws of Miliband, scampering into the victorious yonder.

The media will slowly grasp that key debates are not held on the floor of the House in the theatrical form of Prime Minister's Questions between Cameron and Miliband. They are now between Cameron and Clegg in Downing Street. Because Clegg does not perform at PMQs, the perception is that he has disappeared. This is far from reality, but the truth might only emerge once the coalition has ended, when a balanced assessment can be made of who managed to change Britain most. Or better still, how both parties worked together to transform Britain. Will it be considered a better place than the one Cameron-Clegg found, and better than if it had been run by Cameron alone?

But Clegg will hope for some uplift sooner than that. If the reality of coalition is that the work of government is not accurately reflected in parliament, Clegg will need to find fresh ways to gain public recognition for his private influence. One solution might be insisting on joint press conferences with the Prime Minister—not love-ins like the rose garden scene, but regular, workmanlike, policy-laden sessions where the work of government is spelt out. In time this might come to be seen as the true Prime Minister's Question Time.

Traditionalists will argue that even without such an innovation, coalition gradually sidelines parliament. Which is right up to a point, the point that you remember parliament was sidelined by the executive long before this coalition. Defenders of parliament should also realise that as coalition terms lengthen, rebellions tend to increase in both parties.

How much the new dynamic can be conveyed to the public in one coalition term, I'm unsure. But I would suggest "England" can, in answer to Disraeli, learn to love coalitions. I offer you three reasons.

Firstly, as we have seen, coalitions are not so "un-British" after all, with five elections in the 20th century not delivering a single-party win: January 1910, December 1910, 1923, 1929 and February 1974. It seems 2010 wasn't so exceptional after all. And on none of those occasions was the flag at Buckingham Palace lowered or the White Cliffs of Dover flattened. Moreover, as well as being established in the national system, power-sharing is ever more common lower down and indeed higher up. Local government routinely has coalitions where voters seem happier to keep power out of small cabals. Voters often don't understand why practical problems in their communities cannot be tackled by men and women of goodwill. With devolved government, Scotland, Wales and Northern Ireland are now regularly governed by coalitions. In the European parliament the need to work with rival groupings is assumed, including by those who oppose coalitions and electoral reform in Britain. Even in that bastion of democracy, the House of Lords, votes are often cross-party.

Further, British parties are themselves coalitions in all but name. Blair had scarcely more in common with Tony Benn than he found with Col Gaddafi, yet Labour's warring factions still cobble together manifestos they at least pretend to support. And much the same can be said of Conservatives, where the Edward Heath/ Rab Butler wing never really found ideological soul-mates in the Norman Tebbit/ Enoch Powell wing. They still, by rules of parliamentary convention, used "my honourable friend" to refer to those they must privately have considered dishonourable enemies. Both parties have long been dogged by more rancour than has the Cameron-Clegg "marriage of convenience". Even without the explicit coalition of 2010, where a deal was struck after an election, perhaps our politics is not so routinely different from that of France where parties of differing shades of red or blue fight an election side by side.

And there is a second reason why we might come round to coalitions. And that is because they seem to work. Almost despite himself, Cameron concedes the point, praising in statesmanlike tones the contribution of Liberal Democrats, and even the camaraderie of two parties putting aside petty rivalries for the greater good. Yet as soon as Cameron remembered in the AV debate that he was meant to consider coalitions A Bad Thing, he suddenly trotted out the old banalities about instability.

The true value of coalitions was shown by the Rupert Murdoch scandal. A purely Conservative government might have been in real peril with its closeness to News Corp, not least through the tarnished presence of Andy Coulson, former *News of the World* editor who

Cameron chose as his spin doctor. But Clegg urged a tougher line throughout. Having long warned about press ownership, he had hugely more credibility than Cameron and his "Chipping Norton set". If Cameron's instinct was to hold the line, Clegg argued successfully that the scandal wasn't going away. It was Cameron's ostrich strategy that had allowed the scandal to grow so big. Even if Cameron had tried to block a proper inquiry, Clegg would not have let him. Because when a coalition Prime Minister is so clearly wrong, even a junior partner can mobilise opinion to force his hand. This Clegg did very effectively.

And we have seen the value of two parties working together in other areas. Most obviously this is in dealing with the Gladstonian "emergency of state", the debt crisis. Just imagine how a purely Conservative government would have ripped through the budget, with even more of the burden for spending cuts falling on those least able to bare it.

If the hoary criticism of coalitions is that they pursue policies of the lowest common denominator, the historical experience points the other way. Labour's support helped radicalise Liberals before the Great War, bringing about desperately needed social reform. After that war Lloyd George smuggled numerous Radical measures past the Conservatives, just as Chamberlain had done. The experience is, rather than agreeing a policy mush, parties prefer to have several of their flagship measures adopted, and in return will grant the other party similar license. We see this in the current coalition which even its critics acknowledge is strikingly bold. Lib Dem policies of the pupil premium and tax cuts for the low paid have not only survived, they have become showcase achievements for the entire government.

But if it is too early to judge the effectiveness of this coalition, we should look at precedents from across the Channel. This is recognised by Conservative opponents of coalitions and electoral reform. For although such diehards remain generally oblivious to "abroad", they love dredging up one particular European example: Italy, and the mess it is in, all apparently due to proportional representation and the coalitions that system produces.

Oddly, though, they rarely remember Germany, even though its party system is the one closest to ours, in that it has two larger parties—one centre left, one centre right, and one liberal party. It can only be an oversight, for Germany's post-war history is held up by virtually everyone else as a model of good governance, the stability usually secured by either Social Democrats or Christian Democrats working with Free Democrats to produce consistent economic policies. The results are clear. And if this gives too much power to the centre, when the two larger parties found the Free Democrats too uppity, they formed a "grand alliance": nothing but mutual loathing and stale thought stops Labour and Conservative doing likewise.

So instead opponents focus on Italy, normally with a guffaw. It is always characterised as "unstable" for having more governments since the war than Silvio Berlusconi has (allegedly) enjoyed lady friends. But what this ignores is that in Rome a change of government might consist of, say, the transport minister, as leader of one small party, being replacement by the leader of another minor party. The change in policy has actually been far less than the wild swings of post-war Britain. Arguably the problem with Italian politics is not that it suffers from too much flux, but too little.

So even the "killer argument" against coalitions—Italy—is based on ignorance. Meanwhile, countless countries to the north of Italy have been steered by coalition government, and have enjoyed consistently higher growth and more united societies than Britain.

And this brings us to the third and final major reason I would advance for coalition government, and it is a singularly British consideration. A sustained period of coalition would, I believe, help heal Britain's class divisions. Helped by the presence of Clegg, socially-concerned Conservatives such as Iain Duncan Smith and Gove have sought to tackle modern-day evils such as poverty and poor educational attainment, a marked change for a party traditionally prone to deliver simplistic and splenetic attacks on "benefit scroungers" and "the youth of today". If you put aside the business of dealing with "events", the striking theme running through the policies of this coalition is the desire to increase social mobility. To anyone who believes in classlessness—in people being given the chance to succeed despite their background—there can be no more virtuous ambition in domestic politics.

Coalition government can reduce division, not only by tackling the problems of the underclass but also by reassuring the southern middle class that rather than the politics of envy, this is the politics of opportunity.

Moreover, a consensual approach to government would mean that when a coalition is finally kicked from office, there would be less ideological, class-interested legislation on the statute books for the incoming government to rip up. Governing would be marked by continuity and evolution, not rupture and revolution. And generally, stable societies are more successful than unstable ones.

When Zhou Enlai, the Maoist leader, was asked what the effect of the French Revolution had been, he replied "It is too early to say". If so, we certainly cannot judge this coalition.

But I close this chapter by suggesting three possible consequences to look out for. First, coalitions often cause re-alignments, often several years later. I make no predictions but merely suggest it would be complacent to assume that all three parties will go back to how they were, because historically one party tends to do much better out of a partnership, which changes the tectonic plates. And such realignments are unpredictable. So if the Liberal Democrats appear to be a party of government once more, is it not possible that other progressives make their careers there rather than in the Labour Party?

Second, it seems the greatest danger to coalition comes, not at the point of crisis, but when the crisis has been averted. So perversely the danger for this coalition is not going to be arguments about spending cuts but over spending increases after possible economic recovery. But perhaps this tendency for coalitions to fall apart in the wake of their greatest triumph reflects the political temperament more than structural weakness. The challenge for Clegg and Cameron will be to control the tempers of their parties.

Third, and last, the British enjoy their reputation for fair play and willingness to compromise. That quality will be tested to the maximum by coalition government. Regardless of electoral reform, the voting trend for half a century has suggested a growing desire for politicians to work together. The challenge of the political class is to show the public they were right to want it.

As for the Lib Dems, the historical lesson of coalitions is clear: be bold and enter coalition, but ruthlessly pursue party advantage as rivals surely will, and above all hang together.

British food—along with its teeth and even its plumbing—is much improved. We have to hope the same will prove true of our governance. For all Clegg's disappointment over the AV result, he is cheered by belief that within a decade we will come to see coalitions as eminently British. As British, indeed, as chicken tikka masala.

POSTSCRIPT

IN CONVERSATION WITH NICK CLEGG

From his vast mahogany desk in his vast ministerial office overlooking Horse Guards, Nick Clegg surveys an equally vast modern painting.

It features a narrow path bordered by snow, but in the not so far distance trees burst with summer leaf and even a little light.

In those rare lulls when people in power snatch time to think, Britain's second most influential man must study that painting intently. For it encapsulates both the achievement and the agony of his position. You see, his path from anonymous MP apparently unrecognised in his own corner shop to "most popular leader since Churchill" took just 30 months to tread. Yet he knows if he doesn't reach that distant light in similar speed, his career could be lost in the political tundra.

Clegg has gone through more in a couple of years than most politicians experience in a lifetime. He went from being David Cameron's "favourite joke" to his Deputy Prime Minister, and he did so by becoming a television phenomenon, Britain's first Politician Idol, as the nation was seized by "Clegg-mania". Yet having led his party into government for the first time since the war he has become an object of scorn, even of pity.

He may have faced a media barrage heavy enough to flatten a medium-sized town and seen his effigy hung in makeshift gallows around Parliament Square, but to my intense surprise he comes across as more chipper than chippy. Then again, at school and university he displayed a notable flair for acting.

"I'm not really allowed to say this but I feel much better than I'm supposed to," he smiles, impishly. "I'm quite practical about it. You don't go into politics if you aren't prepared to take quite a few knocks. And the job is also extremely exhilarating."

But the constant flux, he acknowledges, is "extraordinary": "The party has been in opposition for 65 years and is now in government with people it has been tearing strips off. It would be naive not to think it would be difficult. Some [in the Liberal Democrats] find it very uncomfortable. But I still think it's very impressive how they have got on with it." Indeed, Baker has told me that suddenly finding himself a minister of the crown was "Like Tom Brown's School Days, arriving at those big gates for the first time"—only to discover that his first lesson was that there is a full-blown media conspiracy to blast the Lib Dems from government.

Clegg smiles: "Attacks, derision: none of this is new to Liberal Democrats. All that the party has been through does help with resilience."

Indeed, to each new bombardment Clegg appears to have trained his platoon to laugh rather than cry, at least in public. So while some ministers dredge the historical barrel to argue that at least Clegg isn't up on a murder charge like Thorpe, I'm told Huhne privately invoked the name of Dominique Strauss-Kahn over The Scandal of the Missing Points: "At least I'm not up on a rape charge..."

Through this rolling turmoil Clegg seems almost super-naturally calm, confident he has chosen the right path. "As long as people see with the compromises the party has made we are also doing a lot of what we wanted to do, on the environment and the economy, we will be alright. And that is even before we hit the sweet spots I'm aiming for towards the end of this parliament."

This book has revealed that Clegg's early-retirement is already being discussed by certain dis-loyalists within his party. Meanwhile, a list of demands is being drawn up to renegotiate the coalition, providing the Clegg-Cameron axis with its fiercest challenge to date. Yet as Clegg surveys his grand study with his family photos and countless books on his favourite subject of social mobility, he doesn't appear to be going anywhere soon. If coalition government can feel alien to some Britons, to one steeped in the ancient culture of Europe this historic government is Britain's future.

In Clegg Towers, just one aspect of Blairite administration remains: the sofa. Clegg is perched on a rich, squidgy white one sipping tea from a green mug. The atmosphere is relaxed, informal, young. A darkly attractive woman, tall and slim, slips in to remind Clegg of mounting appointments: "Oh, he can wait!" our subject throws up his arms, presumably not about Cameron. There is a striking difference in style between the Prime Minister, a traditional Englishman, and the Deputy Prime Minister, a contemporary European. While Cameron's office is not quite "take dictation, Miss Jones", the Conservative leader displays more reverence for the office and ranks within it. Cameron, I suggest, has the greater appetite for power; Clegg the greater hunger to achieve something with it.

Clegg's outer office contains no more than eight people, none over about 30, so hardly a great empire for Britain's second most important man. From here Clegg runs his department, of Political Reform, while also working to transform the Liberal Democrats from a movement of protest and centre left posturing into a centrist party of government.

Not only is this phenomenally hard to drive, it comes at a cost. Supporters horrified by the deal with the Conservatives ran from the party with a speed that would impress Usain Bolt.

"There is a huge constituency out there for a party more competent economically than Labour with more of a social conscience than the Conservatives, and is without the prejudices of both," he says. "But it will take some time to prove to people that this isn't some nightmare repeat of the eighties."

As we have seen, whether the voters Clegg is courting even exist is growled over in the highest echelons of the party. More immediately, he has to convince those once enthusiastic followers that the Cameron-Clegg beast of government is not Thatcher-Tebbit reborn: "That is the shrill complaint. And my job is to show that this government is very different from that."

Labour figures such as Andrew Adonis have claimed in private that Clegg decided before the election to work with Conservatives in a balanced parliament. Clegg denies this, trotting out his familiar line that it was always for voters to decide as his stated intention was to form a government with the largest party. But he admits the emergence of a young group of Liberal Democrats open to genuinely liberal solutions was an important shift that made Con-Lib Dem coalition possible.

"There was a group of us in the Lib Dems who reacted to years of big state centralism, directed by the Treasury. That was significant. We also had the rabid populism of John Reid [Labour's Home Secretary] who was frothing at the mouth, utterly shameless in spreading fear. So David Davis [Tory home affairs spokesman while Clegg performed a similar role for the Lib Dems] came from different places but ended up in the same place in response to Reid. That was also significant as it crystallised the division with Labour."

This is the closest he has come to suggesting coalition with Cameron was on his mind before the election, though he insists: "I formed a group to produce a paper before the election setting out all the scenarios. I read it, put it away, then didn't think about it. I just concentrated on the campaign."

Where, I ask, does this leave Ashdown's long cherished ambition to re-align the left? Is coalition with the Tories merely a minor detour on that monumental journey? It appears not. "Realignment" is dead: "Talk of realignment on the centre left and centre right misses the point. If we believe in pluralism we must accept the cards dealt us by the British people. You cannot make these grandiose plans about who you would like to go into government with as it diminishes the will of the electorate. And with realignment I don't believe the electorate would like to see two parties ganging up on one."

It is the starkest repudiation I've heard Clegg make of the Ashdown-Kennedy-Campbell project. And this reflects far more than mere tactical difference. For Clegg simply doesn't accept that progressive advance demands Labour's co-operation: "I believe in a Liberal tradition. You can see it in government. It is about giving a child the best start, then supporting the individual to do what they want. Tories are about keeping social patterns as they are. Labour is all about the state."

We meet the day after Barack Obama's visit in the summer of 2011, and while Clegg had a private meeting and listened to the president's address in Westminster Hall on a platform with Messrs

Cameron, Brown, Blair and Major, this was hardly how his role was depicted next day. The cruelly brilliant Peter Brookes of *The Times* has drawn a series of cartoons casting Cameron as head boy of the Westminster Academy with Clegg his fag, and in that day's masterpiece Clegg is bent in the shape of a stool sat on by Cameron—who turns from Obama to hiss at Clegg: "Look, chum, you can be bloody grateful you're in here at all." It is the "chum" that is the killer.

I ask Clegg if he has ever felt like quitting. "No, I've never thought I'd like to be out of it. There are times when I think 'will this work?' and 'should I have done that?'" But his eyes look quite soft, even imploring. I am sure he does relish the job, but I suspect it comes at a human cost.

There has been, I point out, speculation about his future. Will he lead the party beyond the election? "I want to. And without being too pompous I feel a strong sense of duty to the party. This is a risky adventure and I have to see it right."

And what of his domestic coalition? Has that found government a strain? After all, with dog excrement posted through the letter box the job must have lost a little lustre? "Miriam has been amazing," he says, suddenly animated. "It's much more difficult being the husband or wife of a politician than being a politician. At least if you go into it and are paid to do it you know what's in store. She isn't from here, yet has had to fit into the system and be constantly on display. Much more is expected of a political spouse now and they can't answer back." It was a point often raised about royalty, before the Duke of Edinburgh corrected the problem.

Clegg smiles: "It's a miracle she hasn't shared with the world in full Technicolor her views." And he leans back and laughs. In the days he was allowed lunch we would share a joke about marriage to strong-willed Latin women. He asks about my house in the country and when I tell him of the peace it gives me he makes as if to cover my mouth: "alright, that's enough. I don't want to hear any more."

Its good Clegg retains a little of his old humour, and reminds me why I took to him on a personal level when first we met. It is a quality once remarked upon by journalists and politicians alike but which some friends report is now less evident. As the attacks have intensified they say the lightness has gone and Clegg has grown a little "lawyerly", so used is he to defending himself.

How, I wonder, does he rub along with Cameron now? Shortly after the coalition was formed Clegg said at a summer garden party that the PM texted him so regularly Cameron had even messaged to ask how coalition negotiations were progressing in the Clegg household over 2010's World Cup (Miriam's Spain was battling Clegg's Holland). Has their relationship become a bit shoutier? "I've never shouted at him," Clegg says evenly. "We've had intense arguments. We will be tough on each other, but not angry. Because we come from different parties we know there are things we disagree on. In a funny way that takes the emotional edge from it. You have to know when to be firm. There have been occasions we haven't been able to agree for a couple of weeks and we've sat on it, but finally you do have to come together and make a decision."

How does he predict the coalition will pan out? "I'm not a sooth-sayer and life might go pear-shaped. But given the information we have I think we are generally taking the right decisions. There have been errors, particularly presentational issues. But on the big decisions over the economy, deficit, tax changes, the pupil premium, even the early AV referendum were based on sound judgements."

But before tackling those I ask if he regrets any of the iconography of the coalition—the rose garden scene launching the "Nick and Dave Show", to slapping Osborne on the back in the House. Even cabinet colleagues I've spoken to suggest he must wince over what more strident activists would regard as chumming up to the Anti-Christ.

"No, I can't stand this ghastly Westminster wisdom of hindsight," he waves a hand in one of his gestures left over from drama club. "A coalition government had just been formed in extremely difficult circumstances by two party leaders knackered to the bone, and they were prepared to show good humour about it. However David and I might have our differences we will never apologise that the Prime Minister and Deputy Prime Minister can get on."

Nor can he resist pointing out that although this is a coalition, the two figures at the top "get on" considerably better than the last double-act to run a government, even though both were ostensibly of the same party: "Do we want to go back to the soap opera of Brown and Blair? We don't need to create synthetic differences."

However, there will be those in both parties who rather hoped the differences were real. Surely Clegg must regret raising tuition fees? This, more than any policy, damaged Brand Clegg. "Do I regret that lots of young people are directing anger at me? Of course. Believe it or not I don't go out of my way to upset people."

But that is regretting the result, what of the decision? He pauses and scans the room, his eyes fixing on the painting. "I constantly ask if we could have done things differently. But how? We could have cut drastically the number that go to university, but I would hope then people would have gone out in even bigger numbers and protested. Or we could—and I did toy with this for several days—have let the report cogitate for a year and the universities would have gone nuts demanding they receive the funding. Then at least it would have been the universities driving it."

It is a defiant answer, suggesting he only really regrets the tactic. "It's difficult," he reflects "but we should have rolled the pitch better. I totally admit we got the politics wrong, and with hindsight we shouldn't have pushed it through without preparation." A lesson he has learned, he says, is "you have to prepare the ground." A point developed by Francis Fukuyama in his new book *The Origins of Political Order*, which would suggest that if the coalition has a failure it is that it hasn't always set out to win the argument for major change.

Clegg accepts it was photos of him and other Lib Dems signing pledges that highlighted the betrayal: "But when I went round universities during the election, tuition fees wasn't the big issue. On my soap box I was tub thumping about the environment and civil liberties, but myths take hold."

One suggestion is he should have pushed his party to drop the pledge before the election, as I am told he privately wanted. He looks momentarily shocked that I knew his private position, but recovers:

"No, I believe in free university education. But you can't do everything. We have re-allocated almost as much money to early years learning, something which wouldn't have happened if Liberal Democrats weren't in government."

Which leads us to Clegg's greatest problem. While the coalition's unpopular decisions seem to have Liberal Democrat ownership— even the ones, such as tuition fees, which were Conservative built— the triumphs are often claimed by Tories. Investment in early learning should actually reduce educational inequalities far more than tuition fees will raise them, but how many have heard of this achievement? Ditto the pupil premium, providing massively more for the education of disadvantaged nippers? Or tax cuts for those on lower incomes? Or the establishment of the world's first green investment bank?

None are negligible achievements for a year in power as a junior coalition partner but no one is talking about them in Westminster, let alone in West Wittering. At the end of our interview when the spin doctors have departed Clegg draws me aside and says: "Well it's always very nice to talk about myself and you've been asking me how it's going. So how do YOU think it is going?"

Much of what you are doing in government is terrific, I reply. But your public relations are crap.

"Tell me about it," he smiles grimly. "But it's not easy. I also have Chris [Huhne] and Vince [Cable] speaking out and this means that rather than being out there leading the debate as I should be, I'm having to hold it all together."

And "holding it all together" is going to be exceptionally tough when he comes to negotiate the second stage of the coalition agreement. This hasn't really been picked up upon by the media but both parties decided when they went into coalition that they would reconvene half way through the parliament to forge a new pact. And, as we have seen, many senior Lib Dems say privately they want to use those negotiations to find an excuse to pull out.

This, for Clegg, is the most important remaining stop on his gruelling journey. "I agree with you, this is the big debate in the coalition," he admits. "Much will depend on how you divide the spoils of growth." He emits a hollow laugh and looks heaven-wards: first catch your fish. Then he stares at me seriously and says something important: "That discussion will be more fraught than the original coalition agreement. That will be a real fork in the road. Both parties have a very different tax stance and a different spending stance."

Senior Liberal Democrats consider this their opportunity to wrench concessions from Cameron. However, Clegg will anger many as he clearly won't demand a generalised spending splurge in some desperate attempt to buy a feel good factor.

"There will be so many good candidates for further funding and much will depend on the pressure on public spending," he says, before showing that his Liberalism is imbued with a little of Gladstone's steely disapproval of state profligacy: "our reforms are also about making our public services better run so in some areas I hope it won't be necessary to increase spending."

In a further remark that might produce squeals from his left he points out that through Blair's first administration public spending stood at only 35 per cent compared to 40 per cent even after this government's "savage cuts": "Yes its really, really tough but public spending is only down to 2008 levels. To call this some scorched earth policy is nonsense."

He intends to drive a hard bargain with Cameron. He has a close aide, Polly Mackenzie, drawing up a list of demands for the talks. But he does not, unlike some colleagues, see re-negotiation as an excuse to divorce.

"I think that would be an act of political suicide for both parties. If either side engineered a split I think the British people would be quite unforgiving. Clearly people haven't retained that first flush of enthusiasm for the coalition but I think they kind of like the idea of people weathering unpopularity."

How unpopular does he feel? "Most people I meet in a park or on a train are very friendly. Metropolitan England and the north are a bit different. There are very strong visceral memories. They feel personally besieged. I get this a bit in Sheffield. They say 'the Tories attacked us in the eighties—why are you allowing them to do this to us again?' They won't believe me at the moment even if I tell them till I'm blue in the face, but it's not going to be like that this time."

And this is what gets Clegg animated: "Politics is about what helps. It's what delivers social mobility. So I'm obsessed about education for all the obvious reasons."

But the immediate mood of the poorest is going to be determined not by Clegg's ideals but by the deals Clegg has made over Osborne's recovery plan.

On the day we meet the chief economist of the OECD suggests Britain should slow down cuts to draw back from recession. I have barely uttered the letters "OE..." before Clegg leans forward and exclaims: "I have to say something here. The media is hitting consumer confidence. Every day people are told they are going to hell in a handcart and hatchet man Osborne is going to take your school away. It is understandable people are spending less. But the idea you can string out the cuts for another year or two...I would love to ask these economists if they really think this would bring about long-term growth. These cuts are hardly slash and burn."

Nevertheless, some Conservatives regard a small state as a virtue in itself. Have they cut because they want to as well as because they have to? "I've heard this argument [for a small state] made by com- mentators, but not round the Cabinet table. I think this libertarian argument is farcical. Small states can be just as authoritarian as big ones." Whether that truth convinces Conservatives we will see: a small, authoritarian state might sound like paradise to some Tories.

As I leave Clegg asks a final question: "Any big decisions you think we should be making?" I reply that it seems the big one has already been made, cutting rather than spending our way out of the deficit. "Yes, I think that's right. It all comes down to the economy, doesn't it?"

It is a craggy, treacherous path down which he must trudge—but at the end Clegg might find a more forgiving light.

INDEX